THE STRATEGY

GARTH TURNER

THE STRATEGY

A HOMEOWNER'S GUIDE TO WEALTH CREATION

KEY PORTER BOOKS

Canadian Cataloguing in Publication Data

Turner, Garth
   The strategy : a homeowner's guide to wealth creation

Includes index.
ISBN 1-55013-914-2

1. Real estate investment – Canada. I. Title.

HD316.T86   1997   332.63'24'0971
C97-931973-0

The publisher gratefully acknowledges the support of the Canada Council for the Arts and the Ontario Arts Council for its publishing program.

Key Porter Books Limited
70 The Esplanade
Toronto, Ontario
Canada M5E 1R2

THE CANADA COUNCIL | LE CONSEIL DES ARTS
FOR THE ARTS | DU CANADA
SINCE 1957 | DEPUIS 1957

Design: Leah Gryfe
Electronic formatting: Heidi Palfrey

Printed and bound in Canada

97 98 99 00 6 5 4 3 2 1

Contents

Don't let cheap mortgage rates trick you into
buying real estate for the wrong reasons. And
certainly not the wrong kind of real estate, the
kind that has no future.

Stunning changes are about to grip our nation.
In fact, they already have, leading us to a
social, financial, political and emotional
precipice. Don't invest a dollar until you know
what's coming.

We are in an economic boom of unprecedented
strength and importance that will sweep the
value of financial assets higher in a period of
noninflationary growth. It will last until 2010
or longer, followed by what could be
depression-like conditions. There isn't a
moment to lose.

How to turn your real estate into what you will
certainly need in the future—a retirement fund.

If the author is wrong about where interest
rates and stock markets are headed, very.

Caution

This book may not be for you. Many people will have no stomach for the investment strategy outlined here. Indeed, I fully expect some reviewers to call it aggressive or extreme. Some financial advisers will recommend their clients against it, and so they should.

But it needs to be laid before Canadians. For many of them, today in their forties and fifties, with real estate investments in place but without a retirement nest egg equal to the hundreds of thousands of dollars they will require, implementing this strategy could change their financial lives forever. It could save them.

But there is risk. And it certainly does challenge traditional Canadian blind belief in the wisdom of homeownership and the volatility of financial markets.

If you can't bear the thought of investing a large amount of money in something that might fall in value, stop reading.

If laying your paid-for home on the line will keep you awake and in a sweat at night, put this down.

There are other books containing the traditional principles of financial planning on the same shelf as this one. I urge you to select one of them, instead.

Garth Turner

Introduction

Late summer evening, 1987

I walk down the middle of the empty highway opposite my home an hour's drive northwest of downtown Toronto. All I hear is the sound of my boots on the pavement and my dogs scuffing in the ditch. The real estate agent watches me from the side of the road. Over my right shoulder is the boundary post of my new property. Ahead, straight up the highway, as far as I can see into the distance, is my land.

What a rush.

Real estate

I love it. I want it. I have luxuriated in it. Been excessive about it. Owned too much of it. Been blessed by it. Been burned by it. Still can't shake it.

Sold that highway land two years later to a carload of South Korean speculators who paid in cash. Then sold the commercial buildings I owned some miles to the south to a local developer.

I moved on into Parliament and then, after losing my seat at the Cabinet table in 1993, I sold my condominium on the Toronto waterfront to an investor from Liechtenstein. I sold my house in the suburbs to a young family. I sold my home in Ottawa to Prime Minister Jean Chrétien's confidant.

It was then, without real estate for the first time in sixteen years, that I learned The Strategy.

Not a heartbeat too soon.

PART 1

Chapter 1

First, the Bad News

Last year things changed. Traditional real estate kind of went out the window.
—Pam Alexander, Regional Director
Re/Max

It's time for real estate investors to stop listening to the people who are spreading doom and gloom—and to start discovering the real facts.
—David Baxter, Executive Director
The Urban Futures Institute

Real estate has boomed for so long here people seem to grasp at straws to deny the new reality. Local analysts, for example, will point to an increase in sales as proof things are positive, even as prices fall in a market that should be benefiting from near-record-low mortgage rates.
—Miro Cernetig, The Globe and Mail
Vancouver

Just as the definition of "family" is changing, so too must the definition of what we call home.
—Christan Findlay, Vice President
Royal Bank of Canada

This is a book for people who now own real estate and wonder if it's wise to hang on. This is for people who don't have real estate and wonder if this is a good time to buy or what kind to buy. It's definitely for people who suspect that the things their parents did and the views they held about real estate and the future in fact may now be a recipe for disaster.

Of course, there is no shortage of advice on this subject, but be very careful. Most books on real estate in Canada are rewrites of ones first published in the Eighties. The few others that have been produced in the Nineties don't question the basic premise of the earlier ones—namely, that residential real estate is a good investment and you should have some.

Actually, we have this national delusion about houses. We dream about them. When asked what we'd buy if money were no object, we say real estate. We have real estate newspapers, radio and TV shows. We watch "Home Improvement" and spend millions on renovation videotapes. We marvel at the mansions of Rosedale and West Vancouver, Mount Royal and Rockcliffe. We measure social status by address. Success by street name.

In fact, real estate is a cultural obsession. And it's now become extremely dangerous.

Consider these three numbers from the Royal Bank's 1997 Canadian Home Ownership Survey, done by the Angus Reid Group:

Number who think a house is a good investment	80%
Number who have no mortgage	47%
Number who would never borrow against the equity in their home	76%

This is astonishing because it flies in the face of the reality people have experienced. For example, when that survey was conducted in Toronto, local real estate prices had fallen by about a third from their 1989 peak, costing the good people of T.O. about $50 billion in lost equity. The average house price was barely over $200,000, which was about $70,000 less than a few years earlier.

And 80% think a house is a good investment? What are they smoking? Sure, the appreciation in value is tax-free. But how many houses have gained value in the Nineties? And what can we expect in the future, with an aging population, rising stock markets and rapidly changing demographics?

Meanwhile the numbers show us roughly half of all homeowners have no mortgage and three-quarters would never borrow against the equity they have built up in their homes. Why not? When Canadians consistently tell pollsters they don't think they will have enough money in retirement, why are a vast majority of homeowners refusing to use money, which is earning 0% or, more the case in the 1990s, giving them a negative yield, in their homes?

Most Canadians have most of their net worth in real estate. Why are they refusing, in droves, to tap in and make it grow?

Why is a whole financially miserable generation of Baby Boomers clinging to its house-rich and cash-poor philosophy with such passion? And how about today's seniors, struggling to live on 3% GICs while sitting on nonperforming real estate assets? Like the woman who died in her nineties in the house where I now live, likely without enough money to renovate it. She could have had $400,000 in cash—a brand-new condo and money to cruise the world—if she'd done what her kids did immediately after her death, and sold it.

No, this is not a recycled 1980s real estate book. In fact the real estate book I did write in the Eighties I have to disown. Called *Real Wealth*, it was penned at a time when owning real assets (commodities) made sense. But no more. At least, not the same way. That advice was good for a few years, but those years are gone. This book will tell you about the new truths. It will tell you why real estate is now a dangerous commodity, especially in those places—like Vancouver and the Lower Mainland of B.C., Toronto and the Golden Horseshoe—where people have far too much money tied up in residential equity.

It will tell you where your money should be invested today and why. And it is not all in your house. The sooner you realize that, the better your odds for survival.

But don't get me wrong—I love real estate. Always have, always will. It's a rush to close a deal on a unique and exciting property. I've made a lot of money investing in real estate, and I continue to own it. But I own in a different way now, one that lets me enjoy real estate without being financially exposed to it. That's because I have used The Strategy, and I want you to do the same. If you do not, there's an excellent chance you may end up being part of the greatest retirement crisis in Canadian history. It's coming all right. And when it does, about the last thing you will want is too much house.

THE NEW TRUTHS

- Deflation is replacing inflation
- Money is cheap to borrow, rewarding to invest
- Real estate tastes are changing fast
- A retirement crisis is coming
- Your house could be a wealth trap

Be wary of deflation

It's not a concept most people are familiar or comfortable with. And most Canadians have no idea they need to fear this thing. Deflation is when prices go down, instead of up, which makes it the opposite of inflation.

It last happened big time during the Depression of the 1930s, when prices and wages steadily declined. Men like my father were happy to work for a dollar a day, and bread cost a nickel a loaf. Consumer spending dried up because it was cheaper to wait and buy what you needed later, when the price would drop further.

As for houses, they kept going down in value while mortgage debt stayed constant. In fact, with incomes continuously declining, it made that debt harder to service. Finally many people found their houses were worth less than the mortgages on them, so it made no sense to continue owning them. They walked.

That actually happened again briefly during the recession of the Eighties in Alberta, where many homes also dipped below their mortgages and owners gave them up.

Could this happen again? You bet. The seeds are already there. Consider this:

• Most people haven't had a salary increase in years.

• Houses are worth less today than they were in 1990.

• The price of money (interest) has collapsed.

That sounds to me like a pretty decent definition of deflation—at least the start of it, which is disinflation—a time in which the value of commodities falls. It's the opposite of the Eighties, when it made sense to buy the biggest house possible with the largest mortgage, payable in constant dollars, which rising house values and incomes would shrink.

Today mortgages are getting harder to pay, because incomes are going down, but most people don't realize it because the value of money has collapsed. When you can get a mortgage for as little as 4%, there's the illusion of increased affordability. The sneaking, underlying reality is a whole lot more sinister.

Consider these facts from Statistics Canada:

• After inflation and taxes, average family income in Canada fell 5.4% between 1989 and 1995.

• The average income of upper middle-class people earning between $45,500 and $60,500 fell more—by 6.4%. Average annual income dropped almost $3,000.

- Even more shocking, middle-class incomes in Canada in 1995 were 19% lower than they had been 15 years earlier.

There was one very revealing day in the spring of 1997. Bank of Canada Governor Gordon Theissen gave a press conference after releasing the central bank's semiannual monetary policy report, and he said this:

> Monetary conditions, which have been stimulative, are going to have to move to a more neutral setting.

Within minutes the Canadian dollar was rising in value. The buying of the currency became so intense over the next few hours the central bank had to intervene to keep order. By the end of the day the dollar had risen by more than a full cent U.S. It was the greatest single-day advance of the entire decade.

What had Theissen said, and what did it mean?

Well, several years earlier the Bank of Canada had set a target range for inflation of between 1% and 3%—a goal that would have seemed ridiculous during the Eighties. But in the Nineties, it was achieved, allowing interest rates to float down to the lowest levels since 1956. In fact, the bank was too successful.

So Theissen made the above comment moments after Ottawa revealed the national inflation rate had dropped well below 2%. Speaking in code, the governor said this:

> We're now afraid the economy could slip into deflation and so I want the financial markets to understand that interest rates will probably be rising soon. I know that runs counter to our previous policy of cheap interest rates to try to create jobs, but we now have a bigger potential problem than unemployment. It's deflation.

In response, the Canadian dollar suddenly looked like a bargain against the American one, so buyers rushed in.

But maybe it was already too late. Since May 1995 the central bank had been an aggressive rate-slasher, cutting its overnight lending rate 19 times to just 3.25% in a desperate bid to kickstart the economy. Now, by signalling rates would rise, Theissen had swelled the loonie's value, making Canada's exports more expensive, and guaranteeing both the economy and inflation would shrink.

I wondered that day if he knew what he was doing.

CORE INFLATION (LESS DIRECT TAXES)
Year-over-year % change

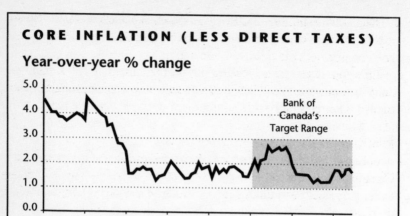

Core inflation has collapsed and has been near the very bottom of the Bank of Canada's target range of 1% to 3% since the beginning of 1996. It was inflation that puffed up real estate values in the Eighties. Now disinflation (maybe even deflation) is housing's enemy.

Source: Bank of Montreal

MONEY'S A LOT EASIER TO GET
Jan. 1987 = 0. Weekly average, in % points

Money has not been this cheap or bountiful for decades. It has made housing affordable and is also the fuel gassing up the fire under financial assets. There is no reason to believe the collapse in interest rates won't last for years to come.

Source: Bank of Montreal

Then, in the summer of 1997, Theissen made good on his word, hiking the Bank of Canada rate in a move that shocked the financial markets, raising both the dollar and the ante.

Inflation, it seems, is dead and buried, and that has got to be inherently bad news for real estate and people who have so much of their money invested in its equity.

Profiting in the days of cheap money

A collapse in inflation has brought a collapse in the cost of money. Canadians have been able to borrow at the prime rate—less than 5%—to invest in stocks and mutual funds, which have been growing at double-digit rates.

Mortgage money has been available for less than 5%, the cheapest it's been in four decades. This has increased housing affordability to the point where in most cities it's actually cheaper to buy a house than rent a decent apartment. And so it does make sense to buy under those conditions, because the cash flow of an owner can be greater than that of a renter.

But that doesn't mean a house is a good investment, or that you are buying low now so you can sell high later. Instead, it's just shelter. And you want to have the cheapest shelter costs possible. Don't make the common and dangerous Canadian mistake—putting your "investments" on one side of the ledger and your "home" on the other. Both are integral parts of your overall financial plan, and the performance of your house as an asset has to come under the same scrutiny you place on the other assets you own.

> *Don't let cheap money trick you into buying real estate for the wrong reasons. And certainly not the wrong kind of real estate, the kind that has no future.*

On one level disinflation has been making real estate more affordable. Prices are vastly below levels of a decade ago, the cost of mortgage money has been cut by more than half and rents have increased. According to the Bank of Montreal's Housing Attractiveness Index, this trend took hold in the middle of 1994, and three years later it cost less to own than rent in every city in Canada except the most dangerous one—Vancouver.

Across the country in 1997 the ongoing costs of financing a starter home were 22% lower than renting equivalent accommodation. That dipped to a 12% advantage in Toronto, where the average house price was over $210,000, and it evaporated in Vancouver, where it was 17%

more costly to own than rent.

Meanwhile financial markets continue to be in overdrive. As I write this the Dow Industrials in New York have flirted with 8,000 and are on their way to 10,000 (but perhaps a visit to 3,000 might occur first). The TSE 300 in Toronto is above 6,000 and perhaps, as futurist Richard Worzel believes, on the way to 30,000 (but again, expect shocks along the way). For long-term investors, there is virtually no risk investing in financial assets, because of what is going to happen over the next ten years.

Today you can borrow money at the same rate your parents did in the Fifties, and you can invest it to earn double-digit rates of return. Some people are doing this. Vast numbers more will be doing it in the future. And as they concentrate on building what they need—a financial nest egg—real estate will suffer.

Some people have written that cheap rates and rising markets will fuel the next real estate boom—a rerun of the Eighties. What a joke. It's the total opposite.

WHAT YOU CAN BUY FOR $150,000

City	Lot size	House size (sq. ft)	Bedrooms
Vancouver	Town house	706	1
Calgary	33 × 110	1,625	3-4
Toronto	Condo	1,100	3
Ottawa	40 × 100	1,400	3
Kingston	60 × 120	1,800	3-4
Montreal	75 × 100	1,500	3-4
Quebec	62 × 114	2,380	4
Halifax	60 × 110	2,300	4
Whitehorse	60 × 140	1,948	3

Source: Century 21 Canada Ltd.

Who wants a Scarlett O'Hara staircase?

Not as many people as in the past, not by a long shot. Real estate tastes are changing fast, because of the times, an aging population and other demographic changes, such as the slow death of the "traditional" family.

Aging alone will bring dramatic changes to real estate, with the number of seniors tripling after 2011. Royal LePage health-care specialist Judy Freeman has been alerting investors to what she thinks is a giant opportunity—the need for more than 30,000 retirement home beds by the year 2006, as the number of people older than 75 mushrooms to 500,000—up almost 50% from 1991 levels.

And I think Freeman has got it right. With Canada-wide cuts to public health-care facilities, there is no way the system will be able to cope with the millions of geriatrics there'll be in fifteen years. Developers and investors who realize this now will be poised to profit considerably.

The latest statistics on the chief killers of Canadians—heart disease and strokes—are stunning. We are dying of these ailments at *half* the rate we were in 1969. Data from Statistics Canada show that cardiovascular disease killed 306.6 Canadian men out of every 100,000 in 1996. In 1969 the disease killed 600 in every 100,000. What will be the number when the Boomers hit 65 years of age in 15 or 20 years? Three hundred? Fifty?

Meanwhile let's not forget the influence of Baby Boomers like me on the national real estate market. We were behind the boom of the Eighties as we formed households and cruised through our consumptive, expansionary and inflationary thirties. In our forties we consolidated, paid off debt, raised families and worried about the economy. Late in that decade of our lives, many of us are selling off those big houses—slowly and often at a substantial loss. Boomers are reassessing their needs.

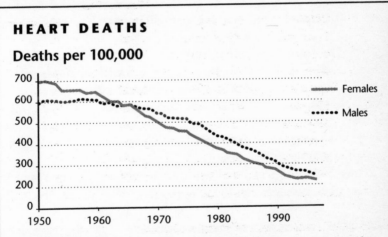

HEART DEATHS

Deaths per 100,000

The number of Canadians who die from cardiovascular disease has been steadily declining since the late Sixties. Life expectancy is rocketing higher, and the advent of nine million Baby Boomer seniors is going to change society and real estate tastes.

Source: Statistics Canada

"Lifestyles have changed," Canadian Real Estate Association president Tom Bosley said in mid-1997. "We've found second- and third-time buyers want smaller houses. They want to go away more."

And in urban Montreal, realtors report that as many as half the sellers of first or second houses elect to become renters—maybe a safe bet until Lucien Bouchard is done holding the province hostage.

This deterioration of interest in the kind of houses people wanted in the Eighties has had a devastating effect on those who didn't see it coming. North of Toronto is a street of homes that all sold for a million dollars or more a decade ago. Today you can easily buy one for about half that amount. All those original buyers made three mistakes. They bought

- the wrong kind of house, at

- the wrong time, and in

- the wrong place.

After a financial seminar I gave in the area early in 1997, a middle-aged couple came up and said they wished they'd heard my views on real estate a couple of years earlier. They have more than $1.4 million invested in their suburban yuppie palace and can get an offer of no more than $600,000 for it. Of course, they have to take it and lose $800,000, because the offers next year will be even lower.

> *The future of certain kinds of real estate is poor. Buyers don't want five bedrooms, outdoor pools or circular staircases in 5,000-square-foot houses on estate lots in the far suburbs anymore.*

And that is precisely the kind of properties that were selling at a huge premium in the Eighties.

Remember what things were like back in 1987? Here's a report from the *Toronto Star* headlined "Frenzy hits as buyers rush luxury rural homes":

About 100 frenzied homebuyers cried, begged and grabbed up proposed luxury homes worth between $500,000 and $900,000 each this week in a York Region subdivision that has yet to be approved.

"It was embarrassing. We had to halt the selling after less than 90 minutes and tell people to calm down," said developer Larry Hoffman, a partner in the Landford Group consortium that plans to build about 50 estate-size homes worth more than $15 million.

Jaguars, Porsches and other expensive automobiles lined rural Woodbine, blocked farm driveways and created havoc for police. Buyers from posh Metro residential areas like the Bridle Path and Post Road ran through mud to swamp the sales pavilion during a preview showing.

They plunked down $10,000 deposits and promised to pay an additional $15,000 before the end of the week on 25 of the homes before sales were halted.

Mostly they were young professionals, 35 and older, with children, one salesperson said. "It was incredible, like cowboys and Indians" in the land-rush days when governments offered a free homestead to the first settler who staked it out.

Prices of the homes were increased $35,000 during the first hour in an unsuccessful attempt to quell the buying tide, which subsided only after the last 10 houses were taken off the sales block.

"We had to do it," Hoffman said. "We were afraid of speculators grabbing them up and the last thing we want is to have people buying in hopes of reselling them for huge profits.

"We never anticipated anything like what happened," Hoffman said. "We just never thought people in the market would be afraid that land was going up faster than even they could afford. When we finally called the sale off, people were begging and crying. It was unbelievable. We didn't want that."

Geez. What a difference a decade makes. Today you can buy massive luxury homes in the same area for far below the cost of construction. And buyers are scarce. For some houses, nonexistent.

And, of course, along with changing real estate tastes come changing demographics. According to Statistics Canada:

- The average household size will drop from 2.7 people in 1991 to 2.4 people in 2016.

- The number of people living alone will soar by 70%, from 2.3 million in 1991 to 3.9 million in 2016, when they will comprise up to 26% of all households.

- The number of two-person families will shoot higher, from just over 3 million to almost 6 million in 2016, comprising a whopping 55% of all families.

- There will be at least a million and a half single-parent families, 50% more than today, most of them headed by women and 60% living below the poverty line.

Clearly the universe of potential buyers for "traditional" real estate is crumbling, a trend that will accelerate as time goes on, and that will likely torpedo the values of vast amounts of existing residential real estate.

What will become of all those large houses in the suburbs? You'll be able to get a deal on monster homes—no one will want them.

—Sharon Chisholm, Executive Director
Canadian Housing and Renewal Association

Already there is a lot of evidence that the kind of real estate people will want is changing quickly. According to the Royal Bank's Home Ownership survey, one in four Canadians expects their parents will live with them as they get older. And because there is also concern about the fate of the health care system, real estate buying considerations are bound to evolve. No need for a house close to a school. And no stairs, please.

"Whether building, modifying or renovating a home or condominium," the report concludes, "in the future Canadians will have to take into consideration the accessibility and layout of the living space as more and more citizens grow older and need to adapt to a different, and potentially more dependent, lifestyle."

Now entering the mainstream are concepts like the "accessory apartment" for a widowed mother of Baby Boomers. Built into their home, ideally it is "age-proofed," including features like contrasting colours on walls and counters, higher-wattage lighting, levers instead of door handles and repositioned light switches and outlets. "People fear age-proofing means an institutional look that may lower a home's resale value," gerontologist and designer Lori Molnar told *Chatelaine* magazine, "but it's not true."

Just wait a while—and "age-proofed" will be the hottest selling feature a piece of real estate has.

And then there is the issue of the "home office," the emerging workspace of the millennium. Today about 17% of us work from home. In ten years that could easily be a third of the population, especially as technology races ahead, making us more productive and turning traditional offices into expensive-to-maintain dinosaurs.

High-tech compatibility will be as sexy a feature for residential real estate in the New Century as size and gold-plated faucets were in the last decade. Lots of people will want to buy a house on a street where Mr. Rogers has provided his Wave. Coaxial Internet access will be what living on a bus route used to be.

Will you be a part of the retirement crisis?

I first predicted this in my 1995 book, *2015: After the Boom*, which shocked me by going on to sell almost 100,000 copies. To this day I am deluged with mail from people who have read it and suddenly realized they will be part of a retirement crisis that will affect millions of unsuspecting people.

This crisis is going to hit after the year 2011, when the Baby Boomers are turning 65. It will be the result of:

- The shocking investment habits of most Canadians, who have $650 billion in GICs earning less than 5% and who, in 1996, bought $5.7 billion worth of Canada Savings Bonds paying 3% in the first year and 6.2% for an entire decade.

- The failure even to come close to maximizing the tax-saving and investment-pumping potential of North America's best tax shelter, the RRSP.

- The collapse of the Canada Pension Plan, even after contributions were raised by 70%.

- The dramatic increase in life expectancy, especially for women. By 2017 almost 40% of the entire Canadian population will be over 50 years old, and just a quarter will be younger than 22. The average Baby Boomer today can look forward to spending about 30 years in retirement. To do that comfortably will take savings of about $800,000, which is roughly $750,000 more than average Boomers have today.

- The plunge in interest rates, taking the yield on fixed-income investments down to the lowest point in a generation. And with a deflationary environment building, there is no reason to believe rates will return to higher levels anytime soon. That means all those Canadians who thought they could get ahead by saving money can't. Savers can no longer cut it. They will run out of time unless they understand they need to become investors.

- The residential real estate meltdown that is now around the corner. Most people do not see it because current boomlike conditions in many markets have them hoping against hope the heady days of the Eighties will come back, excusing their bad investment habits and their miscue about where the housing market was headed.

Your house could be a wealth trap

The Eighties are not coming back. For all the reasons I have outlined, there is simply no chance that traditional residential real estate in most markets of Canada will avoid the decline.

In the future it could just be impossible to sell your house. There will be a glut of properties and not enough buyers. If things don't change quickly, millions of 60-year-old Baby Boomers will face the stark reality that the asset in which they had put the bulk of their net worth is evaporating.

> *Imagine what happened to a few thousand Bre-X shareholders in 1997 happening to millions of Boomers in 2011. Their wealth trapped in an asset free-falling in value, and for which there are few takers.*

This is why you need to know about The Strategy. Now. And you need to start using it immediately if you hope to avoid the coming real estate wealth trap. The good news is that today's financial conditions are ideal for a recovery from the real estate mistake. Interest rates are low, banks and trust companies are willing partners, and most of the population is totally unaware of the impending crisis. That means there still are ways for you to rescue the equity you have built up over the past years.

But you cannot delay. The evidence is everywhere, and it is suffocating.

Chapter 2

All the Rules Just Changed

When their parents or their friends bought their first homes, they typically bought more house than they could comfortably afford because they assumed that prices would increase year after year and their jobs would be secure forever. These young people take a more calculated approach.
—Don Lawby, President
Century 21 Real Estate Canada

Does anyone really need to wonder why many Canadians have been feeling more anxious about their financial condition in the 1990s?
—The Globe and Mail, May 19, 1997

My finances preoccupy me, more than the pressures of my job.
—RCMP Constable Christina Humphreys
Vancouver

Residential designers are already taking advantage of the growing wave of aging Baby Boomers by making light switches and electrical outlets more accessible, and adding seats and grab bars to bathtubs and showers.
—Residential Real Estate Report, Century 21

Y ou can't escape the fact that the most dominant features of Canadian society these days are financial anxiety and the greying of the Baby Boom generation. Just look at the bookshelf you pulled this volume from: Bestsellers of the past year have been David Foot's *Boom, Bust and Echo*, along with David Cork's *The Pig and the Python* and my own *2015: After the Boom.*

Why are books about demographics on the bestseller list? The same reason people are making a lot of money selling hair replacements, Redux and glasses with seamless bifocal lenses. The Canadian population is getting a lot older fast. And an aging population is disinflationary, as many more people are savers rather than borrowers.

That means inflation will continue to be subdued or even change to deflation. In turn, interest rates will stay low and commodities like gold, oil and real estate will languish.

Stunning changes are about to grip our nation. In fact, they already have, leading us to a social, financial, political and emotional precipice few are prepared to look over, let alone leap over. When the Bank of Montreal chose a Bob Dylan song to launch its electronic subsidiary, mbanx, it knew exactly what it was doing. The same for the world's biggest mutual fund company, Fidelity, selling its new funds to the music of Buffalo Springfield.

The Boomers are just not ready for what is happening to them. So our popular culture is spinning backwards as the Boomers search for familiar things. Randy Bachman, Mick Jagger and Rod Stewart are still on tour. So is Bob Dylan, competing with his own son's new rock group. Unfortunately this is just going to make the intergenerational wars even worse.

I think we know what lies ahead:

• More taxes

• Fewer services

• Pension tension

• Rising health-care costs

• Intergenerational warfare

• A retirement crisis

• Plunging values for traditional residential real estate

But at the same time we can also expect:

- Little or no inflation
- Cheap, cheap interest rates
- Surging corporate profits
- Soaring stock markets
- A massive inflow into mutual funds
- Rising values for New Century real estate (see page 44)

Let's look at each of these, then put them together and understand why they all point to one plan—I call it The Strategy—that makes the most sense for middle-class, middle-aged Baby Boomers anxious to secure their financial future.

1. Taxes. The assault on your wealth is already relentless and debilitating. But it is going to get a lot worse. The cost of health care will increase by 50% as the number of seniors grows by threefold. The Canada Pension Plan will collapse unless supported by more tax dollars. Every day, until the federal and provincial deficits are reduced to zero, the amount of public debt is increasing, and how will we be able to service that in 15 or 20 years when the economy slows dramatically because of the drag 9.8 million seniors will create?

Already Canadians pay up to 54.2% of their incomes in taxes to the federal and provincial governments, and that top tax rate clicks in at just $60,000 in income. In the United States taxpayers don't start paying the top rate of just 39% until they are earning more than $200,000.

You may think that we are at the tax wall, that it is simply impossible to squeeze more out of middle-class people whose real incomes have been eroded for more than a decade. But that is exactly what's going to happen.

- Ottawa has already decided that Canada Pension Plan contributions will increase by more than 70% to buy the scheme some time. That will cost us about $10 billion, as well as increase the payroll tax employers must cough up.

- The Seniors' Benefit, scheduled to replace Old Age Security (OAS) and the Guaranteed Income Supplement (GIS) starting in 2001, will seriously raise the taxes on middle-income Canadians, saving

Ottawa about $8 billion but reducing after-tax income for middle-class Canadians by between $3,000 and $7,000 a year.

2. Services. The planned move to the Seniors' Benefit officially signals the death of universal social programs—benefits that were once conferred on everyone. Under the new system, people who never save a cent for retirement will receive up to $18,400 per couple, tax-free, in the form of a guaranteed annual income. But people who do save for retirement and have an income stream from RRSPs or other investments will now pay more tax.

That means the system suddenly has a built-in disincentive to save. At the same time Ottawa has restricted your ability to sock money away into RRSPs, by reducing the period you can save by two years, and freezing the contribution limits right into the next century.

Expect more changes. The age at which the Canada Pension Plan pays benefits will probably be moved to 67. The amount you receive will be less than it is today. User fees are going to riddle your daily life, from use of the toll highway to visiting the emergency room.

3. Pension Tension. The majority of Canadians do not have a company pension plan. The Canada Pension Plan is teetering on the brink of insolvency. The average amount saved in an RRSP is just $31,000, and half the people in the country don't have one.

More than nine million people in Canada will be turning fifty over the next few years. The fastest-growing segment of the population over the next three years will be people between 45 and 54. Within two years there will be 400,000 more middle-aged Canadians. The fastest-growing age group over the next 20 years will be eighty-year-olds.

When today's youngest Boomers are retiring, the largest group in the population will be women aged 65. The second-largest group will be women aged 70. There will be more 75-year-old women than girls under ten.

Meanwhile the average RRSP contribution is a mere $4,000 yearly, and in 1997 we saved just 15% of what the rules allowed.

Pension tension? Soon you'll be able to cut it with a knife.

What does this have to do with real estate? Just about everything.

4. Health-care costs. An aging population cannot escape this fact of life because, on average, we consume more health care in the final six months of our existence than in all the years that go before.

According to the Canadian Institute of Actuaries, future costs of the current medical system are simply "unaffordable," estimated to rise by half. And already we cannot finance the system we have, as witnessed by hospital closures and the laying off of health-care workers across Canada.

The actuaries have called for a rationing of health care, along with a rush into preventative medicine and major cost control by government. As with the public pension plan, our pay-as-you-go health-care system is poised to plunge into crisis. Today's working Boomers are paying for the costly care of their parents. Soon it will be the GenXers facing a huge bill as the Boomers get plastic knees, heart valves and prostate therapy. Today people over 65 will cost the system $369 billion, so thank goodness the huge Baby Boom generation is in place to pay it.

But the health-care bill for the Boomers could be $1 trillion.

Who, exactly, will pay that?

5. Intergenerational warfare.

> **Why are there cuts in the education budget to the provinces when our kids will need more training to get good jobs in the future?**
> —*Voter Rita Caluori to Finance Minister Paul Martin during the 1997 election campaign*

That's an easy one—so Baby Boomers can have 6% mortgages. Actually Paul Martin told Ms. Caluori it was the provinces that had cut spending on schools, but that was a political answer.

Ottawa has done exactly what the largest single voting group in the population has wanted—cut the deficit so monetary policy can be eased, bringing interest rates down to a 40-year low and ensuring stable financial markets for all those people worried about retirement assets. The cost of the central bank's insistence on rock-bottom inflation was 1.4 million unemployed. But most of those were the children of the Boomers, not the Boom itself, with youth joblessness running at a stunning 16% nationally.

> **Make no mistake, this has resulted in one of the most promising overall economies of the entire twentieth century in Canada. As I will detail in the next section of this book, you are standing on the brink of the best economic years of your entire**

adult life. But they will only be golden if you have the assets and the experience to mine that gold, and they will come to an end sometime around 2010, just when GenX is hitting middle age.

We already know the system is incredibly tilted in favour of the Boomers, who control our political system. According to the Institute for Research on Public Policy, today's 20-year-olds will pay hundreds of thousands of dollars more in taxes than they will ever collect in benefits, while today's retirees will, on average, receive $121,000 more than they contribute.

This is not going to change anytime soon. Look, for example, at the Parliament Canadians elected in June 1997—almost 80% of the MPs are Baby Boomers or just slightly older!

BABY BOOMER PARLIAMENT

Age bracket	Number of MPs
Twenties	9
Thirties	32
Forties	114
Fifties	118
Sixties	24
Seventies	4

If today's next-in-line generation has to face what I believe is coming—an economic meltdown at the end of the next decade caused by the crushing weight of an aging population—just when they need to prepare for their own retirement, there will be intense anger. And that anger could come just when GenXers are in control of the political levers. Will they be willing to pay substantially more in taxes to support the aging Boomers?

How could they, especially in lean years for the economy? Who will take up the slack?

According to the Institute for Research on Public Policy, to correct the intergenerational imbalance now would mean slashing seniors' benefits, raising taxes permanently and downsizing government in a big way. But today's mainstream political parties, both federal and provincial, are building support with agendas of tax cuts, guarantees for seniors and guarantees of social programs. After all, guess where the votes are.

We are ignoring the reality that a population so lopsided as ours cannot sustain pay-as-you-go social programs like our health care and public pensions. It is unfair, indeed immoral, for us to bury our heads in the sand and pretend we can't see what's coming.

6. Retirement crisis. It will hit shortly after the second decade of the new century arrives. Then 9.8 million Boomers will want to retire. Those who can, will. But most won't be able to.

So, laws dictating mandatory retirement ages will be repealed and many Boomers will work until they no longer can. There will be a lot more extended families living under one roof. Health care will be rationed at first, then you will have to pay for it. Getting sick after 2010 is going to be an expensive proposition.

Government pension benefits will be available only to those who have no other income. The introduction of the Seniors' Benefit in 2001 will start that process, as it guarantees liveable government income only to those with family incomes of less than $26,000. The Canada Pension Plan, the other leg of retirement income, probably will not survive past 2010 despite the reforms Ottawa made to it in the late Nineties, jacking up the premiums and investing pension assets in the financial markets.

We have to face the fact that most Canadians do not have a corporate pension, and that Baby Boomers today—actually most Canadians—are vastly behind in their retirement savings. The average RRSP is less than $35,000, and yet it will clearly take a retirement nest egg of well over $600,000 to finance 25 or 30 years of retirement, as life expectancy explodes higher.

Ironically we're in a period now when many Boomers could easily grow the assets they need to finance their later years and avoid being part of the crisis, if they knew how. They would stop investing in the wrong assets: guaranteed investment certificates, savings bonds and money market funds. They would use the hundreds of billions in home equity, which is now paying them no return whatsoever and which, of course, is now at extreme danger of being lost.

7. Plunging real estate.

> *In Toronto, when a listing comes out on a Tuesday, you don't wait until Friday. You go within the hour, or it will be gone.*
> —Ruslana Wrzesnewskyj, Re/Max Professionals, Toronto

Don't panic if you lose a bidding war. Take a deep breath—another will come along.

—*Judy Ludwig, Realty World-Tempo, Calgary*

You bet, real estate is finishing the decade on a high. In fact, it is the best market of the entire 1990s—the product of pent-up demand, job growth, cheap mortgage rates and prices that by early 1996 had plunged as much as 40% in some markets from levels set in the late Eighties.

It's now clear prices overcorrected. In 1996, for example, more resale homes changed hands than ever before in Canadian history, and yet nationally prices were lower by 2%. They dropped 1% in Toronto and 9% in Vancouver.

In 1997 prices jumped higher—up 11% in the country's largest housing market, the GTA (Greater Toronto Area), which accounts for more than 30% of all Canadian sales. Even recreational property took off, with Re/Max reporting sales of cottages 10% to 50% higher in the first half of 1997, with prices jumping 20% from the year earlier.

"I think you are seeing a case of more disposable income heading to cottage country," says Re/Max's Pamela Alexander. "The reason is

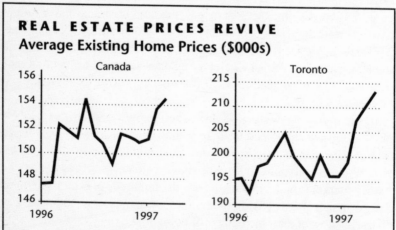

REAL ESTATE PRICES REVIVE
Average Existing Home Prices ($000s)

Cheap mortgage rates, a good economy and rising consumer confidence have modestly boosted real estate prices from their depressed state of the mid-1990s. Many people will be deceived into thinking 1980s-like conditions are returning. Those who buy expecting that will be sadly disappointed.

Source: Nesbitt Burns

consumer confidence. And maybe people have made a lot of money in the stock market and are thinking it's time to buy a cottage right now."

And that would be a huge mistake, unless you go into it with your eyes wide open to the fact that this is a lifestyle choice, not a wise investment decision.

Real estate once again has spun its web over a generation that grew up believing a home equalled financial security. The lowest mortgage rates in four decades made it seem reasonable to borrow $300,000. After all, the cost is just $1,900 a month at 6%, only a few bucks more than renting a three-bedroom apartment in Toronto or Vancouver.

But few have realized that if the same amount of money was used to leverage, or pay the interest on, an investment loan, you could borrow $450,000 at 5% to invest in mutual funds earning 12%—building wealth by $54,000 a year with all the interest payments tax-deductible.

Instead, the Nineties are finishing with legions of people walking into significant mortgage debt that will have to be paid off in after-tax dollars over the next twenty years, just as real estate enters a phase of serious decline.

This is because there will be too much of the wrong kind of residential real estate for sale in the next century. Too many people will have too much of their net worth tied up in housing that will be increasingly difficult to sell. Millions of Boomers will be trying to cash out their home equity at the same time, just as the universe of potential buyers shrinks. House prices will fall. People will look back at the buying frenzy that characterized the last 36 months of the Nineties and shake their heads.

How could they have been so foolish?

Why did they miss the obvious fact that the makeup of the population made residential real estate—at least the traditional kind of real estate everybody wanted—such a bad idea? Why didn't the experts tell them that in the future people wouldn't want that kind of real estate, that instead they would want, and need, financial assets? Wasn't it apparent that inflation and interest rates were so low because we had an aging population, which is exactly what diminishes the value of real assets like real estate over time?

How could it be that other real assets like gold and oil were half the value they were during the Eighties, and yet real estate values were rising? Wasn't this a clear sign of a speculative market based on false assumptions?

Almost 20 years after the last real estate bubble burst, how could it be happening again? And this time, sadly, when most of the people putting their wealth into residential real estate would not have time to recover.

If this picture frightens you, then you understand perfectly the dangers on the road ahead. But there are also opportunities, and in my mind they outweigh the problems for those who are ripe to take action.

If you know what to do, your real estate can protect you from the coming adversity that will cause a retirement crisis for millions of people. In fact, for most of us, it is the last and best hope for achieving a decent and carefree retirement. Real estate can be the source of capital that allows you to build wealth surely and swiftly in the environment that is, mercifully, on our doorstep.

Could the demographers be wrong?

There exists no evidence in either the academic literature or through a presentation of the stylized facts on demographics that would lead one to conclude that demographics deserves anywhere near the attention it has attracted as an explanation for much of what has been witnessed in the 1990s concerning the overall Canadian economy.

—*Derek Holt, Economist*
Royal Bank

Is the impact of demographics overblown? Is it a fad? Are people who believe the makeup of the population affects things like the housing market misleading us into wrong investment decisions?

Bank economist Derek Holt thinks so. His 1997 economic report charts new housing starts to debunk the theory that Boomers have had a profound impact on real estate. Holt concludes that because starts soared in the Seventies, when Boomers were too young to buy, and dropped in the Nineties, when they should have been buying, shows other factors are more important—like interest rates, consumer confidence, unemployment and real incomes.

He also wonders how it could be that if the Boomers today are flooding money into mutual funds and stocks, the personal savings

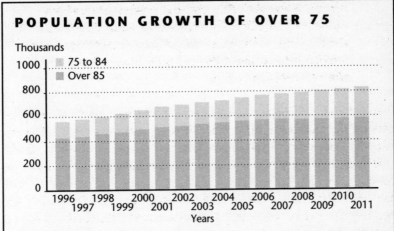

POPULATION GROWTH OF OVER 75

The Baby Boomers start retiring in droves after the year 2011. But already by that time, the number of people older than 75 will have vaulted higher. The Canadian population is greying as never before, and housing needs are going to change dramatically.

Source: Care Planning Partners Inc. and Statistics Canada

rate is going down, not up. More evidence, he says, that other factors are more important—namely low inflation, low interest rates, employment and income. As for booming stock markets, we're told they are the result of low rates and rising corporate profits, not Boomer investment dollars chasing mutual funds.

Finally Holt compares the Canadian and American populations, which are quite similar in age groups. The fact that U.S. economic growth and housing construction has far outstripped ours also lends weight to the theory that demographics plays only a bit part when it comes to moving the economy.

His conclusion: "Looking into the future, the outlook for the housing market and consumer expenditures remains favourable as low interest rates and job gains will continue to feed growth in this sector of the economy."

And, in the short term, I think he's right. Real estate values probably will continue to climb as the 1990s come to an end, thanks to cheap mortgage rates, rising employment and more buyer confidence. There is no reason to believe rates will jump anytime in the next decade, nor inflation, either. These factors are bullish for housing values.

But I believe economists who miss factoring in the *soul* of the economy don't give us a clear picture of what has really happened, or what will. The Baby Boomers today control corporate Canada, Parliament and, especially, the media. When they start to feel old, it will have a debilitating effect on the economy, just as fifteen years ago it was the opposite. Then the 30-something Boomers did have a dramatic impact on real estate, despite rising interest rates, runaway inflation and unaffordable home prices.

Fifteen years from now, real estate will still have a future, but in a radically different way—again, because of the Boomers. It is critical to know what kind to sell or drain the wealth out of, and what to buy or hold. I detail that in Chapter 7.

Meanwhile it is time to build wealth.

Chapter 3

The Coming Boom Is Here!

That's right, the best economy so far. Better than the swinging Sixties or the earnest Fifties or even the roaring Twenties—eras people think of as golden ages. It's now: 1997.

—Fortune *magazine, June 9, 1997*

There are short-term profits in real estate. The market has been all but abandoned for five years, and exceptional bargains exist. But properties bought today should be sold within five years.

—2015: After the Boom, *October 1995*

As I write this, I sense most Canadians have absolutely no clear idea what has happened to the North American economy, what is about to happen or how long it will last. Most people are afraid of the economic future, which is why they have been making disastrous decisions about their money. How else can you explain $650 billion tied up in GICs that pay less than 5%? Or Canadians rushing to snap up $5.7 billion worth of Canada Savings Bonds in the autumn of 1996—bonds that pay just 3% in the first year and just 6.2% if held for a decade?

They don't get it. They think losing money in a volatile investment that may decline in value is the greatest risk possible, when an even greater risk is that most people—especially Canadians my age (48), women in particular, because of today's stunning life expectancy—will run out of money.

Canadians are so preoccupied with trying to avoid risk that they are seriously at risk. And that preoccupation has kept them from looking up and seeing a golden age unfolding.

We are in an economic boom of unprecedented strength and importance, one that will sweep the value of financial assets higher in a period of non-inflationary growth. It will likely last all the way to 2010 or longer, when a period of decline will lead to depressionlike conditions after 2015. Between now and then, there is not a moment to lose.

Let's review the climate that exists right now:

1. There is no inflation. In fact, as I have already argued, we are closer to deflation than inflation. The core inflation rate is hovering somewhere near 1.5% in Canada and a point higher in the United States. Part of the reason is demographics, as our aging population focuses on saving rather than borrowing, reducing the demand for money.

The result: money is cheap. The value of financial assets will continue to rise sharply. Savers will run out of time to accumulate the retirement assets they need. The value of commodities will continue to be depressed. The fuel of the real estate boom of the 1990s—rising prices—is simply absent from the economy this time around. The current hot market is a false one.

But little inflation and cheap money guarantee economic growth, rising corporate profits and soaring stock markets. Is this not a dream scenario for investors in financial assets? Do you *really* want to be diverting most of your money into mortgage payments on a property that might only decrease in value?

2. Interest rates will not rise. Not substantially, and not for years. We are not going back to double-digit rates. Don't expect in your lifetime to see a 10% GIC again. Or a 10% mortgage. The cost of money has collapsed—because of inflation, because of demographics, because the burden of government is falling, because of global trade, because of powerful and unstoppable trends.

These cheap rates have accomplished what everything else could not—the creation of hundreds of thousands of new jobs for the Canadian economy. By the end of 1998 the jobless rate should be in

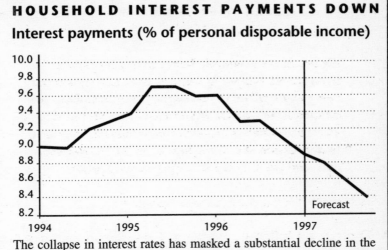

HOUSEHOLD INTEREST PAYMENTS DOWN

Interest payments (% of personal disposable income)

The collapse in interest rates has masked a substantial decline in the personal savings rate. Cheaper mortgages and credit card balances are easier on household finances and bullish for the economy.

Source: Nesbitt Burns

the 8% range and on its way down. As employment increases, so does consumer confidence, spending in durable goods and economic growth. It is the kind of virtuous circle economists dream about.

- Canadian household expenditures began to revive in early 1996 after falling behind the rest of the economy since 1990. According to Nesbitt Burns economists David Rosenberg and Doug Porter, household spending on goods, services and housing will grow almost 10% by the end of 1998.

- Collapsed interest rates mean household debt is a lot easier to pay and so the domestic balance sheet is vastly improved. And while lower savings rates hit older Canadians, they put more spending power into the hands of younger borrowers—and that is positive for the economy.

- Canadians are growing their assets faster. Households now own more than three dollars of financial assets for every dollar they owe in consumer and mortgage debt.

- All this translates into confidence. Already business confidence is at a record high, and consumer confidence will soon join it as new jobs pop up. And that means . . .

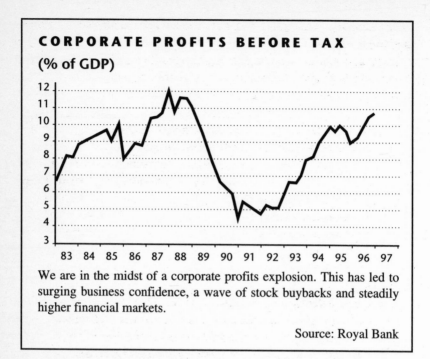

CORPORATE PROFITS BEFORE TAX
(% of GDP)

We are in the midst of a corporate profits explosion. This has led to surging business confidence, a wave of stock buybacks and steadily higher financial markets.

Source: Royal Bank

3. Corporate profits will keep surging. Canadian corporate earnings are at record levels. In the first quarter of 1997, for example, they totalled more than $25.5 billion. The six major Canadian banks are now routinely generating annual earnings exceeding $6 billion. American corporate after-tax profits also hit a record level in 1996 of $378 billion, and that was three times the profits seen in the booming Vietnam-war-fed Sixties.

A mid-1997 survey of the National Federation of Independent Business found small U.S. companies had the highest levels of optimism in the history of the 23-year-old poll.

Convinced both sales and profits will surge higher, corporations on both sides of the border have been buying their own shares back on the open market in unprecedented numbers. Companies like the CIBC, Royal Bank, IBM, Canadian Tire, Shell Canada, Imperial Oil and others are doing it. In the first few months of 1997 American corporations announced spending of almost $30 billion to buy their shares back.

Why? Simply because they know share values are going to rise, and this is a path to corporate wealth.

It seems unthinkable anybody could go wrong buying up the shares of Canadian banks, with combined profits of more than $6 billion and rising steadily. Why would you put money *in* the bank, when you can *buy* the bank?

And, of course, record profits combined with a growing demand for financial assets by Baby Boomers will guarantee that.

CORPORATE CANADA ON A ROLL

Total non-financial industries in Canada

	First Quarter 1997 (billion $)	% Change from 1996
Operating Revenues	329.3	6.1
Operating Expenses	310.2	5.9
Operating Profits	19.1	9.9
Net Profits	9.8	27.1
Cash Flow	23.2	16.0

Low inflation and interest rates, rising employment and income, as well as a super-charged U.S. economy and declining Canadian dollar combined to energize both the domestic and export sectors. Stronger activity was particularly noticeable in new housing construction, retail trade and manufacturing. On the foreign trade side, merchandise exports broke yet another record during the quarter. The healthy economic environment created excellent conditions for Canadian businesses.

—Bank of Montreal
Business Financial Performance, June 1997

4. Stock markets will soar. Maybe as never before. In fact, it's already happening, isn't it? The Dow Jones Industrials rushed 5,000, then 6,000, then 7,000, then 8,000 with nothing more than a 10% correction in early 1997 that was erased in just weeks. On Bay Street the TSE 300 has also risen to record levels, despite the threat of Quebec separatism.

The market is being fuelled by low inflation, cheap rates, rising corporate profits and the raging torrent of money starting to flow from people cashing in their low-yield fixed-income investments like GICs and savings bonds.

It is going higher. Vastly higher.

In his latest book, *The Next Twenty Years of Your Life*, futurist Richard Worzel predicts that

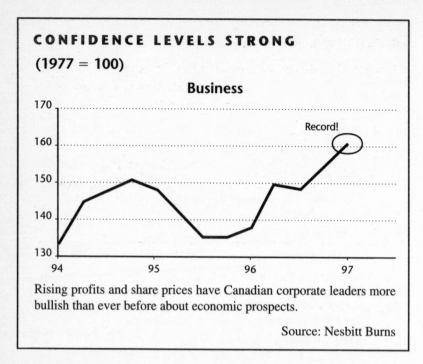

CONFIDENCE LEVELS STRONG

(1977 = 100)

Business

Rising profits and share prices have Canadian corporate leaders more bullish than ever before about economic prospects.

Source: Nesbitt Burns

when the leading edge of the Boomer generation reaches age 70 and the trailing edge reaches age 50, the TSE 300 will likely have punched through the 30,000 mark—an increase of almost five times its current level. Indices in the United States, such as the Dow Industrials and the S&P 500, will experience similar explosions owing to similar demographic trends. Accordingly, you should have a significant portion of your assets invested in stocks.

That's for sure. And as stock values explode higher (taking mutual funds along with them), the idea of sitting on a large amount of your net worth in residential real estate will become bizarre—especially when that real estate begins again to decline in value.

As Worzel rightly points out, most of the stock market explosion is likely to take place within the next ten years, meaning the investment decisions you make now will be the most important ones of your entire life.

But could the market suffer severe volatility on its ride higher? And what about twenty years from now? Could there be a crash when all the Boomers take their money out?

Well, expect volatility for sure. Another 1987-style crash is a distinct possibility. In fact, as markets climb, the odds of a 500-point, single-day

OVERTIME HOURS WORKED

3-month moving average of y/y % change

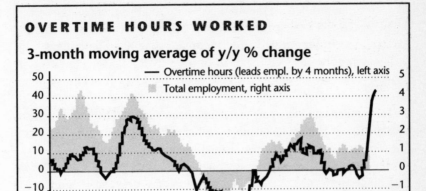

The number of overtime hours worked in early 1997 soared dramatically and, according to Royal Bank chief economist John McCallum, that presages an explosion in new jobs—700,000 by the end of 1998.

Source: Royal Bank

correction become much greater. But remember, only those people who sell will take a loss. Those who hang on will see the value of their investments eventually recover, then appreciate further. Too many Canadians are not aware of just how temporary most bear markets turn out to be.

SIX DECADES OF BEAR MARKETS

Years	Market decline	Duration (months)
1941-2	32%	16
1946-7	28%	13
1948-9	18%	13
1956-7	20%	20
1961-2	28%	7
1966	22%	8
1973-4	48%	22
1976-8	19%	16
1980-2	27%	22
1987	33%	5
1990	19%	5

Source: *The Mutual Fund Letter*

As for a meltdown on the markets when the Boomers start to retire in droves? I don't think it will happen, because interest rates will stay low and the Boomers will need income to live on. That means they will stay highly invested for most of their lives, and the markets will remain relatively strong for the better part of twenty, if not thirty, years to come.

The sooner you are a part of it, the more secure your future. I believe that for long-term investors there is virtually no risk in the stock market. The real danger lies in *not* investing there.

But there are certainly those who disagree. I deal with some of their arguments in the next chapter, but be warned, it's very scary stuff. And, I think, very wrong.

5. Some real estate will be in great demand. But not the traditional kind. The future of big family-type houses with lots of little bedrooms and swimming pools is a bleak one. The market is glutted with this kind of real estate, and it will be selling for pennies on the dollar in a decade's time.

If you own a house like that and your kids have left home, then you should leave home, too. Sell now in this relatively good market. Sell while you can—it could be your last chance.

In the future people will still want to own real estate, but as the Boomers age, they will dictate that different kinds of properties are in demand. I call this New Century real estate and it will include:

• Urban low-rise condominiums

• Bungalows in established residential areas

• Duplexes jointly owned with children or friends

• Retirement communities in smaller cities designed around golf courses and artistic venues

• Time-share apartments and beach homes in the sunbelt

• Independent living units with universal control centres for appliances, lights, drapes and security systems; integrated Internet access; home offices; and room service

Real estate does have a future. In fact, a bright one. But the way we think about housing is going to change, along with the makeup of the

EXISTING HOME SALES

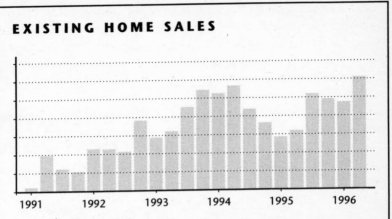

The collapse in mortgage rates has coincided with a surge in resales across Canada. More homes sold in 1996 than in any previous year, and yet the average price declined because a preponderance were first-time buyers. That later changed as more move-up buyers began to believe a real estate "cycle" was beginning. It wasn't.

Source: Nesbitt Burns

population. There will be more couples without children, more singles, more single-parent families and a lot more older Canadians. The demand for the kind of real estate most people have today will evaporate, along with the equity they have in it.

It's time everybody knew about The Strategy.

PART 2

Chapter 4

The Strategy
1998–2010

This is certainly the simplest real estate and investment strategy in the country. It has two parts, the first of which just about every Canadian knows, if not follows, the second of which more people will have to learn and execute:

In the first half of your life, build equity.
In the second half of your life, use that equity.

In the following pages I will explain The Strategy and show you how to implement it.

- If you do not own real estate now, I'll show you how to buy the right kind at the right price and with the right mortgage. This advice can save you tens of thousands of dollars. It can also prevent you from making a horrible mistake—putting hundreds of thousands of dollars into the kind of real estate that has no future.

- If you do own real estate, I will give you winning strategies on how to sell it, taking advantage of today's best housing market in a decade. Do not delay. As I write this, the residential real estate market is hot just about everywhere with low mortgage rates and rising investor confidence. The time to strike is now.

- If you don't want to sell, or can't, I will show you how to use the equity in your house to build financial assets, increase your net worth and seriously reduce your tax burden. If you're over 40, you must do this. The consequences of sitting on your equity, believing today's rising real estate values will continue, are extreme. You must take action while it is still possible. In fact, there could hardly be a better time.

Imagine, wealth virtually without risk. It's now possible thanks to the amazing convergence of low interest rates, solidly rising financial markets and an economic rebound in North America that will last well into the new millennium, in fact, for a dozen golden years. Today you can dip into your real estate equity and put that money into financial assets with confidence, as long as you are a long-term investor. I will show you how to do that, and where to put the money.

Remember: you must have confidence and determination, and the ability to see beyond the short-term fears of others. There are many who will caution you to turn back, because they see risks in this strategy.

They may be people from your parents' generation, who see real estate as something completely different from what it has become. To them a house is a "real" asset, one you can touch, paint, be proud of and live in. Because it is physical, it has value. It exists. Meanwhile many older people view financial assets with intense suspicion, and financial markets with raw fear. The only paper assets they are comfortable with are ones with a guarantee—GICs, savings bonds, term deposits—those that today pay virtually no rate of return because the old laws no longer apply.

Today, as I have already stated, the value of real assets is declining and financial assets rising. I cannot imagine the conditions under which this trend would be reversed. The largest generation in Canadian history is now past its real estate–crazy years and is focused on building wealth. The amount of money going into financial assets like mutual funds is turning from a trickle into a torrent. The kind of housing that people will need, and want, is changing fast. The old rules of real estate investing—buy big, pay it off completely and hold on for capital growth—have been swept away. In their place . . .

The new rules of real estate
1. It is now just shelter, not an investment. Buy it if it lowers your shelter costs.
What you ultimately want and need is wealth, not a house. In the future you will be able to buy fabulous real estate for a fraction of its price today. So the game plan is to live wherever you can lead a pleasant life at the lowest shelter cost, which will free up more of your income to invest in financial assets.

So when, and where, it makes more sense to buy, go and buy. Where it's cheaper to rent, then rent.

Right now, in just about every major market in Canada, it costs less to buy a home with a minimum down payment and to carry it at today's mortgage rates than it does to rent. In Toronto, for example, the average 1997 selling price is just over $210,000. With a 25% down payment ($52,500) and a 6% mortgage, the house will carry for $1,000 a month. To rent an equivalent three-bedroom apartment would cost $1,500 a month. With 5% down (just $10,500), the house carries for $1,280 a month—still cheaper than rent.

Today this is also the case in Halifax, (especially) Montreal, Winnipeg, Regina, Saskatoon, Calgary and Edmonton. Across the country, according to the Bank of Montreal, the costs of financing a home are about 22% lower than the rental costs of equivalent accommodation—because of mortgage rates, higher rents and falling real estate values.

Only Vancouver breaks the mould, where the highest real estate values in Canada mean homeowners still face costs about 17% higher than renting.

So obviously owning real estate in Vancouver is a bad idea, especially given what's been happening there. The anticipated great boom of 1997 did not materialize, and now this is the most dangerous real estate market in Canada. A flood of new investment money from Hong Kong never arrived, as Asian investors decided they could live with the Chinese takeover of that former British colony on July 1, 1997.

As Miro Cernetig accurately reported in *The Globe and Mail*:

> Go down almost any street on Vancouver's west side today and you will find For Sale signs on the new stucco mansions that Caucasian Vancouverites label monster homes. Many are empty. Their owners, who, after seeing their original cash investments double or more in the past decade, are liquidating real estate to put the capital back into high-growth investments in Asia . . .
>
> As the real estate board now likes to say, it's a buyer's market on the west side. Where the bottom is, however, is still anybody's guess.

Danger, danger, danger.

2. Buy the kind of real estate people will want.
This much is obvious—the real estate market will continue to be dominated by demographics, and that means the Baby Boom generation.

Boomers' families are growing up and moving out. So the number of two-people households is going to mushroom, and traditional multibedroom homes will be tough to sell.

What will the Boomers be looking for in real estate?

- *Independent living, convenience and comfort.* That means low-maintenance and a good location. Look for a revival of urban condominiums.

- *Activity.* This is a self-centred generation of egomaniacs, after all, who will wear blue jeans and listen to rock music into their eighties. They will refuse to age gracefully or feel old. So at an age when their parents were eyeing retirement homes, the Boomers will be hot to have bungalows on golf courses.

- *High tech.* The home-office revolution is just taking off. Half of all the jobs created in 1997 were the result of self-employment. Boomers will want to live where there is good Internet access and a mall nearby with a Business Depot and Future Shop in it.

- *Security.* The number of single seniors has exploded and will continue to explode. Canadians have the second-longest life expectancy in the world (after the Japanese). Baby Boom women will routinely reach 90 or 95 and be the healthiest seniors in human history, living alone and very concerned about personal protection. Developments and buildings offering elaborate security measures will be in high demand. Already the gated communities are appearing. In fact, Tridel's high-security development in Toronto—Mondeo—made national headlines when its units first opened behind the barriers and the guardhouse.

- *Flexibility.* Families are changing. Today's Boomers are having to deal with elderly parents, typically widowed moms, and many of them do not like the experience and will not want to repeat it. The Boomers are witnessing parents doing the wrong things and suffering because of it, such as hanging on to the family home for decades after it was appropriate. Often a father's death forces the sale of the house, with his widow then having to find rented accommodations and suddenly coping with an entirely different lifestyle—underground parking garages, apartment corridors, no garden and no front porch to sit on.

The Boomers will do it differently. Semis, duplexes and bungalows have an awesome future.

3. Sell the kind of real estate with no future.

The Baby Boom generation is just about finished with its suburban multibedroom housing, although most of its members don't realize that yet. If you own this type of house, the kind that is now increasingly expensive and time-consuming to maintain, then sell. The market in the future will be glutted, with few takers.

Also bail out of recreational properties that are not the very best in their class. The overall market for cottages and hobby farms will shrink drastically, but there will always be buyers for the best stuff, at Whistler or on Lake Joseph. The rest will go cheaply, partly because buyers will have increasing difficulty finding lenders to mortgage such properties.

I have serious reservations, too, about one of the newest real estate crazes—lofts. These are most often residential units in converted industrial or commercial buildings in the city core. They are appealing now to younger buyers and the alternative-lifestyle crowd, but they have the smell of a short-lived fad all over them. Remember granny flats?

4. Don't keep more money than you have to in an underperforming asset.

This should be a self-evident truth to everybody, but it is amazing how many people deny reality. Most residential real estate is not going up in value, which means owners are not benefiting from the tax-free capital gains that residential real estate can provide. So why keep money there? The return on the equity is zero if your house is not climbing in value month over month. At the same time, by using The Strategy, you can take that equity out, invest it to increase your wealth and write the interest off against taxes you already pay from other sources of income.

Face it. The old reason to pay off your house and then just sit on it has ended. Inflation is dead and most residential real estate values are about to go into a long and steady decline. Your house is likely an underperforming asset and chances are you simply can't afford to be making a 0% return on it. After all, if you're like most Canadians, most of your net worth is sitting in that house.

What happens when you can't sell it ten years from now?

Well, if you had taken the equity out and invested it for those ten years while getting a break on your taxes, you likely won't care. But if you hadn't, it might be a disaster.

5. Don't be daunted.

I know, the doomsayers are all around us, and a number of reviewers in the financial press will call me a radical. They will use that word "leverage" to describe my strategy, a word that has negative connotations for lots of people, especially those who attach it to the stock market and then hark back to the generational meltdown of wealth that took place in 1929.

But this is not 1929, and today there are solid reasons for believing the old "safe" investment strategies are actually fraught with risk.

I have great respect for financial writer Gordon Pape, but his strategies are among those that now alarm me greatly. He counsels people to be intensely risk-averse at a time when too many Canadians will end up being both old and poor because they did exactly what he advises.

Consider his recent advice on leveraging, published in many Canadian daily newspapers:

On the Money with Gordon Pape
Leveraging – a dangerous road to riches

PAPE'S TIP: *Borrowing to invest can be hard on your bank account.*

When the stock market rises, people become interested in borrowing to invest – leveraging, as it's called. New loan options, such as home equity lines of credit, have made large amounts of locked-in money available. You can increase your profits, but you can also lose big time.

Pros

- Money is cheap right now, so borrowing costs are low.
- Interest on money borrowed to invest is tax deductible.
- Leveraging allows you to earn substantially higher capital gains in a rising stock market.
- Investing in a portfolio of high-quality mutual funds will limit downside risk.

Cons

- Most loans used for this purpose have their rates adjusted monthly. If rates move higher, the cost goes up.
- Leveraging will expose you to greater losses in any market correction.
- Unless you invest in a guaranteed product, stocks and mutual funds are subject to potentially heavy losses.
- The anxiety could affect your health.

If you do use leveraging...

- Understand all the risks involved and make sure your health and financial well-being won't be adversely affected if markets move against you.
- Take a long-term view. Have a plan with at least a five-year time horizon.
- Consider using a guaranteed product that will protect you from loss, e.g. stock-indexed GICs. The new Guaranteed Investment Funds (GIFs) offered by Manulife are another possibility, but you must hold for at least 10 years for the guarantee.

TIP: Use leveraging to make up any unused RRSP contribution room. You won't be able to deduct the interest, but the tax refund helps reduce your investment risk.

Source: *The Toronto Star*

Here are some counterpoints about leveraging, or borrowing against the equity in your home, you must remember when pondering advice like Gordon Pape's:

- Leveraging is not the same as borrowing money from a broker to buy stocks or mutual funds on margin. When you do that, and the market value of those securities falls below the loan amount, you face a "margin call," and have to cough up the money.

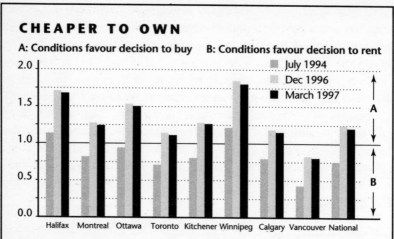

CHEAPER TO OWN

A: Conditions favour decision to buy   B: Conditions favour decision to rent

In just about every city in Canada, lower mortgage rates in the late Nineties mean it is cheaper to buy a home than rent a comparable one. The single exception is Vancouver, the most dangerous real estate market in the country.

Source: Bank of Montreal

That will never happen with a home equity loan, because the loan is against your real estate, not your investments. If your stocks or mutual funds go down in value, so what? You trigger no loss unless you sell, and even then, you are not required to pay off your home equity loan.

And if your real estate falls in value, to the point where the home equity loan is greater than the worth of your home, you can always take a walk. Then it's the bank's problem.

- Yes, interest rates could rise. And your interest-only home equity loan payment could also rise. But let's remember that the likelihood of a substantial rate increase—taking the cost of money above 10% again—is close to nil as long as inflation stays below 2% and society is dominated by savers, rather than borrowers.

  In any case, the interest on your home loan is tax-deductible. So what downside can there be if rates rise, when you can just use that increase to reduce the income taxes you pay?

- Using a home equity loan will not expose you to greater losses in any market correction, even if you unwisely decided to sell your investments at a low point. Then you would still owe exactly what you borrowed, not more.

- You cannot rationally borrow money against your home at, say 6%, to invest in a guaranteed product (such as a GIC) paying 3% or 4%, because the interest on the loan is no longer tax-deductible. After all, how can Revenue Canada classify it as an "investment loan," when you are losing money by taking it?

  You are only allowed to deduct interest on a loan if the money is invested for a "reasonable expectation of profit." That means investing in mutual funds that might go down qualifies, because they also might go up. But investing in a guaranteed investment that will not give you a profit because its yield is guaranteed to be less than the loan cost does not qualify.

- **As for the anxiety that borrowing against your home might bring, in case your investments temporarily decline, consider the anxiety of running out of money before you run out of life.**

  For most Canadians, especially those who refuse to manage risk, that is a far more likely event.

Chapter 5

How Dangerous Is This?

When the bubble bursts it will hurt all of us. The savings of this generation could easily be slashed by 50%. It could even be worse.

—Harry D. Schultz
U.S. bear market analyst

Let's make sure we all understand what it is I'm suggesting you do: borrow money against the equity you have built up in your house over all the years it took to pay off the mortgage, and use that money to buy financial assets like mutual funds or stocks.

There are three clear advantages:

- You insulate yourself from the coming crash in values of traditional-family real estate because you withdraw equity now while the house still has a higher value. This limits the losses that are coming for millions of homeowners. Remember, the threat is deflation, and deflation kills real estate.

- You take money sitting in your equity—which is earning you 0% because, despite some hot pockets, most real estate values are stagnant or hardly outpacing inflation—and you put it to work, building wealth. If you can invest in mutual funds growing at the rate of 12% a year, you double your money every six years. So $100,000 borrowed against your equity in 1997 will turn into $800,000 by the year 2015 if you can maintain that rate of return. (And I suspect that won't be too hard to accomplish.)

- You are going to save a lot of money on taxes. That's because a home equity loan is considered the same as an investment loan, so the interest is tax-deductible. If you borrow $100,000 at 5%, the annual interest cost will be $5,000 (and you take an interest-only loan, of course, because you never want to pay a home equity loan back). That $5,000 you can deduct directly from your taxable income. If you are in the 54% tax bracket, that saves you $2,700 a year in tax.

> *So, borrowing against your equity to invest makes a lot of sense. In fact, for a lot of middle-aged and middle-class people like me, this is probably the sanest thing you can do. After all, the days of steadily rising real estate prices are history. I just wish more people would realize that before they run out of time.*

But what of the dangers?

The faint of heart will point to the potential for rising interest rates and plunging financial markets. If rates jump, then it costs you more to service the home equity loan. Will that happen? Could we go back to the mid-1980s when loans were 20%? And what about a stock market crash? After all, stocks tanked in 1929 and stayed low for years and years. Then in 1987 the Dow Industrials fell more than 500 points in a day, wiping out the wealth of people who had just bought stocks and mutual funds, and then had to sell them off to cover loans.

Could either of these things happen again? Exactly how much risk *is* there?

Where interest rates are going and why

Interest rates will remain low for years.

> *The Eighties are not coming back and the economy will have strong noninflationary growth for more than a decade. Then things will fall off a cliff.*

That is why this book focuses on the crucial period between 1998 and 2010—the best years to build your wealth through investing in financial assets, and using real estate to do it.

Money is a commodity and its price is interest. That price is affected by supply and demand, so when there is a surge of borrowing, the price goes up.

And so we had the Eighties, when the Baby Boomers were forming households and gorging on mortgage money. The level of mortgage debt exploded, and the cost of money did, too, with interest rates rising through the 20% mark, accompanied by a surge in inflation.

Today the Boomers are rapidly turning into savers and investors, not borrowers. Instead of asking for money, they are lending their money—to RRSPs, to the banks, to companies in exchange for shares and to mutual funds in return for units. And because close to 100 million people in North America are in this age group and doing the same thing, the demand for money has collapsed and so has its price.

Are things likely to change?

What could possibly happen in the next twelve years to stimulate enough demand for money that the price shoots higher? What incredible event could take place that would reinflate the economy? In the second half of the Nineties corporate profits have come roaring back, along with job creation, consumer confidence and spending; yet we've had no inflation and even lower interest rates. The fact remains that in the U.S. alone 42 million jobs disappeared thanks to corporate downsizing. That's hardly inflationary.

Those who warn you that interest rates could explode are the Chicken Littles of the millennium.

Where the stock market is headed and why

There are many people who believe stock and mutual fund values could collapse. One of the scariest scenarios was painted by entrepreneur and investor Andy Sarlos in the book *Fear, Greed and the End of the Rainbow*, published right around the time of his death in mid-1997 by Key Porter Books.

Similar sentiments were echoed by legendary investors Warren Buffet and John Templeton as the market soared near the 8,000 mark in New York, outpacing all but the most extreme bull-market predictions.

They are all wise and successful men, for sure, but they also all appear to have become market timers—people who seek to ratchet their wealth higher by trying to anticipate market gains and declines. If you are, say, Warren Buffet, with $18 billion to preserve, this might make sense. But for the average Canadian, trying to build wealth, market timing can be dangerous indeed. Just about every survey shows long-term investors are better off to buy and hold, rising through the inevitable market corrections.

Then there are charts like the following, which can strike terror into the heart of anyone. It traces the ominous parallels between today's market action and what took place in the 1920s, which led to a financial meltdown in October 1929. Wealth was erased, and the market declined for years. In fact, the Dow did not regain its 1929 high until 1950! Combined with other factors, it all resulted in the century's worst economic conditions, which we now know as the Great Depression.

Could it happen again?

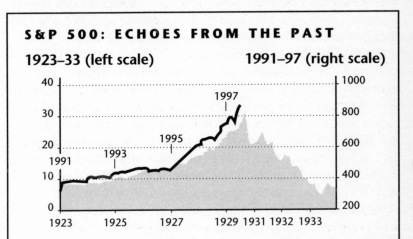

S&P 500: ECHOES FROM THE PAST

1923–33 (left scale)   **1991–97 (right scale)**

Could the run-up in financial markets of the late Nineties be just an echo of the run-up that preceded the crash of 1929? This chart suggests it's possible, but the U.S. economy is not in recession, the way it was at the end of the Twenties.

Source: Argus Research Corp., New York

This chart is the product of New York–based Argus Research Corporation. Jim Solloway is the co-president and research director, and he told *Financial Post* columnist William Hanely that, yes, there are worrisome parallels, but history is not about to repeat itself.

The demand for equities (stocks) took on manic proportions in 1928 and 1929, and threatens to do so now. Indeed, by some measures, the stock market is more overvalued in 1997 than it was in the late 1920s.

While the parallels are fascinating, the differences are even more compelling. When the market collapsed in October 1929, the U.S. economy had already been in recession for two months, although no one knew at the time.

As we now know, that recession turned into depression when combined with international trade protectionism, bad monetary policy and the worst climactic conditions in decades, which fostered an agricultural collapse.

Today there is no economic downturn. In fact, growth in the late 1990s is exceptional and shows every sign of continuing well into the new century. The Royal Bank and Bank of Montreal are forecasting massive job growth. The move towards government tax cuts is growing. Bank profits are at record levels. Consumer spending has come roaring back. And then there are those Baby Boomers . . .

In a single month in 1997 Canadians poured in excess of $10 billion into mutual funds—more than any month ever before. That was February and it was RRSP season. This scene is going to be repeated for many Februaries to come, as the Boomers pour unprecedented amounts of money into these financial assets, which in turn invest largely in stocks. After all, with someone turning fifty every seven seconds for the next ten years, the need to grow retirement assets is intense.

This is the future, and it is one reason stock values will continue to rise. Where else is money going to go when guaranteed investment certificates and Canada Savings Bonds pay just 6% interest for a ten-year investment? And that could soon look like a good deal!

Now look at the next chart from the seminal 1993 work by American Harry Dent, called *The Great Boom Ahead*. Dent has done something very arresting and sensible—taken the birthrate in the U.S., lagged it by 49 years and then imposed the stock market's performance since 1920. The result is dramatic, showing that markets rise and fall in almost an identical way, further emphasizing the impact of demographics on financial assets.

If Dent's analysis is correct, the stock market has just embarked on an explosive path higher. It could be a monstrous decade-long rally that will see the value of financial assets peak somewhere around 2010, before dropping substantially to a trough around 2020, which will herald another twenty-year-long bull market.

There are powerful reasons to believe this will happen. In fact, this is already where we are—on the side of the mountain, climbing higher.

The whole foundation of The Strategy is that there's a lot more upside potential for financial assets (stocks, mutual funds, bonds) than there is for real assets (gold, oil, real estate). In fact, money left in the equity of residential real estate could be lost as the Baby Boom generation in particular turns its attention to wealth creation through those financial assets.

THE SPENDING WAVE EXTENDED

The 49-Year Economic Forecast

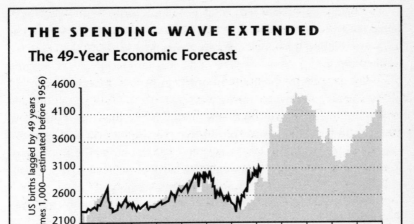

Futurist Harry Dent's superimposition of births over the stock market's path lends weight to the theory demographics moves markets. If he's right, the greatest boom, then one of the worst crashes, lie before us.

Source: *The Great Boom Ahead*

Those who question this, or raise fears that money could leap in value and financial markets plunge, are still traumatized by the experience of the Eighties, which is exactly what happened then.

But the Eighties are dead and buried. They are not going to return. Inflation is finished, the cost of money will stay low and the rush into financial assets will not peak until about the year 2000. You might as well peak with it.

But what if I'm wrong?

My belief is that the great bull run of the 1990s will come to a crashing halt as the supports propping it up crumble from the sheer weight of a 7500 or 8000 Dow. What remains to be seen is whether a normal market break becomes a mega-crash. If millions of novice fund investors panic, they will trigger an avalanche of selling not seen before.

—*Andy Sarlos*
Fear, Greed and the End of the Rainbow

During his lifetime Andy Sarlos made and lost fortunes as a stock trader, and was at one time manager of $6 billion. His death in 1997 left us with a prediction that stock markets were about to plunge in a crash of biblical proportions, erasing 50% of the market's worth and destroying the retirement savings of Baby Boomers and everyone else. Yup, 1929 all over again. This time, maybe worse.

His argument is that too much money is chasing too little value. Companies would rather use profits to buy back their own shares, raising the value, than use the money to expand and create more jobs. Lemminglike Boomers, all moving in a herd, plough money into financial assets without understanding the consequences.

Market value erases real value, as people do things like pay $574,400 for the late John F. Kennedy's cigar humidor at a Sotheby's auction. Sarlos saw a world gone mad with more money tied up in stocks and bonds—about $65 trillion—than the actual value of the world economy. He was worried interest rates might rise, causing inflation, or the cost of living would suddenly drop, causing deflation. But either way, with overvalued markets, an event like that would trigger collapse.

And then a wave of selling would hit mutual funds like a tidal wave—funds that are cash-poor and cannot cope with so many redemptions. Sarlos predicted that by the time this financial Armageddon was over, 60% of those mutual funds would have disappeared. A meltdown, pure and simple.

And in his 1997 book, *Fear, Greed and the End of the Rainbow*, he has this to say about people like me:

> Indeed, some advice gurus are actually telling their audiences to remortgage their houses to invest in the stock market, playing on the boomers' fears about eating dog food in their old age. They call it an "adventurous" investment strategy. I call it dangerous. We are in the last leg of this bull, and no one can say how far it will go because we are in the midst of craziness. This sort of thing—telling homeowners to "suck the equity out of your home and play the market"—proves how insane it actually is.

Andy Sarlos died believing in a real estate renaissance, and also that history moves in cycles, with commodity prices about to make a comeback as financial assets hit the skids.

Well, what do we make of all this?
As I have already stated, it is entirely conceivable, maybe even likely, that we could have another 1987, with the Dow Industrials and the TSE plunging by 15% or more in a single day. After all, in the past six years there has only been one market correction of 10%, and that took place in the first half of 1997. Hardly much for a market that has gained a stunning 900% since its low point in August 1982.

So the key is this: would a 1987-style dump turn out to be another brief violent correction (and a buying opportunity), or the start of a grinding, multiyear meltdown (definitely a time to sell)?

Nobody knows for sure, but increasingly I do not believe the Baby Boom generation is as gullible or financially naive as Sarlos states. My experience across Canada at the front of seminar rooms packed with people shows me the interest in financial information and the thirst for it. This is likely the most financially literate and astute generation ever, exhibiting a growing sophistication and understanding of risk. Would everybody bolt for the exits if there was another 1987-type crash?

Sarlos argues that the last time we all had more money in real estate than in stocks, so the impact of the crash was muted. This time, he says, stock assets exceed real estate assets, which is not a true statement. Canadians have $270 billion in mutual funds and more than $600 billion in bank deposits and guaranteed investment certificates. Real estate holdings run into the trillions.

In addition, he ignores, I feel, the awesome advance in the public's understanding of how financial markets work in the decade that separates us from the last crash.

But then there is Bre-X
And Timbuktu, Delgratia, Cartaway and other junior resource companies that investors pushed into the stratosphere in the late Nineties, only to see them collapse in scandal and disgrace. But the story was not the collapse itself, but rather how investors almost willed the share values higher, adding enormous value on the flimsiest of information, often just wild rumour.

In saying this is a sign of danger, Sarlos and others are absolutely correct. Value was added to those companies by investors who were acting out of greed instead of knowledge. And if the Bre-X factor is at play in large parts of the market, then we certainly have much to fear.

The worst case scenario

It's something like this: not a Sarlos-style meltdown, robbing the wealth of an entire generation, but another 1987-style market crash caused by an overvaluation of stocks and a disregard for the market fundamentals, but this time taking two years or so to regain the lost ground.

This is not a disaster for people currently ten or fifteen (or even five) years from retirement, because as long as they do not sell, they will not take a loss of capital. It will just take a little longer to dust away the effects of the sell-off.

The market will recover for all the reasons outlined here, including:

- No inflation and continued low interest rates

- The lack of investment alternatives

- The overarching need for millions of people to achieve growth in their financial assets

- The longevity explosion

- A rising tide of corporate profits and solid noninflationary economic growth in North America

- The power of demographics

- Smart investors like you

PART 3

Chapter 6

_____●

In the First Half
of Your Life . . .

I t's been the Canadian thing: buy a house, pay off the mortgage as fast as you can and build equity. Equity means ownership, and as you pay down the mortgage principal, the amount of equity grows. It's the difference between what you owe and what the piece of property is worth.

People buy real estate for different reasons. For some it's to get the lifestyle they want, whether that's in a downtown condo in the swing of things on Vancouver's glorious Robson Street or an acreage on the sea in Nova Scotia. For others an address gives them identity—Mount Royal, Rosedale or Shaughnessy. Some folks have an incredible emotional attachment to their homes and believe that people who rent rather than own are shifty fly-by-nighters who probably don't vote, either.

A lot of Canadians treat home ownership like sex—they do it without really thinking why. It's just a part of life, this powerful drive to own some dirt.

Most people buy badly, though. They don't know cardinal rules like selecting the worst house on the best street or considering resale appeal. Buyers choose houses based on the most personal needs—proximity to work, lifestyle and family needs. Those are important considerations, for sure, but the house is also an asset as well as a place to live, and at some point you will need to unload it.

There is nothing wrong with buying a house, as long as you have an overall financial plan. After all, you need a place to live, and real estate is shelter. If you can get that shelter more cheaply by buying than renting, then there is no question that you should buy.

But buying a home properly requires a lot of care and research. Paying it off in the most efficient way is critical. And never before has it been so important to buy the right kind of house. Fail on any one of these points, and real estate can turn into an enemy of your wealth.

In 1996 residential real estate entered the miniboom that I predicted a year earlier would happen. As I spelled out in *2015*, it would be the result of cheap mortgage rates, better economic news and pent-up demand. The boom first hit starter homes, as legions of renters suddenly realized they could own for the cost of leasing. Sales took off, but because it was mostly lower-end real estate selling, overall prices in 1996 actually went down, as the middle and top ends of the market languished.

In 1997 the first-time sales subsided and more of a move-up market developed. Prices started to increase as the miniboom matured. As I write this, there are relatively few buyers across the country for the top end of the market. In fact, in Vancouver it has tanked, while in Toronto there is not much offered for sale, with the priciest digs—like former retail czar Robert Campeau's Bridle Path mansion (yours for $6 million) —taking three years to sell.

My view has not changed since 1996 when I wrote: "How long will this boomlet last? Maybe a couple of years, maybe less. It will not signal the start of another cyclical run-up or bull market for housing, but rather something more short-term. For astute Baby Boomers, it will be an opportunity to sell—not to buy."

But that does not mean in any way that real estate is a black hole and people without houses today should stay renters. I am convinced it is quite possible to make major tax-free capital gains in real estate today if you know what to buy and what to avoid.

Real estate markets across Canada

FIRST HALF OF 1997			
City	**Sales change from 1996**	**Price**	**Change from 1996**
Victoria	1.1%	$214,882	0.6%
Vancouver	8.5%	285,323	−2.8
Calgary	32.8%	141,128	4.1
Edmonton	13.1%	110,495	1.1
Saskatoon	0.5%	96,766	14.6
Regina	−11.1%	82,927	10.9
Winnipeg	14.5%	84,804	−1.2
Toronto	26.1%	208,163	6.1
Ottawa	10.6%	141,506	2.0
St. John's	25.0%	93,503	2.4
Saint John	−7.6%	89,758	15.3
Halifax	5.1%	107,190	3.7
Canada	16.5%	162,721	2.7

Source: Canadian Real Estate Association

The new rules of real estate buying

1. Only buy when it decreases your living costs

With money invested in financial markets giving returns of between 10% and 20%, and with the stunning need for most people to build retirement assets, it's hard to justify putting cash into real estate that, if you are wildly fortunate (as the previous chart shows), might appreciate at 5% a year.

Yes, the capital gains made on residential real estate are tax-free while capital gains made on stocks and mutual funds are taxable. But don't forget that you'll lose a large chunk of your real estate equity in commission when you sell, and also that real estate, unlike financial assets, is illiquid. It can take months or years to sell, while stocks and funds can be converted into cash in hours.

And, as I argue here, with an aging population and a shrinking universe of homebuyers, real estate values may be headed for a long decline after the premillennium miniboom we are now in has run its course.

So why buy a house?

Only if it makes your life cheaper than renting. Period. That's it—even (and maybe, especially) for today's first-time buyers.

Affordability of housing nears a record

37 per cent of renters could buy

high of 38.6 per cent set in 1985, the federal housing agency said yesterday.

months of the year by taking out a record number of loans under the First Home Loan In-

would mean that a record 4 per cent of renters could aff starter homes.

Source: *Canadian Press*

I realize that for most young couples, owning a home is still a dream, because it was ever thus for their Boomer parents, and their parents' parents before them. But that was then, and this is now. Today's young people should only tie up money in real estate as long as it increases their cash flow.

That is a new reality—and a big change. It used to be that you threw everything you had into a down payment, got a long five-year mortgage term and spent the next 10 or 15 years trying to pay down the principal and living off Kraft Dinner.

Today that is a recipe for disaster for young people. Why? Because of what's going to happen to the economy. As the Boomers start to retire after 2011, it will slow dramatically because of the drag nine million cranky, egocentric, demanding and expensive seniors will create.

But, as I have also argued, the time between now and then should be wonderful—ideal years to create wealth by investing in financial assets. So the last thing young new buyers should do is waste those years feeding a mortgage on a property that may be worth a lot less in 2015 than it was in 1998.

Only buy when it gives you more cash flow than renting, and then plough that extra cash into financial assets. Fortunately right now in just about every major city (except Vancouver) you can own more cheaply than you can rent. So do it. And remember:

- Buy with the minimum down payment—5%.

- Don't cash in your RRSPs for the down payment, even though this may look attractive under the Homebuyer's Plan. Better by far to leave the money in your RRSP and properly invested in growth-oriented equity mutual funds.

- Take the shortest cheapest mortgage. Don't lock in for five years, although this is the traditional logic because a long-term loan stabilizes financing costs. With rates stable and, if anything, falling, going short is the best bet. Study after study shows that over the long haul borrowing short saves money.

2. *Know what you can afford before you look*

The down payment plus the amount you qualify to borrow determines the price of the house you can buy. In general the house should not cost more than two and a half times your gross earnings. And the mortgage payment, plus realty taxes, should not exceed about 30% of your income.

The simplest, most effective and smartest move is to be preapproved for a mortgage. That way you know precisely how much the bank will advance. More on preapprovals later in this chapter.

3. *Buy the worst house on the best street*

Location, location and location. These are the three most eternal and important things about real estate. By its very nature, real estate is immovable. It's worth what it's worth because of where it is.

For that reason you should pay much more attention to where the house is situated than to its condition, because anything that's wrong with it can be fixed. But a bad location will live with you as long as you hold the asset.

So always buy the worst house on the best street, not the other way around. Buy in the middle of the block, instead of on a corner, because you will have more privacy and less traffic. Buy in an established neighbourhood instead of a transitional area. Buy into a "demand" area rather than a cheap one. There's usually a very good reason why it's in demand.

Schools and transportation services are important to most people, so buy where there is good access to them. But not beside them. A home next to a school or a bus stop will sell at a discount to one a few houses away, because of the nuisance and noise factor. A condo on the first floor will sell more cheaply than one on the twenty-first floor, because it gives you a view and more quiet—a better location.

Don't buy a house next to a service station or dry cleaner or certain industrial operations, for obvious environmental reasons. Anywhere near a hospital or fire hall, land values will fall because of the sirens and disruption. Treed neighbourhoods carry a premium over newly developed—and treeless—ones.

Then there is the question of urban or rural or something in between. I definitely believe city homes will command a sharp premium over suburban ones as the population ages. And I completely disagree with David Foot's prediction that there will be a big boom in rural and recreational properties down the road. To the contrary, I believe aging Baby Boomers will want to cocoon in the city, not invest in $5,000 garden tractors and live a half hour's drive from the nearest bottle of chardonnay or video store, let alone emergency room.

Condos on transit lines, bungalows by a golf course, gated retirement communities, infill garden homes—just some of the types of real estate with a future, and how much future depends on the precise location: city, neighbourhood, street, block and lot.

4. Buy what you can sell later

The day you buy should be the day you start preparing to sell, because selling some kinds of real estate in the future is going to be next to impossible. Canadians live in one house for an average of seven years, which is not all that long. And now, with an aging population and far too much of the wrong kind of real estate about to come on the market, resale should be at the top of every buyer's mind.

This is another reason not to buy the most expensive house on the street, because it's probably about as developed as it's going to get, with limited upside for appreciation. Better to buy something you think is a bargain, because the next guy is likely to think the same way.

How big a house? Well, the traditional thinking was to buy as many bedrooms as you could afford—four or, even better, five. But that has changed. Now with the number of two-people families set to explode, five bedrooms will be a liability, not an asset. After all, in the future buyers will want one to sleep in, perhaps one for a guest room and, most important, a home office.

Parking is important. So is a property with no easements or rights of way—which can lead to legal nightmares. Detached homes will continue to command a premium over semis and town houses. Buyers want front and back yards; however, the trend will be to smaller spaces, more meticulously planted and landscaped.

Imagine yourself seven years older. What would you look for in the ideal home? Then buy it.

5. Use the new technologies

> **Gone are the days when people had countless hours to spend leisurely perusing neighbourhoods for open houses and For Sale signs.**
>
> —Simon Dean, President
> Royal LePage residential

The Internet is revolutionizing real estate. Royal LePage says its web site helped to sell more than $15 million worth of real estate in the first year of its existence. The first day the Toronto Real Estate Board's site was operational, it was swamped with close to 30,000 hits. As I write this paragraph, I just did a search on the Net under the query heading of "real estate," and more than 1,359,900 entries popped up!

The World Wide Web has turned into an unbelievably useful tool for preshopping the market. Most major real estate companies have their own web sites, crammed with listings. Many also offer mortgage calculators so you can immediately determine the cost of carrying a home.

Real estate boards are now putting their whole multiple listing service (MLS) inventory on line. For example, the Toronto board (www.real estate.ca/toronto) now has the largest number of local listings in North America, as well as a sophisticated search engine that lets you find properties based on their asking prices, location, type and features.

The MLS also has a site (www.mls.ca/), which contains more than 130,000 listings, also with a search function. The site will eventually include both video and audio information.

One of the Web leaders is Royal LePage (www.royallepage.com). It already offers a demonstration of what's to come—QuickTime VR (virtual reality), which gives you a 360-degree view of a property you can move through, using your mouse. (It does require the download of a 2.5 megabyte browser, which can take a half-hour.) LePage is also about to launch virtual tours of properties on its web site, the first major company to do so.

Equally exciting is the ability to get a mortgage over the Internet. In fact, now you can instantly preapprove 24 hours a day. One great service is the Online Mortgage Explorer, which offers instant access to a number of lenders, as well as valuable borrowing information. Web site address: http://www.mortgage-explorer.com.

And the banks themselves are jumping into Internet service, offering a plethora of on-line mortgage services. A leader here has been the Bank of Montreal (www.bmo.com). Its site will help you calculate how much you can afford to pay for a house, how to sell, how to determine closing costs and, of course, how to apply on-line for money. It takes about 15 minutes to find the right mortgage, after going through a series of options, and then another 30 minutes to complete the application.

Other resources include the Canada Mortgage and Housing site (www.cmhc-schl.gc.ca/cmhc.html), The Mortgage Store (www. mortgage-store.com) and Cebra (www.themortgage.com).

So it is now possible to preshop the real estate market and view in a hour more properties than you could see in a week from the back seat of an agent's car. You can instantly determine the carrying costs and then move to another site and actually secure the financing. This means when you actually do hit the market, you'll be an effective and powerful shopper.

Never before has such empowerment been available to real estate consumers. Use it.

> *How to buy a good home at a decent price, stabilize your housing costs and have potential for a tax-free capital gain (which are the only reasons to buy).*

The object is to get the right kind of house in the right place at the right price to minimize your exposure to long-term declines. To achieve that, you don't have to know half the things that are in other how-to real estate books.

All the questions you need answered

How do you choose an agent?

Real estate agents suffer a reputation similar to used-car salesmen, and it is almost always unjustified. A good agent is indispensable for finding good real estate. You cannot go through this process alone, and there is absolutely no need to. After all, the agent costs you nothing, because it's the seller who pays the commission, not the buyer.

> *It's simply amazing the amount of work a good agent will put into finding you the right house, without earning a dollar in return until the whole operation is complete. This is why you must be loyal to the agent you select and not two-time him or her by shopping the market on your own while the agent does the same thing.*

Sure, search the Internet for interesting listings, but don't go to an open house without your agent, or certainly not without stating at the door that you have an agent and giving his or her name. Failure to do so would cut your agent off from receiving any of the commission when it's paid upon closing.

A good agent will:

• Find out what you're looking for, what kind of house in what price range and in what neighbourhood.

- Search the market, going through computerized MLS listings, driving key streets, seeking willing buyers and polling colleagues about potential and actual listings.

- Immediately notify you of any relevant new listings hitting or about to hit the market.

- Prescreen properties on the market, usually in special agent open houses before offers are accepted.

- Provide you with "comparables" to properties you're interested in— similar houses in comparable locations or price ranges that have sold recently.

- Give you the selling history of properties, so you can gauge whether the sellers themselves bought high or low, how much they may have invested and their expectations.

- Inform you of the length of time a property has been on the market, so you know whether the seller is just out of the gate or has been on the market for months and is hot to dicker.

- Give background information on the neighbourhood, schools, services, transportation, shopping, population mix, traffic patterns and development plans.

- Help you determine the condition of the house and what repairs may be needed, at what cost.

- Advise you on market conditions and suggest what an offer might contain in terms of price and conditional clauses.

- Help write and deliver the offer to the seller, then stay and negotiate on your behalf with the seller and the seller's agent. Then your agent will bring the offer back if there are changes, and advise you on how to proceed.

- If asked, help arrange mortgage financing, find a home inspector, a mover or a contractor.

- Be there when it's time to sell, knowing the property's strengths and weaknesses and lining up potential buyers.

In short, the agent is central to everything. I know, when I get into my agent's white Cadillac, he will have the latest listings with him, the price history of each and comparables. I know he has prescreened the properties to be viewed and can give me information on local market conditions I could never get on the Internet or from any book. He is a road warrior in the marketplace and my best defence against buying the wrong property or paying more than is absolutely necessary.

But how do you find this person?

Well, like finding a good financial adviser, this is not an exact science. The quality can vary widely. You have to shop around, so here are a few suggestions:

- *Get an agent who knows the area in which you want to live.* This is crucial, because he or she needs to be a local expert. You can drive around and see who seems to be active in the area, judging from names on For Sale signs. Or drop into a couple of local real estate offices, ask for the manager and ask for help in finding the kind of person you're looking for.

- *Ask around.* Often the best recommendations come from friends or people at work who have recently bought or sold.

- *Go to open houses* in the area you're interested in and meet the agents hosting them. They might be interested in helping you or have a colleague who will do so.

- *Use the Internet* to preshop your future neighbourhood and see who the movers and shakers seem to be. You can E-mail a few agents, giving them some details of what you're looking for, then judge the quality and depth of their responses.

- *Interview a few agents*, being up-front and telling them the process you're going through.

- *Contact the local real estate board* and ask for some names of people it recommends in the area (although this does not guarantee integrity or quality).

If all this seems like a lot of work, then you are getting the point perfectly: The agent is absolutely key to your real estate strategy's success. He or she can save you tens of thousands of dollars in negotiations and even hundreds of thousands in steering you towards the right property. The agent is your eyes and ears in an unfamiliar place, where you need all the good intelligence you can get. He or she is the one representing your interests in what can often be hostile dealings with the vendor. Take some care.

After you find an agent and start looking at houses, be very specific about what you do and do not like with each. This allows the agent to focus on those properties most likely to meet your needs and goals, so everybody's time is not wasted.

Finally, be aware that in most areas the real estate agent is legally working for the seller, even if he or she has been recruited by you. This normally doesn't affect anything that your agent will do on your behalf, but the agent has a legal responsibility to tell the seller anything that might affect the decision to accept or amend your offer. So, if you told your agent you were really willing to offer more money than you initially did, that info could be passed on. However, in some jurisdictions, an agent can now *exclusively* represent the buyer, so make sure you check with the real estate board.

How do you choose a lawyer?

Again, carefully. This is another person that can save, or cost, you a lot of money. The sad reality is you can't buy a house without a lawyer, except in B.C. or Quebec, where the deal can be handled by a notary.

Now, a lot of what lawyers do would be totally unnecessary if it weren't demanded by other lawyers. So expect a blizzard of paper when the deal closes, along with a few extra charges. The lawyer's role is .to make sure you end up with clear title to the property and not inherit any problems.

Why get a lawyer before you submit the initial offer to purchase?

- It's a good idea to have the lawyer review your offer before you submit it to the seller, because he or she might recommend a clause or two to protect your interests. If the property is a condo, with its associated complexity, then you definitely need the lawyer involved at this point.

- Once your offer is accepted, the deal could close in as little as 30 days. During that period a great deal of legal work has to take place, so if you burn up a week or so finding a lawyer, you could end up with a rushed, and therefore sloppy, job.

Why is a lawyer essential, and what needs to be done to close the deal?

- You need to get clear title to the land on which the house is located. If you are taking out a mortgage on the house, there won't be any choice about it—the lender isn't going to fork over a lot of money without assurances you have clear title to the property. So any claims or liens against that title have to be discovered and dealt with before closing. The lawyer will have somebody go to the local land registry office and search the records to see what gives. On closing, you can expect your lawyer to give you a history of the property, based on that search.

- The lawyer will contact all the utilities to see if the vendor has paid all bills. If the vendor hasn't, then the amount owing can come off the selling price. Ditto for municipal taxes, and the lawyer will obtain a certificate saying they're up-to-date and also that the property meets zoning requirements.

- You need to make sure that the house is on the lot and that nobody else's home is encroaching on your land. For this you need a survey. The lawyer uses it to confirm that fences are indeed on the lot lines and to discover any easements or rights of way that would give a neighbour, the municipality, hydro or the gas company the right to use part of your land now or in the future.

    Because things like that can cause hassles, they also affect the property's value. You might not want to complete a deal once you've seen the survey; you might at least want to renegotiate it. Your offer should stipulate that the seller provide you with an up-to-date survey, at his or her expense. If there is no survey, then don't do the deal—unless you're willing to pay a few hundred dollars to have the survey done yourself.

- You need to be the legally registered owner of the property. The lawyer will register you, your spouse, both of you or anyone else on title. In a marriage situation, this is usually not that important because provincial family law acts stipulate assets like real estate are equally divided if there's separation or divorce. If you and your spouse decide to both be owners, the lawyer will register joint tenancy, which means if one person dies, the survivor will automatically gain ownership, regardless of what any will stipulates.

- On closing day or just prior to it, the lawyer will have you come in to sign a lot of bewildering documents and give you the bad news about closing costs, which usually amount to about 2% of the purchase price. The lawyer is responsible for dealing with the vendor's lawyer, the bank giving the mortgage, the insurer (if mortgage insurance is involved) and handling any problems that arise.

The two lawyers meet to square things away. The new owner's name is recorded in the land registry office, and keys are released, usually to your lawyer, after closing. Within a few weeks a fat envelope will arrive in the mail, and inside will be the lawyer's complete accounting of everything, including the statement of adjustments and, of course, the fee.

How much does the lawyer cost?

Most lawyers will charge you a standard flat fee for a normal residential real estate transaction, usually in the $500 to $700 range. But there may be more to pay if the deal runs into complications or is out of town. And then there are all those irritating charges many lawyers pile on for things most people in business would never dream of charging extra for—telephone calls, mileage, parking and (most irritating of all) photocopy fees.

Make sure you discuss up front what it's going to cost you in legal fees, and if the lawyer won't disclose it, find another lawyer. By the way, legal fees are not carved in stone and are always negotiable.

As for finding a good lawyer, many of the same rules as finding a good agent apply: ask people you know for recommendations. Ask your agent. Ask the local law society for a list of names. Make sure the lawyers you talk to are real estate specialists, because experience is all-important.

> **And never try to save money by using the same lawyer as the seller. This is a blatant conflict of interest, because the buyer and the seller have completely different agendas.**

Do you need a home inspector?

Can you recognize a termite tube? Do you know what a 220 amp service looks like? Can you tell when an asphalt roof needs replacing? Would you know urea formaldehyde insulation if you fell over it?

No? Then you need a home inspector. And there are very few conditions under which you should make an offer without a clause stating that the offer is conditional on a satisfactory (to you) home inspection at your own expense.

Houses are complicated structures, and getting more so with the advance of technology.

You cannot make a judgement about the structural soundness of a place in the typical 15 or 20 minutes you have to view it. And in a steamy real estate market, that may be all the time you get before submitting an offer.

So you need an inspector. That means inserting a clause into the offer saying it is conditional upon your receiving a satisfactory report within a few days after the offer is accepted. If the seller balks at this, then he or she probably has something to hide, like a major drainage problem outside a foundation wall that has just been hidden by a new coat of waterproof paint. A little item like that can cost you $7,000 to repair.

Some points to remember:

• Home inspectors are not licenced by anybody, so references are crucial. Ask your agent and lawyer for some names. Find out how long the company has been in business, if it has insurance, and ask to see a sample of the reports it generates.

• You will need to act quickly, so line up an inspector before you make the offer. The inspection typically will have to be completed, with the report in your hands, within three to five days.

• This is going to cost you at least two or three hundred bucks, more if you ask for special testing to detect radon gas in the basement or the quality of the drinking water.

On the day of inspection, be there. Do the whole thing with the inspector, because in addition to discovering the condition of the house, this is a great chance to learn how things work. You'll be thankful, once you move in, that you know where the central water shutoff valve is or key electrical circuit breakers.

A good home inspection covers all kinds of things, including the foundation, roof, electrical and plumbing systems, furnace and air conditioner, ceilings and floors, insulation, sewer and septic, basement and attic, kitchen and bathroom fixtures, windows, chimney, drainage patterns, porches, driveway and brickwork.

The inspector will not tell you what the property is worth, nor offer to make any repairs (at least, he shouldn't). During the inspection you will get a verbal report, followed immediately by the written one.

And if there are problems?
Then you have some options:

- You can walk away from the deal if the report reveals a problem too big or expensive to deal with.

- You can renegotiate the deal. If the place needs foundation work, then you can ask that it be done prior to close at the vendor's expense; or the price can be altered to reflect the cost of the work you'll have done after closing.

- In general, give the seller a chance to make the repairs because, especially in a weak real estate market with few buyers around, his or her lawyer may accuse you of using the inspection clause solely to cancel the deal.

Unlike new houses, resale homes have no guarantees. What you buy is what you get, so get some help.

TEN QUESTIONS TO ASK YOUR HOME INSPECTOR

1. Do you have a list of clients I can contact for a reference?
2. Are you a member of a recognized industry association and does it have a standards code?
3. Are you affiliated with a contractor or renovation company?
4. How many homes have you inspected?
5. How much experience do you have with homes in this particular location?
6. What kind of a report will you provide: written or checklist?
7. How quickly after the inspection will you provide the report?
8. How long will the inspection take?
9. Do you have Errors or Omissions insurance and for what amount per house?
10. Can I come along during the inspection?

Source: Century 21 Canada

How tough can your offer be?
As tough as you want. The buyer is almost always in the driver's seat, unless the market is sizzling and bidding wars erupt for prime properties. That is occasionally the case, but not usually.

This is the time for the adrenalin rush. It is the second-sexiest moment of the whole process, just a little less exciting than the moment you push the key into the front door lock for the first time.

The offer is your weapon, your sword. The first strike is critically important in setting the scene for the duel with the seller. And it *is* a confrontational situation—because you have radically different goals. The seller wants out at the highest possible price with the biggest down payment and the fewest complications. The buyer wants in at the lowest price with nothing gambled and the most protection.

The right offer will elicit the sign-back you want. It will draw the seller out, forcing him or her to respond to you, and once you have the sign-back, you are again in control. More tingles.

Of course, the offer is a complicated legal document, and real estate lawyers have been known to write entire books about its various elements. But forget all that, because you are going to show your offer to your lawyer before presenting it. Besides, the key player here is your agent, who will help you craft the right deal—depending on three things: the vendor's situation, market conditions and your desire to get the house.

• If the vendor is highly motivated, your offer can be a lowball one that tries to scoop the property at a very cheap price. Or you can go for all kinds of extras—things in the house you want included in the deal (and everything is up for grabs). But if the vendor is just fishing the market to see what offers will surface, or if there's a lot of competition among bidders, then the offer has to be instantly appealing—no conditions and a good price.

• Market conditions are critical. In sellers' markets prices are higher and buyers have to pounce to get the place they want. In buyers' markets prices decline and sellers are happy to see an offer, allowing more flexibility.

  In the early to mid-Nineties, it was a buyer's market in Canada, with the exception of the Lower Mainland of B.C., where things were hopping. As the decade closes, the situation has been reversed. The market is active almost everywhere (especially Alberta and southern Ontario), except in the Lower Mainland, where it's become squishy.

• And the offer will reflect your intensity as a buyer. If you really have to win that house (a bad attitude to have), then you will give the seller what he wants. If you are a realist (lots more houses will come along), then you will take care to stick to your price range and not be pulled higher in a battle of wills with the vendor.

There is no limit on how many times an offer can go back and forth between the parties. Each time changes are made and initialled, and a new deadline (called the irrevocable date) is established. At some point you will either cut a deal or decide to take a walk. If you don't get the price you want, you can always just let the offer expire and go in with a new one days or weeks later.

Your agent is the person who orchestrates all this, delivering the offer, presenting its contents and arguing your position. The agent will bring you the sign-back, discuss the seller's position and counsel you on how to respond. At the end, if there is a deal, the agent will deliver copies of it to your lawyer, lender and home inspector.

Killer negotiating tips

• **Put in conditions so you can remove them later.** The offer can be conditional on anything you want—getting financing, having a successful home inspection, being able to assume the seller's mortgage or selling or mortgaging an existing property. Sometimes it makes sense to include lots of these conditions in an initial offer just so you can drop them during a sign-back, to show you are serious and willing to sacrifice things (that you didn't care about anyway). This tactic could save you a few thousand on the price.

• **Ask for absolutely everything you want.** The drapes, the light fixtures, the rugs, the dog—virtually anything can be included in the sale price. It is assumed some items (wall-to-wall carpeting, the furnace, garage-door opener) go with the house because they are nailed down, screwed in or otherwise installed. Lawyers, of course, have a word for these things—fixtures. And the lawyer word for the other stuff—that can be moved—is chattel.

But is a stove a fixture or a chattel? How about a freezer, as opposed to a television set? A satellite dish? Some of these things may be quite portable, some not. So whatever you want, write it in the offer. And the more you write in, the more you can take out during the negotiation period.

• **Don't drag out the process.** The period you give the seller to respond should be short—perhaps just a few hours. Reality is the seller will respond mentally and emotionally within minutes, so it's pointless to have the offer flying around between the parties for a week.

• **Offer a surprising amount.** This is the trickiest part of the offer, of course, and it's what the vendor's eye will light upon first. The price colours everything else—the closing date, the deposit, the conditions, the fixtures and chattels. Everything.

  First, know your limit, which is why you got preapproved for a mortgage at the bank. Don't exceed it. And obviously don't offer everything you can on the first shot. Leave some room to manoeuvre.

  Also, know the mood and situation of the seller. Know what comparable houses in the area have sold for and how long it took—the seller certainly will have that information. If the market is hot, you may actually have to offer more than the asking price. In fact, in a sizzling market, sellers often will ask less than market value in order to stimulate a bidding war. If the market is cool, go for a low amount, perhaps making the offer "clean"—no conditions, short closing time and a whopping deposit. Make a cheap price as easy to swallow as possible.

• **The deposit can influence the seller.** No deposit should be made under $5,000, and the real estate agent will want to see enough of a deposit to cover the commission the deal will generate. And while the seller does not get any of the deposit money until the deal actually closes, this is a psychological thing. A big deposit will impress the vendor with your seriousness and perhaps with visions of getting that money as a windfall if the deal doesn't go through (although this hardly ever happens).

  In any case, if the closing date is more than 30 days away, ask for interest to be paid on that money. I know, I know—short-term interest rates are minuscule these days and likely to stay that way, but asking for this does leave the impression you have some financial savvy. Intimidation. It is, as Martha Stewart says, a good thing.

• **So can the closing date.** If you are a first-time buyer, then you probably have a lot of flexibility here, so give the seller what he or she wants in the closing date as a tradeoff for getting the price you can afford. If you have a house to sell, or if you're trying to coordinate the closing date on your existing home sale with a purchase, life can get tricky. Make sure you've lined up some bridge financing, in case there's a gap of a few days or weeks.

Your lawyer is going to want at least 30 days to make sure the deal is properly handled. It takes time to thoroughly search the title and to write the municipality and utility companies to ensure there are no liens or outstanding bills. Don't make the closing date a Friday, weekend day, holiday or the end of a month, for various reasons. You may have trouble getting mortgage funds advanced or finding an available mover or having your lawyer register title at a busy registry office.

- *Ask to visit the house before closing.* Don't forget this, because chances are you'll need to get in there at least once to measure for window coverings, or to meet a contractor to discuss repairs or renovations, or simply to map out rooms to know if the grand piano is going to fit.

  Don't rely on the seller's gentle nature to allow this access, because in many cases he or she will be fearful you might discover the basement fills up every time it rains and try to walk away from the deal.

  So, the offer should contain a clause setting out the right to enter the premises before closing a specified number of times and for a specified set of reasons, like measuring.

- *Get a warranty.* The offer should include a clause that the seller warrants that everything about the property, including the fixtures and chattels you write in, are in good working repair on the day of closing. This is an assurance that the seller will repair all those little things that inevitably wear out, and if he doesn't, you have some legal recourse.

Strategies for hot and cold markets

Buying a house when prices are rising and everybody is shopping can be a harrowing experience. Buying into a market where listings have languished and vendors are desperate can be a religious one. At any given moment, of course, many different markets can exist. Edmonton can be hot and Montreal frosty. The market for urban property can be torrid, while rural mansions are selling for far below the replacement cost. You have to do considerable research to know where the market has come from and where it's headed.

Many factors affect the market, but the biggies are mortgage rates, supply and consumer confidence.

- *Mortgage rates.* These have been at generational lows in the last years of the Nineties and are likely to stay there. Low rates have made housing the most affordable it's been in years. They've made it cheaper for most Canadians to buy than to rent. And they have freed up gobs of cash flow for people to thankfully and mercifully invest in financial assets and save their retirement hides.

  Low rates will keep most markets active, with prices rising modestly through to the millennium before buyer demand peters out.

- *Supply.* This is a constantly fluctuating thing, and your agent will keep you informed of what's selling, in what price range and with what level of interest. More people list their homes for sale when they perceive prices and demand are rising. But there are always vendors who must sell—because of family changes like death or divorce, because they've bought firm elsewhere or because of a job transfer.

  And there are times when a great deal of action can result from a rare listing. For example, a home came up for sale in Toronto's fashionable Lawrence Park area. It was in need of renovation and listed at $729,000. Since it was the only listing in the area, it was viewed 24 times on the day it appeared and was gone by sundown for full price. The successful buyer needed to be ready for immediate action.

- *Consumer confidence.* This is elusive and fluctuating. It is closely related to the general perception of the economy, and that is changing rapidly. Through most of the Nineties, Canadians perceived the economy to be in bad shape and getting worse. This was a false impression because it was based on just one thing—jobs, or the lack of them. Actually the economic fundamentals were very good and the future a brilliant one, but that was not widely seen until the decade was almost over.

  Strong employment growth, rising technologies, low rates and surging profits and financial markets have finally convinced people that the time to make big-ticket purchases like houses has finally returned. That mood is likely to be sustained through the fin-du-siècle period leading up to the millennium. So, a seller's market.

Tips to buying in a seller's market

- *Be there first.* In a hot market, houses sell in hours. Some sell even without being viewed, if you can believe it. That means you have to be ready to take action within a very short period of time and then be psychologically prepared to make an immediate offer. You could possibly spend hundreds of thousands of dollars in far less time than you would buying new jeans.

- *Be ready to take action.* That means having a preapproved mortgage, which will eliminate the need for a messy financial condition. It also means having a home inspector and a lawyer lined up, along with setting aside money for closing costs and having enough money in your bank account for a fat deposit in the form of a certified cheque.

- *Go with a clean offer.* In fact, the fewer conditions you have on the offer, the better it will look to the seller. And be flexible about the closing date, because this is something many sellers are particular about. You can always arrange some bridge financing if you have a house of your own to sell.

- *Waive the home inspection.* This will impress the seller, but obviously put you at more risk. How can you protect yourself? Take a home inspector with you when you view the property and before you make the offer. This will cost you a few hundred dollars, but it's money well spent.

- *Offer more than the asking price.* This might help you avoid a bidding war, which is the last thing you want to be involved in. There are people who "won" bidding wars in Toronto in the late 1980s who are still stinging, and who may never see the value of their properties approach what they paid. Make the first offer and make it high, and you just might settle the thing fast.

- *Know your true limit.* If you do become part of a war, set your limit and stick to it. You could end up in your agent's car parked outside the seller's property, with several other bidders parked behind you, with emotions running amuck. Be cool about things, and when the price jumps too high, drive to a McDonald's.

- *Force the seller to respond quickly.* Put pressure on him or her to sign back the offer within a short period of time—certainly no more than 24 hours. Subsequent sign-backs can be shorter and shorter, going down to a couple of hours. Again, this may settle things fast and keep you out of a war.

- *Chill out and find another house if you don't get the one you wanted.* It's just a piece of property, after all, and more will become available. Markets change. Things happen. Lots of people bought the wrong house in the wrong place in the late Eighties because of a sense that home ownership was about to pass them by forever. Give me a break.

Tips for buying in a buyer's market

- **Bargain hard.** After all, this is the flipside of the bidding-war market, and you are in complete control. Likely yours is the only offer the vendor will receive, so you can go after everything that you want—low prices, lots of inclusions like drapes, carpets and appliances, a convenient closing date, modest deposit and conditions for financing and home inspection.

- **Know the seller.** Why is this person selling a house when both of you know the market is bad? It must be a forced sale of some kind, and knowing the conditions will help you be an even more ruthless buyer. Hey, sometimes it feels good.

When's the best time to buy?

I bought my last property on Canada Day, and that was a good thing. This house would normally command many bids, but mine was the only one because of the holiday and, as a consequence, I saved a few thousand dollars. I was also the first buyer, showing up the day before the property went on the MLS. That shows what an excellent agent can do, operating with lightning speed on word-of-mouth information.

So there is some wisdom in shopping and buying in the real estate offseasons (July–August, December–January), but increasingly the market seems to be less seasonal than ever. Certainly you can anticipate the really busy times, which are spring and fall, when the number of listings and buyers explodes. That means far more choice of houses, but also more competition and maybe higher prices.

Some other timing tips to remember:

- Avoid locking in a mortgage during the six hot weeks of RRSP season—from about the second week in January to mid-February. That's when tens of billions of dollars in GICs come up for renewal—money the banks want to keep their hands on, instead of seeing it migrate into mutual funds. So it's no coincidence that interest rates on both GIC yields and mortgages tend to rise during that time. After the first of March you have a better shot at a lower rate.

- For lots of buyers, the school year dominates their lives, which means they need to move between the end of June and Labour Day. This can be helpful to bear in mind when making an offer on a house where children reside. Make the closing date as convenient as possible, and you might get a break on price.

- Watch out for some millennial madness. Everything is going to be affected in one way or another by the turning of the century, especially because it coincides with the fiftieth birthday of tens of millions of North Americans, many of whom are just getting ready to ditch their multibedroom family homes. If that's the kind of house you want, wait—you will be drowning in both choice and falling prices.

Should you buy new or resale?

There is absolutely no question that buyers of resale homes get a better deal—more house for the money and usually a better location. They are also buying history, because the house exists and has likely been sold before, sometimes dozens of times. This gives it a kind of track record and you can then judge what it's future resale appeal is likely to be.

But not with a new home, which is really only worth the value of the construction materials and the lot, plus a little profit for the builder. It has no track record, something scores of unhappy new homeowners came to discover in the past couple of years as they were forced to bail out of houses that had become unfashionable and—as new homes—cost a small fortune in the late Eighties.

Of course, a new house gives you new appliances, straight walls, shiny floors, big closets and a nice garage. For many buyers, that spells peace of mind. But it usually also comes with a sterile streetscape, boring architecture, a very small lot and a long commute. Certainly there are exceptions, and new urban infill projects now feature front porches and rear-entry garages in an attempt to recapture lost human synergy. But those kinds of projects are expensive, and the resale potential is untested.

So new materials and worry-free maintenance costs may not outweigh a new home's obvious problems, including:

- A higher price.

- Less bargaining room with a builder whose margins are already squeezed.

- A very uncertain closing date because of inevitable delays with materials and labour.

- Long and complicated nightmarish contracts, which put major restrictions on new owners and contain endless extra charges.

- Defects that have to be fixed after occupancy often by a builder who wants to move on and make money building new homes, not wasting time fixing yours. And while new homes usually come with a warranty, it doesn't shield you from hours on the telephone trying to get service and satisfaction.

Furthermore, a new home typically does not exist on the day you buy it, which means taking a leap of faith. For that reason the builder is a critically important issue, and you must research the company's background, reliability, reputation and financial strength.

Again, no such problem with a resale. And when you buy an existing house, using a home inspector before the deal is firm, you should avoid buying into any major repair problems.

Other advantages of buying a resale:

- Extras. Your can write the drapes, light fixtures, garden tools or whatever else you want into the offer, because the stuff is already there. There are an amazing number of things you need to spend money on after moving into a brand-new dwelling.

- You know exactly when it is going to close. That means you can plan your life in a way that's usually impossible with a to-be-built house.

- You get an established neighbourhood. With an unbuilt new home in a community that doesn't exist yet, it's impossible to know who your next-door neighbours will be or the age or ethnic mix of the neighbourhood. If, for example, homogeneity is important to you, this could be a problem.

- You will get thousands of dollars in landscaping, driveway paving and decorating that a new home usually does not offer.

But if you do opt for new digs . . .
Buying a new house involves a lot more work than a resale, and you should be prepared for delays, frustration, hassles with the builder and, at the end of the process, hopefully, the home of your dreams.

The process involves active participation by three parties: you, your agent and your killer lawyer.

Your role:

- First you have to spend a lot of time reading the new-home ads in the newspaper, visiting sales pavilions and driving and driving and driving. Most new homes are built in distant suburbs, and you simply have to visit all the sites to know if they might be acceptable. Also judge the commuting time to work, and the proximity to shopping and major transportation routes.

- Visit the municipal offices and find out what the official plan spells out for the area around the new development. After all, you are buying something that does not yet exist, which means attention has to be given to the surrounding environment. And don't neglect to get an opinion on what the property taxes will be.

- Now you have to investigate the builder. A good reputation and track record are essential. The builder should belong to the local homebuilders' association. The builder's rep at the sales pavilion should be gushing to help you with references—giving you locations of past projects. Then go there, knock on a few doors and ask if the owners are happy with their homes and were satisfied with the builder during construction and afterwards.

- If all that checks out, you have to select a plan for the houses and then a lot within the subdivision. Both of those decisions will dramatically affect the unit's future resale value, so they must not be taken lightly.

  I believe the most important item is the lot because, as I've said before, location is the only thing about real estate you cannot change. So shun corner lots (not enough privacy). Opt for a cul-de-sac or other quiet street over a major one. Be careful about what the lot backs onto, because an arterial road behind could cost you tens of thousands off the future resale value. Make sure existing trees on the lot are preserved, or find out the fate of ones near the property. Mature trees add major value to resales.

  And there is nothing like a view. Of open fields. Water. Forests. The city skyline. Always go for the view, even when it might mean ordering less house on the best lot.

Your agent:

Some buyers think they don't need an agent or that the person in the sales trailer will work with them and represent their interests to the builder. Bad decision. *You always need an agent.* In fact, using one could save you thousands of dollars and gobs of aggravation.

The reason is simple: the agent is a professional negotiator who knows the rules of real estate. You, the buyer, are an emotional amateur who, after selecting your dream home, turns into putty in the builder's hands. Meanwhile the person at the sales site is likely a commissioned salesperson, with a vested interest in getting the best deal for the builder.

The builder or his rep may tell you independent agents are not allowed, but ignore that. If they really want to sell you a house, they will work with your agent and pay him or her a commission, as they should do. Experienced builders are happy to work with buyers who have agents, because it shows the buyers are serious about proceeding, are not just tire-kickers looking for decorating ideas in the model home.

These are some of the goals your agent will work towards accomplishing during the negotiating process:

- Price. All prices are negotiable, just like with a resale home. When you make an offer, the negotiating process starts.

- Closing date. Again, you tell the builder when you want the house, instead of the other way around. But be aware, all new home contracts contain builder-friendly clauses allowing the closing date to be extended for a host of reasons.

- The mortgage. Try to get the builder to buy down the mortgage rate. I know mortgages are cheap now, but even a quarter point will help you out with cash flow. Or you could ask for some help defraying closing costs.

- Upgrades. You can negotiate for a better quality of bricks or shingles, kitchen cupboards or trim. How about getting a paved driveway or landscaping included, or a free fireplace?

- Special deals. Your agent might advise you to buy an already built model home, which you can rent back to the builder until he's finished with it. The builder gets cash for an asset he's already had to build, and you get a house that invariably features top-of-the-line finishings, hopefully at a reduced price. Or maybe you might buy the last unit in a development at a discount, because the builder has already made most of his money and may be more flexible on price. Or how about buying one of the first units? Early buyers can get deals from builders anxious to advertise that their development is selling out fast.

In short your agent will do all he or she can to get you the best house for the least amount of money and on the best terms. To accomplish that, emotion has to be checked at the door, and most buyers simply cannot do that.

Your lawyer:
Buying a new home is complicated, so the choice of lawyer is important. The house could be subject to all kinds of potential delays and problems, so get a real estate specialist, one with lots of new-house experience.

Show the offer to the lawyer before you present it. Make sure it allows you the right to regularly inspect the site during construction and gives you a final walk-through before closing. If you close before everything's the way you want it, you might have a hard time getting repairs made. Ensure they're done before a dollar changes hands. Be on the lookout for any substitutions made from the model home or changes to the floor plan.

Provision for all these things should be in the agreement, along with verification that whatever new-home warranties are available in your province apply to this house. (In Ontario, all new homes are covered, but the warranty is optional elsewhere.) Part of your lawyer's job is to go over all these documents with you and to fight for your interests during any construction delays or problems.

Will that be freehold or condo?
A home you own completely, whether detached, semidetached or row (town) house is freehold. With a freehold house, you own the bricks, shingles, grass, glass and everything from one lot line to the other.

A condo is completely different. In a condominium unit, you own the air space between the walls of that unit, basically between the layers of paint, from the floor to the ceiling, while also sharing in the ownership of all the common elements with everyone else in the condominium. Those common elements include the structure itself, the walkways, elevators, landscaping, parking garage, pool and so on.

And condos don't just come in the shape of apartment buildings. Anything can be a condominium, because the term really just refers to a form of ownership. There are condo developments consisting of town houses and detached houses, even entire rural communities with acres and acres of grounds surrounding them.

Some parts of the common elements that everyone owns can be used by the owner as if they were freehold. The balcony of a condo in a highrise building, for example, would be owned by all but used by that unit's owner alone. These are called "exclusive use" areas and can also include lockers, parking spaces, garages and back yards.

Condos are bought, sold and mortgaged just like freehold properties. But they are typically insured like apartment units—for contents only, since you do not own the walls. The condominium corporation, representing all the owners, carries insurance on the structure, paid for as part of the monthly condo fees.

In a condo I once owned, pipes froze and burst one winter after the heating-oil company neglected to fill the tank when I was out of town. The oil company's liability was zero since my heating contract required someone to enter the house and check it every day (which I naturally discovered after the disaster). But the condominium corporation's insurance policy did cover the $7,000 in repairs, since it owned the floors, which buckled, and the ceiling, which collapsed.

Like resale and new homes, condos come in all sizes and price ranges. There are scads of entry-level condos in all major Canadian cities, selling for $50,000 or less. And then there are condo palaces, like The Cheddington in midtown Toronto, where the average selling price is $1 million (and all the units sold out quickly prior to construction).

As with all the interesting things in life, there are advantages and disadvantages to condominium ownership, no matter the size or price or shape.

Condo Advantages:

• No maintenance. No snow to shovel, no grass to cut, no roof to replace, no shutters to paint. Since everyone owns the structure, grounds and recreational facilities together, this work is contracted out. That means a condo lifestyle can be dramatically different from a freehold one—ideal for people who like to travel or for seniors or young couples married to their jobs.

• Stable operating costs. The monthly condo fees take care of insurance, maintenance and repairs. They are predictable, so you can budget for them.

- Price. Often it costs far less to buy a nice condo in a desirable residential area than it does to get a freehold property there. Yet you can still enjoy the same streets, shopping, proximity to work or ambience as you would if you'd purchased a home.

- Facilities. Imagine what it would cost to buy a house with a swimming pool, games room, squash court, library or art gallery. Many condo owners get access to all these, and often more, because they are affordable when everyone owns a chunk.

Condo Disadvantages:

- Loss of personal freedom. Remember, you don't own the actual structure, and this means you don't control it. So while it is liberating not to have to worry about the condition of the roof, it also means you can't paint your balcony a different colour or maybe not even remodel your bathroom without permission.

  Condos are governed not only by the same laws freehold homeowners have to abide by, but also by rules adopted by the board of directors of the condominium corporation. So you are part owner and part tenant.

  The board is made up of condo owners and can pretty well decide what it wants. The law requires it maintain a reserve of money for maintenance, but the board can authorize that extra money be collected from each owner for major repairs. If you don't pay, a lien can be put against your property. If that happens, you can't sell the unit and may, in fact, lose it.

- There is sometimes less privacy, especially in apartment condominiums. So choose a building carefully and visit the unit a few different times in the day to get a feel for how much your space will be compromised.

- Reselling is sometimes tricky. Condos tend to be the first to go down in value when real estate markets decline, and they are often overbuilt when the market advances. Both of these trends keep prices in check. It also takes longer to sell a condo than a freehold, at least it has in the past, but that may change thanks to demographics and a growing demand for condo living.

- Responsibility may be unclear. Are you responsible for maintaining and repairing your exclusive-use area? Can you trim a tree in your exclusive-use back yard? Is the parking space owned as part of your unit, given as exclusive use or just allocated? Does the condo board have the right to change your locker space or force you to move to another locker? Find the answers to questions like these before you buy.

- Rights are restricted. The condo rules may prevent you from owning a dog, for example. A Toronto couple spent a lot of money taking their condo board to court over a no-pet rule, and they ultimately lost.

Make sure you have your lawyer examine both the rules and regulations of the condo corporation, and also its constitution, because both can set out restrictions you might not want to live with. If you want a dog, then your offer has to spell that out. So if the offer comes back striking that out, you can take a walk instead of finding out later that Fido is doomed!

Condo tips to remember:
- Find out the financial status of the condo corporation. Get a copy of the statement. Find out if any major repairs are pending or if owners have been forced to pay any special assessments for repairs in the past.

- See if the condo is well managed and properly maintained. After all, one of the big advantages of condo living is leaving this to somebody else to do.

- How many units are vacant? How many are rented? What does this say about the entire development?

- Pay careful attention to the location of your proposed parking space and locker. Is the security adequate? If you don't require a parking spot, can you sell or lease it? Are their restrictions on your leasing your condo?

- And, after you buy, it's always a good idea to seek a seat on the condo board. After all, this is the government of the condo and its actions can affect both your lifestyle and the resale value of your unit. Naked self-interest requires action.

What does it cost to close a deal?
Probably more than you thought, or budgeted for. In general you should be ready to cough up an amount on closing equal to roughly 2% of the purchase price. That's right—$4,000 on a $200,000 property.

So, what on earth does all this money go for?

Well, the list is a long one, and some charges are arcane while others constitute gouging, sometimes by lawyers, always by government. A good lawyer will tell you far in advance how much money you will actually need to have on the day of closing. And always remember that all these costs must be paid on that day, in cash, or the deal may not happen. Here's what you will be dinged with:

- *Legal fees.* This is the money your lawyer will charge for everything he or she has done, from meeting with you to reviewing your offer, to handling the transaction itself. You should have already discussed this and know the amount, which will typically be a few hundred dollars.

- *Disbursements.* These are payments the lawyer has made on your behalf to various agencies. For example, the municipality needs money to issue certificates saying taxes and utilities are paid up and there are no work orders outstanding. The province needs to be paid for the title search and deed registration. The local registry office needs to be paid for a certificate saying there are no judgments against the buyer or seller. And with a new home you need an occupancy permit, issued by the municipality.

- *Nickel and dimers.* Also expect to pay the lawyer every time he makes a phone call, uses his photocopier or calls Purolator to pick up a package. This is a unique lawyer thing and it's irritating, but most do it.

- *Taxes.* The biggest will be the land-transfer tax, which is one of the most unjust taxes in existence. Every time a piece of property changes hands, whether value has been added to it or not, the provincial government has to be paid this ransom—which is an escalating tax, rising with the price of the property. If it is not paid up front, the deed will not be registered and the deal will collapse.

  There may also be retail sales taxes to pay on the chattels included in the sale (like appliances). But often these can be ignored without consequence, because it's impossible to assign any meaningful value to used appliances.

- *Adjustments.* After the deal is done, you will get a Statement of Adjustments showing exactly how the money changed hands on closing day and where it went. You'll also see from the statement that the vendor was credited with things like how much money was paid up to the day of closing in realty taxes, how much oil was in the furnace tank, how much water and sewer charges were paid. Then there are the charges for the survey, appraisal, insurance, home inspection, any bridge financing and miscellaneous mortgage costs.

Clearly this is not a cheap process and the key is full disclosure. Before you even sign an offer to purchase, make sure you fully understand how much actual cash will be required on the day of closing. This will affect the amount you need to borrow and the amount of house you can afford.

How to find the right mortgage

In the first half of your life, when you're a real estate consumer, you want the right mortgage at the right rate with the proper strategy for paying it down, because the interest on this is coming directly out of your after-tax income.

In the second half of your life, when you are a real estate user, the mortgage you place on your paid-off house to use for investment purposes is tax-deductible. Therefore, you don't care if you ever pay it off, because it is saving you income.

So clearly, paying the least interest is important in the early years and less important later on. But human nature dictates that no matter what stage of life people are at, they want the cheapest mortgage rate they can get. That brings us first to the question I am asked the most:

Should you borrow long or short?

There are a lot of costs involved with buying a new home, and the last thing you want is to be worried about an interest rate risk.

—Mike Braid, Vice-President
Toronto Dominion Bank

They're prepared to take the risk and so far it's been a good strategy. You mitigate that risk by paying off the loan faster.

—Tom Alton, President
Bank of Montreal Mortgage Corp.

A lot of Canadians, especially the Boomers who were the most affected, remember August 1981. That's when the cost of a five-year mortgage topped out at 21.25%.

Homeowners with mortgages coming up for renewal were in complete shock. Many lenders stopped making five-year loans. Some people walked away from their real estate. Others lost their homes when the lenders demanded rates that were simply unpayable. On the flip side people with money to invest got huge returns without taking any risk.

Me, I was on Parliament Hill, a tabloid journalist in corduroy jeans leading a protest of several thousand people against the Bank of Canada policies that had resulted in that situation. The Peace Tower was circled by RCMP in riot gear, but we got to meet the housing minister, who went on national TV a few hours later to declare the government was imposing a moratorium on house foreclosures.

The sting of superhigh rates is still felt by many. In fact, in the early Nineties a long-term mortgage spiked again around 14%. And it's only been as the decade comes to an inconclusive close that the cost of money has collapsed.

As I write this a short-term mortgage can be yours for less than 5%, while it costs just over 7% to lock up the rate for five years.

Which should you choose?

There is no question at all. You should borrow short, either putting the extra cash into paying down the loan faster or using it to invest in financial assets. The last thing you want to do is pay the extra to the bank in interest.

Some people say they're willing to make the higher payments for a long-term loan as "insurance" against being shocked by another 1980s-style rate explosion. But this is financially insane.

• Consider $100,000 borrowed at 5% on a short-term or variable-rate loan amortized over 25 years. Over five years you will pay $35,000 less interest than on the same loan locked in for five years at 7%. That's got to be the most expensive insurance in the world! And imagine how much better that borrower would be to simply pay down the principal by $35,000. That would increase the equity, hastening the day when you can borrow against that equity to invest.

But what if rates rise?
And they might. The estimates vary, with economists predicting interest rates could increase by 2% by, say, the middle of 1998 or the begin-

THE COST OF LOCKING IN YOUR MORTGAGE

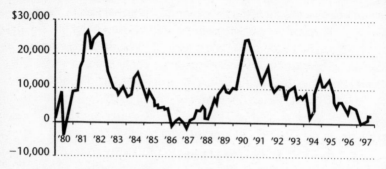

This chart illustrates how long-term mortgages have been more expensive than short-term ones. For any given date it shows the difference between the total interest paid over five years using a five-year mortgage and the interest payments on one-year fixed mortgages rolled over from year to year. For almost the entire time between 1980 and 1993, you would have been ahead staying short.

The values for the 1993–97 period assume long-term rates will climb 2% in 1998 (although that is not at all assured or likely), and short-term rates will rise a little faster. Rates will drift down over the following years.

Source: Peter Norman, Bank of Montreal community banking and real estate group economist, and *The Globe and Mail*.

ning of 1999. But there's also general agreement the long-term economic fundamentals are unlikely to change, and that means strong growth with little inflation.

In short the Eighties are not coming back. Interest costs could rise a little from where they are today, which is hardly a disaster, since today we are enjoying the cheapest money since the mid-1950s. And—dare we think it?—there is real hope among some economists that modern capitalist society may have found the way to end boom-and-bust cycles that result in interest-rate gyrations.

In the current economic expansion, which began back in 1991, we've enjoyed strong growth but without inflation. This is thanks mostly to global free trade, which heightens competition and reduces costs, and the explosion of new technologies, which have actually cut

Source: *The Financial Post*

manufacturing overhead. At the centre of the new thinking is American economist Daniel E. Sichel, who says that with the right policies governments can now stop recessions before they start and extend expansions indefinitely.

Downturns, he says, will only take place if the government pulls the wrong economic levers or there is an external shock, like an oil crisis or an international financial collapse.

If this is true and American and Canadian central bankers get it right (which they seem to be doing), then the odds of good growth, little inflation and stable interest rates are excellent. So there is no question of what kind of mortgage to get, just as there's no reason to fear a stock market meltdown.

Meanwhile historical data show us that even during years of rate volatility, you are still a winner to take a short-term mortgage. Canada Mortgage and Housing Corporation found in a study that one-year terms were the best financial choice 85% of the time between 1980 and 1994. Another study, done by Bank of Montreal economist Peter Norman, looked at the rate experience between 1980 and 1991 and concluded the short borrowers were better off 91% of the time.

So why in the autumn of 1997 were 60% of new home buyers at the TD Bank opting for five-year mortgages? Probably because they got bad advice from loans officers or friends and didn't bother to work out the best game plan; or they are typical first-time buyers, terrified at taking on a huge amount of mortgage debt and facing a rate shock in the first few years.

Well, there's no rate shock coming. Today's interest rates are going to stick for a long time, and this is a godsend to the one million households in Canada who will renew a mortgage within the next twelve months. When they took out those mortgages in 1992 and 1993, they were paying 10% for their money and can renew today at half that. On a $100,000 mortgage, that constitutes a saving of more than $400 a month—money that can be put into financial assets that have the potential of doubling in value every six years.

Besides, the mortgage rates banks post are always negotiable. Good customers coming up for renewal can get a reduction of between a quarter and three-quarters of a point, adding further to the windfall.

Don't be afraid to ask for a break and don't delay. This last strong real estate rally of the century, narrowing rate spreads and an improving economy may soon spell the end of discounted mortgages. But money will remain cheap.

Of course, borrowing short means getting a commitment for money at a fixed price for one year, for six months or for no period at all with a variable rate loan. An open loan can either be paid out or rolled over into a new mortgage without any penalty, but generally has a slightly higher rate than a closed loan. And a convertible loan is just that—you get a term of, say, six months, and at any time during that period you can convert it into a longer-term mortgage without penalty should interest rates start to rise.

So which of these is the best option?

• If you share my views, you will get the cheapest possible mortgage available, because there is little upside risk for rates. That means a **variable-rate loan**, which rises or falls with the cost of money.

But if you are leery of any increase at all, you could always compromise by taking one of the hybrid mortgages offered by the banks. You can get a variable-rate mortgage that offers some protection from hikes over a five-year term at banks like the Royal. Or you can sign up for a three-year term at the Bank of Montreal and opt to switch to a lower rate on anniversaries, if mortgage costs decrease. The mortgage business is highly competitive (because it's highly profitable), so shop around before accepting anything, and get the lenders to bid for your business.

More options:

- An **Internet mortgage**, such as with the Citizens' Bank of Canada. The country's first true virtual bank (no branches), has broken ground by offering no-dicker loans at a fixed price substantially below that offered by brick-and-mortar lenders. The latest reduction: .75% off the big boys' rates.

- A **closed five-year loan with a six-month variable rate**. National Trust pioneered this, giving borrowers the current six-month rate, which is revised twice a year but guaranteed not to exceed the five-year rate at the time you took the loan. So if rates stay low, you get to enjoy them, and if rates rage higher, your upside is protected. It's a great product.

What if I'm wrong, and you have to renew your mortgage at a higher rate?

- **You could just extend the amortization period** of the loan, say, from 25 years to 35 years. This means it will take you a decade longer to repay the mortgage, and the interest costs will be vastly higher. But the monthly payment will be lower, so you could weather a mortgage-rate increase on a temporary basis. However, this is not a good idea.

Are there options for locked-in mortgages when rates are falling?

Of course. A couple of things you can do are:

- **Blend and extend**. This means rolling your existing mortgage into a new loan with a longer term. If you have three years left on an 8% mortgage, then create a new five-year mortgage. The interest will be a prorated blend of the old rate and the current lower one for the next five years.

    Some lenders will charge you a penalty for doing this, one equal to the amount of interest they lose until the end of the original term. But you are still probably better off.

    Or, as Tony Hunble of Online Mortgage Explorer suggests, you can bribe the bank into waiving the penalty by bringing some new business into that branch. It could be transferring RRSP money, borrowing to make this year's RRSP contribution or taking out a line of credit.

• **Break the mortgage**. In this instance you are asking the bank to let you out of your long-term commitment to take advantage of substantially lower rates—for which you will pay a penalty. This strategy generally works best if you have two years or less to go. Longer than that and the penalty will probably negate any gain.

How much will the penalty be?

Depends on the size of your lender's heart, because there are no rules. Under the terms of your mortgage, believe it or not, a lender doesn't have to let you out of a mortgage with a term of less than five years for any reason whatsoever—even if you need to sell your house. Of course, just about every lender will break a mortgage, but the penalties are all over the map, something the Canadian Real Estate Association has been trying to change for years.

In general expect one of two things: a penalty equal to three months' interest or one equal to the interest-rate differential—the amount of interest between the rate and the current one on the amount you borrowed and over the period of time left in your mortgage. And you're right—that's paying the same amount to get out as if you'd stayed in. No advantage there.

My experience has shown me the best deals usually come from dealing with small humane neighbourhood lenders or one of the Big Six banks. The worst are medium-size trust companies. Beware. It always pay to discuss mortgage payout options before you sign for the loan in the first place.

Should you get preapproved?

Absolutely and without a doubt. Banks and trust companies routinely approve mortgage loans before the funds are released. You can do it now in the branch, over the phone, on your PC using dial-up numbers or over the Internet.

This will accomplish several things:

• You'll know precisely how much you qualify to borrow. So you'll know how much house you can afford to buy.

• You lock in an interest rate for a defined period of time, typically 60 days. So if rates rise, you don't get caught.

• You can eliminate the need for a clause on financing, which strengthens your offer. That can mean a lot in a hot market, where you're likely to be in competition with others.

And there is absolutely no downside for you as the borrower. The preapproval costs nothing. You are under no obligation to work with that lender. You can get multiple preapprovals from competing institutions—in fact, this is exactly what you should do.

Shopping the market is essential if you want the best possible mortgage features, like portability (the ability to take your mortgage with you when you move), prepayments (the right to pay off regular chunks of the principal), split-level (the ability to carve the mortgage into different terms with different rates) or weekly payments (paying every seven days instead of every month, thereby seriously shortening the time it takes to pay the loan off and saving you big time). When you get preapproval, ask about more than just the interest rate and make sure you deal with the lender offering the greatest flexibility.

How much can you borrow?

- First, understand that a conventional mortgage will cover only 75% of the price of a house. More than that, and it's called "high ratio," which is no big deal except it needs to be insured, and that costs extra. So to get a conventional mortgage, you have to come up with 25% of the equity.

- Second, the amount the bank will give you depends on your ability to repay it. The rule is no more than about 30% of your gross family earnings should be applied to the PIT—principal, interest and taxes.

How can you pay it off faster?

The cardinal rule about mortgages and financial planning goal number one was always this: pay it off as fast as you can. Nothing is more important than getting a debt-free house. You must scrimp and save and shovel all the cash you've got into achieving that.

In part that still holds true, but not in exactly the same terms.

First, **if you are without a house now**, only buy one if you can justify the purchase because it reduces your housing costs. Otherwise, if you live more cheaply renting, continue to rent and invest your money in financial assets. Over the next 10 or 15 years, you will come out ahead, because rising markets, no inflation and an aging population will bring housing values down.

If you do own a house and have it paid off, then borrow against it to invest the money in growth assets, for all the reasons already articulated in this book.

If you own a home with a mortgage on it, then you can reduce the size of the mortgage so you can increase your equity and give yourself more financial options by using several techniques:

- Making regular lump-sum payments off the principle. Several lenders allow this on an annual basis with no penalty.

- Shortening the amortization period from the standard 25 years. This will result in substantial interest savings and higher payments.

- Increasing monthly payments. "Step-up" features with some lenders let you increase your payments each year by a set percentage.

- Taking a weekly mortgage.

Do it weekly. In my view there is only one useful technique here, and that is the weekly mortgage. Why? Because of the way mortgage interest is calculated and because this is the option that preserves most of your cash flow for where it should be going—into growth financial assets like equity mutual funds within your RRSP.

Making lump-sum payments, shortening the amortization and hiking monthly payments will all drop the mortgage faster, but leave you with less money to invest. And if what I am forecasting comes to pass—10 or 15 great years for the economy and financial markets, followed by years of economic downturn and a retirement crisis—you do not want to spend the next decade shovelling money into a mortgage furnace.

After all, you might end up in, say, 2017 with a mortgage-free house that is plunging in value after having spent the past 20 years paying off the mortgage. That's a lose-lose scenario I fear a lot of young people today are bound to play out, following without question the real-estate-is-good, debt-is-bad philosophy of their Boomer parents. Well, forget what your parents told you. Only nuke a mortgage the right way, and that's weekly payment.

The concept is simple. Take a regular monthly mortgage payment and divide it into four. Now make that payment every week and you will reduce the time it takes to pay it off by about a quarter, saving thousands of dollars in interest.

Why does this work so well?

Two reasons:

- Because there are more than four weeks in most months, you end up making the equivalent of an extra month's mortgage payment each year, which speeds up repayment.

- By making that extra payment early in the life of the mortgage you are accelerating the reduction of the principal. Because it's lowered in size faster than with a monthly payment, the compounding effect of the interest is reduced.

  Remember, in the early years of a mortgage, virtually all of your payments are interest. So if you can make payments more frequently, the small amount of principal being repaid is dramatically increased, dropping the future interest charges on it.

A word of caution . . .
Not all weekly mortgages are created equal. The ones that kill off the mortgage in record time are equal to one-quarter of a monthly payment made each week. Some lenders offer weekly mortgages that are equivalent to the total annual mortgage payment, divided by 52. Have none of that. There is absolutely no advantage at all, except to the lender, who gets the same amount on interest as with a monthly mortgage, but gets it more frequently.

All you need to know about mortgages

Mortgages are complicated, boring and necessary. Fortunately lenders have become enlightened over the past few years, coming up with a host of innovative ways to finance real estate. They are also extremely competitive, a fact that is lost on a lot of the mindless bank-bashing critics.

Right now you can have a mortgage that is cheap, portable, split-level and tax-deductible. Done properly, you can make money on the house that also gives you shelter. Use The Strategy—taking the bank's money at 6%, using it to earn 15% on financial assets, reducing income taxes and living in a nice place. (Using your equity to build wealth in the second half of your life is part two of The Strategy, and I'll describe it in more detail shortly.)

In the first half of your life, though, the object is to build equity. But with the uncertain future of residential real estate, you must avoid becoming a slave to your mortgage. That was a strategy that worked in the Eighties, when inflation made mortgages easier to pay off and artificially boosted house values. But those days are gone, and with them the traditional wisdom that paying the mortgage off is the single most important thing you can do.

Forget that. When mortgages are so cheap and flexible, having one isn't a bad idea at all. Here's a summary of how you should borrow:

- *Go short.*
  Get the cheapest, shortest loan on the market. Interest rates are going to stay where they are for years, so there's no need to waste money on insuring yourself against an increase.

- *Go weekly.*
  Shun monthly payments and go with a weekly mortgage. That will help you retire the loan about 20% faster, saving thousands in interest and not putting a major dent in your cash flow.

- *Get preapproved.*
  You'll know how much you can easily repay, you'll secure a rate and your hand is strengthened when you come to making an offer. Like life's best stuff, it doesn't cost anything, either.

- *Shop the market. Shop on-line.*
  Lenders are locked in bitter competition for your business, so get a few of them bidding on your new mortgage. Take advantage of the new technology, using the Internet to get on-line quotes and preapproval.

- *Be innovative.*
  Your mortgage should be portable so you can take it to another property. It could be split-level so you can hedge against any rate increase, breaking it into different hunks with different maturity dates.

- *Forget your parents.*
  They're full of helpful tips like, "If mortgage rates come down, keep the same payment as before so you can pay off the loan faster." So ignore that and, if rates fall, drop your mortgage payment and invest the difference. The future is in financial assets (even if the markets take a dive for a while), not in residential real estate.

- *Don't waste money.*
  On mortgage insurance, for example; it's expensive and largely unnecessary, only suitable for people who are pretty convinced they will lose a job or become gravely ill. Also on the insurance you're charged for a high-ratio mortgage; this costs a small fortune and you're better off in many cases to get a second mortgage. At all costs, don't take the advice of most lenders and throw the one-time insurance premium on your mortgage principal—it will get amortized higher, and you'll end up paying it back three times over.

- *And when it's paid off . . .*
  Go and borrow again, using your home's equity to get investment capital. This time you want an interest-only loan, because paying it back it not important. After all, the interest is tax-deductible, which means as long as you have the mortgage, you are saving money.

Mortgages are financial tools, just like residential real estate. Both are a means to an end, not ends in themselves. The goal is no longer to die in a paid-off home so your kids can sell it and enjoy the money. The goal is for you to enjoy the money and to avoid the inevitable decline in real estate values I believe is coming.

The greatest threat facing North Americans is not having enough capital to finance decades in retirement. And one of the greatest assets you have for fighting that threat is your home. It can help save you, but only if you follow The Strategy.

Chapter 7

What to Buy

A ctually, first, what *not* to buy. Some kinds of residential real estate have a bleak future. Why? Because the number of people who will want that type of housing is plunging as the population ages, as real estate tastes change, as technology advances and as North American culture continues to urbanize.

As part of my research for this book, I shopped for real estate. Now, this is something I love to do, because I love real estate. I shopped in Ontario, Nova Scotia, Quebec and British Columbia, and there were some stunning bargains to be had.

- A gorgeous small hotel in Pictou, Nova Scotia, for $330,000 with an income that would carry it with nothing down.

- A mansion in Montreal for $629,000 that would cost $2 million to build.

- A 4,000-square-foot turn-of-the century restored executive home on the water outside Kingston, Ontario, listed at $695,000. The owners put $1.1 million into its renovation.

- A huge house north of Toronto on a two-acre lot with nanny's quarters, beside a golf course. It cost $1.2 million to build and is for sale at $529,000.

- A monster home in West Vancouver that sold three years ago for $2.1 million, now selling for a million less.

By contrast, consider two houses that sold in Toronto in mid-1997. One is a dated stone home in upscale Lawrence Park, on a less-than-desirable corner lot, that needs about $80,000 worth of work. It was

A waterfront wonder near Kingston

What: Five bedrooms, in 4,000 square feet on a five-acre lot with 385 feet of shoreline.

Where: On the Bay of Quinte, 35 minutes by car and one hour by boat to downtown Kingston; 30 minutes from Kingston Airport.

Amenities: Whether you're after country living, access to the St. Lawrence Seaway, or an elegant executive home, this place, built by a prosperous farmer in the early 1870s, has it all.

If you're into sailing or powerboating, you'll be on a waterway that can take you along the Great Lakes and the St. Lawrence to the mighty Atlantic Ocean, and Europe, if you so desire. And you can keep your sea-

cate mouldings and spacious dining room. An oak-panelled "gentleman's bar" (sorry ladies, but that's what it was called a century ago), is perfect for cigars and a glass of port after dinner.

Homework: The owner has invested $1.1-million in the home, close to double the asking price, so it's a property worth investigating. But it has been on the market for more than a year, with nary an offer. There are seven waterfront properties listed in the area, all with less waterfront and on smaller lots, priced from $598,000 to $1.5-million. A small home on a much smaller waterfront lot recently sold for $427,000. Entrepreneurs take note: The h...

More than a million dollars invested. Yours for 60 cents on the dollar.

Source: *The Globe & Mail*

listed on a Monday morning for $729,000, was shown 25 times that day and sold by six o'clock for $729,000.

Another is a more modest house in centrally located Leaside on a little 30-foot-wide lot. The two-storey brick home was listed at $409,000 and sold for $422,000 in 48 hours with no conditions. And another house nearby actually made it onto the front page of the *Toronto Star* because it sold for $83,000 more than the asking price.

What gives real estate value?

There is only one answer, and that is buyer appeal. And what appeals to buyers is constantly changing, affected by everything from demographics to newspaper headlines. The population is aging, and that will have a massive impact on real estate. Canadians are getting more security-conscious, anxious to protect themselves against home invasions and sexual assault; this, too, will affect real estate. A new generation of buyers is emerging who want the latest technologies built into their homes, and the market is adapting to that. Finally the population of urban areas, especially Vancouver, Calgary and Toronto, is literally exploding, and this is already having huge positive and negative effects on real estate both inside and outside those centres.

One of the easiest predictions to make in the 1980s was that monster homes would become the white elephants of the 1990s, which is exactly what's happened.

That house on the golf course north of Toronto is a classic example. When I first inquired about the listing, the home was offered at $779,000. It caught my eye because that seemed like a bargain price for a huge 6,000-square-foot custom-built home with heated cobblestone tiles in the gourmet kitchen, a Scarlett O'Hara staircase, four-car garage, guest suite, library and more, sitting on two acres within easy driving distance of King and Bay.

One month later I saw an ad stating the price had just been dropped by $250,000, and the place had to be sold—at whatever price—within five weeks, because of a corporate relocation.

Now, at just $500,000 or so, the house was selling for less than fifty cents on the dollar, and as I write this, there are literally hundreds of similar luxury properties to choose from. These gorgeous homes were built or bought within the last ten years by people who spared no expense in creating architectural masterpieces sitting in picturesque and sometimes dramatic settings.

But there are no buyers, even when the places are being virtually given away. The owners are forced to watch as hundreds of thousands of dollars in equity evaporates before their very eyes, just as if they'd gambled their money on a junior gold-mining company listed on the

DISTRESS SALE. REDUCED OVER $250,000
CORPORATE RELOCATION - OPEN HOUSE SUNDAY 2:00 - 5:00
11 URQUHART COURT, AURORA - ONLY $529,000
Stunning architectural masterpiece. Custom built by owner. Walls of south facing windows with golf course view. Heated cobblestone tiles in state-of-the-art kitchen. Scarlett O'Hara staircase, nanny's suite, private office – all situated on a secluded 1.89 acre lot. Easy commute to Toronto.

Distress sale, indeed. This kind of real estate has no future. The market for monster homes in the far burbs has collapsed, because of rapidly changing real estate tastes.

Alberta Stock Exchange that one day plunged in value. And they're shocked. Because they never ever considered residential real estate— especially expensive, crafted, luxurious real estate—to be a risky investment.

> ***This is a glimpse of the future. And anyone today buying the wrong kind of real estate has to be prepared for the same experience.***

Why are there no buyers for these homes? Because they are the wrong size, in the wrong place and there are no greater fools. The appetite for huge homes is largely gone as the makeup of the population changes. Large families are on the decline. The number of two-person families is surging, along with an explosion of single-parent families. And the number of people willing to pour money into the maintenance, insurance and taxes homes like that generate, at a time when financial markets are giving double-digit returns, is falling fast.

Location is the guiding principle of real estate, and many of these homes have got the wrong one. Increasingly people want access to hospitals, clinics, schools and other services. Rural properties are going to suffer and decline in value as the population continues to age and as the Boomers pass the fifty mark.

Also, homes in the country are weak links on the information highway, often simply because there is no Internet service provider handy without having to incur long-distance phone charges. In most of rural Canada, there's also no cable television, and as you and Bill Gates know, cable is going to be the dominant medium of accessing the Internet within a very short time.

And there are few greater fools left.

The greater-fool theory is simply this: you buy an asset at an inflated price because you know you can sell it to a greater fool than you later, at an even higher price. But when you run out of greater fools, you truly (because you *began* as a greater fool) become one.

Today what appeals to buyers has changed radically. They want location, and that means urban convenience. They want access to services. They want reasonably sized and flexible houses. They want technology. They want safety, quality and value. Buy real estate with those defining characteristics, and it will retain its value for the next decade. It might even rise in value, yielding a tax-free capital gain.

Real estate with a future

Aging Baby Boomers want quality living and a maintenance-free lifestyle. They want to get away from the hustle and bustle and don't want to see their neighbour's kitchen when they look out the window.
—*Mark Bedard*
Heritage Pointe Golf and Country Club
Calgary

Location, quality and services. Size, convenience and flexibility. Technology, safety and value. These are the hallmarks of New Century real estate, which is already being built and recycled across the country. Some of the ideas are new, some old.

There is a reason tiny sixty-year-old 800-square-foot bungalows along the forested streets of midtown Toronto sell for $300,000, while new housing in the suburbs, three times the size, commands less money. Those bungalows simply have what many people want, and will want in the future—neighbourhood, access to transportation and health care services and ease of maintenance. There is no need for a car when you can walk to the grocery store, the library or the bank. Property taxes are low. The WheelTrans bus can come to your door, and your house is wheelchair-friendly. Is it any wonder that this kind of housing sells in hours? Or that an area with the highest proportion of seniors per capita in Canada is so hot with young buyers?

The future is a bungalow.

Some of them will be urban, some in the near country. This housing form is already making a huge comeback, after being shunned and ridiculed in the Seventies and Eighties. Bungalows, especially "executive" ones, will command a much higher price than the two-storey homes that have dominated for the past two and a half decades.

Boomers will want the independent-living features that this kind of housing provides—no stairs, easy access to your vehicle, only two or three bedrooms, open concept living and entertaining areas and energy efficiency. They will also want quality, yet in a manageable space—1,200- or 1,500-square-foot residences with vaulted or cathedral ceilings, gleaming ceramic kitchens, en suite bathrooms, heated tile floors, porches—and views.

The future is golf. It's a small town.

The Baby Boom generation will not age gracefully or quickly, so physical activity will remain important and golf will make a major comeback. Of course, that trend has already started. You can see it in the media fawning afforded that 1997 hero, Tiger Williams. You can also see it in the golf-theme communities taking the great urban centres of Toronto, Calgary and Vancouver by storm.

Many Boomers are children of the suburbs. They are used to cars, space and frontage. But in the future they will not want the upkeep associated with large lots. Gardening isn't recreational—it's a pain. Better to be on the golf course with your friends beside you and your digital PCS device in your bag.

One solution for many will be freehold homes on condominium land surrounding executive golf courses; they will also be within commuting distance of the city. Those kinds of communities are starting to be built now, aiming at the affluent early retirees.

Ontario's finest lakefront golf course adult lifestyle community is now ready to Preview!

CANTERBURY COMMON IN PORT PERRY
LAKEFRONT GOLF COURSE COUNTRY BUNGALOWS FROM $189,900 TO $215,900.

Real estate with a future: bungalow on the links. Aging and active Boomers will be happy to live in exactly this, golfing while the condo people cut the grass.

Millcroft in Burlington, Ontario, is an example, with condo apartments going for $160,000 and executive homes for $450,000. At Calgary's Heritage Pointe, first-phase homes have been marketed for between $225,000 and $500,000—far more expensive than the city's average home price of $140,000.

There's Morgan Creek in South Surrey, where the typical house sells for $600,000 on a third of an acre. And in rural and near-urban Ontario, new developments like the Lake Joseph Club and the Angus Glen Golf Club broke ground in 1997. There will be lots more, many of them giving their owners club memberships. Expect an active resale market, which will keep the value of these homes high until the Boomers start losing their legs. That should happen about 2020.

"We think the demographics of golf course communities are right for the times," Monarch Development vice-president David George told a reporter. "These developments appeal to homebuyers because of the open space, the fact that someone else is cutting the grass and the proximity of the golf course amenity."

Pure Boomer. Quality, convenience, service and location.

The pattern will be repeated in smaller centres, as well. Kamloops. Guelph. Port Perry. This second tier of golf community features smaller, more affordable homes in tranquil settings, but also just minutes away from essential services, like hospitals and banks.

The future is a condo.

The big condo comeback started happening in the first half of 1997 in the Toronto area. Toronto Homebuilders' Association executives were surprised to see the numbers; condo sales had shot higher, representing about 40% of all new homes. "Typically condominiums command a 29–30% market share with condominium town homes representing at least half of the total," Tridel Corporation vice-president Jim Ritchie said. "It is very interesting to note that condominium apartments outsold town homes by almost three to one."

Interesting indeed, and a trend that will continue as condos increasingly become a favoured housing alternative. After all, the advantages are obvious—carefree living with no maintenance concerns, superior security systems, worry-free travel, elaborate recreational facilities, a warm parking spot and a generally lower purchase price than a freehold home, which means more money invested in those precious financial assets.

Anticipate the emergence of condo communities, geared to seniors who will want both convenience and independence. Typical is a European-style development outside Toronto in Woodbridge. Villa Giardino offers residents five acres of gardens around their condos, along with valued amenities like a café, lounge with fireplace and solarium, a bank, medical service, beauty salon and even a fresh-food market. Optional services include housekeeping and laundry and room service. There is also security, with the entire development monitored by cameras; owners can view the front entrance on a dedicated television channel. Each suite also features an emergency communication system.

The ownership aspect of a condominium. The ambiance of a small village. The safety of a fortress. The lifestyle of a hotel. This is going to appeal to a lot of people in the twenty-first century.

The future is flexible.

We Canadians train ourselves to start life in 2,000 square feet, but Europeans are grateful to live in 800 square feet.

—Avi Friedman, architect
Montreal

Families are changing, blending, extending, redefining. That means in the future, housing will have to be more flexible. This will also change the face of real estate, altering what buyers value.

Active adult lifestyle communities are already starting to make a big impact on the market. Making this one attractive are the things people care most about when it comes to real estate—"the friendship of couples our age," along with easy access to health care, regional shopping centres and highway transportation.

The changes taking place in the population base of Canada, indeed North America, are stunning. According to the Vanier Institute of the Family:

- The proportion of children over the past 25 years has dropped, while the proportion of seniors has doubled.

- Marriage is an endangered institution, plunging 39% between 1981 and 1994. In Quebec the marriage rate collapsed 58%.

- Divorce is exploding. In 1951 one couple in 24 divorced. Now it's one in two.

- The size of families is falling fast. In 1961 the average family had four people. Today the average family has just 2.72 people.

The implications for real estate are clear: demand for traditional housing will melt away. It was built for two parents with two kids and earning two incomes. But in the future a "family" is likely to be a single parent with one child, a childless couple, a young couple living with a parent or two Boomers with a 30-year-old daughter at home who has no intention of leaving.

Inevitable demographic changes will lead to parents and children sharing spaces—in duplexes, semis and self-contained accessory apartments.

To Canada Mortgage and Housing officials, these changes also mean the dawn of "FlexHousing," a concept that could revolutionize the real estate choices facing future buyers.

CHANGING TIMES, CHANGING FAMILIES

Canadians expecting their parents to move in:	24%
Boomers expecting their children to move in:	21%
Canadians now working from home:	17%

Source: Royal Bank home ownership survey

One of the most important changes in families over the past few decades is their declining size.

—Canada's Families—They Count
Vanier Institute

Flexible houses may be modular. They'll be wired for home offices because self-employment and home employment are the two hottest labour-market trends. They will be age-proofed, a feature that will add thousands of dollars and buyer appeal to properties as the Boomers start to retire after 2011.

Some aspects of age-proofing:

- Wider doors and hallways to accommodate wheelchairs, walkers and other mobility devices.

- Contrasting colours to highlight surface changes, to make counter-tops stand out, to delineate the junction of walls and floor and the edge of the bathtub.

- Lots more light to assist older eyes.

- Bathroom handles and railings. Textured steps into the tub.

- Greater use of open spaces, fewer walls, less clutter.

- Broadloom and hardwood or tile, instead of area rugs that can buckle or slip.

- Few, if any, stairs. And where they exist, handrails that extend beyond the last step and slip-resistant carpeting.

- Levers replacing hard-to-twist doorknobs.

- A dedicated emergency communications system.

- Electrical outlets within easy reach.

- Visual fire alarms.

- Raised characters beside elevator buttons.

- Telephone and data jacks in every living space.

- Voice-activated home-management software that can work appliances and phone for assistance.

Already the very form of real estate is starting to change. McGill architecture professor Avi Friedman has designed the "Grow Home" with movable interior partitions. The "Next Home" is already being sold in Montreal's Mount Royal area, a three-and-a-half-storey pre-fabricated town-house structure that allows buyers to choose one or two or all three floors and then customize the spaces. Future buyers can then tailor the space to their own needs. And the good news is, construction costs are about half the traditional home.

A prototype in Montreal uses the ground floor for a retired person, the second floor for a childless couple and the top for a single mom with two teenagers. The entry level "Next Home" sells for an affordable $89,000.

The market for this kind of housing may be small today, but it will doubtless increase, because there's no fundamental reason to believe the massive changes taking place to Canadian families are going to end. Beaver Cleaver's all grown up now. Probably divorced and living in a loft.

The integration of real estate and interactive information technologies has begun. It won't be stopping. Ninety-eight per cent of Canadian homes have telephones, which will be largely replaced by appliances integrating phone, computer and Internet capabilities.

The future is secure and interactive.
Gated communities will be popular, even though the urban critics decry them as undemocratic and unfriendly. Toronto's Mondeo project has set a new standard for community security, with an armed gatehouse, closed-circuit television, dedicated security channels on the cable TV service and perimeter cameras. As well, each town house has its own security system. Mondeo was a big seller from the day the sales pavilion opened in late 1996.

Future buyers will also put a premium on access to the information highway. Houses on streets serviced by Rogers Wave will actually sell for more than those where inhabitants will have to communicate with the world over twisted copper strands.

In Newmarket north of Toronto, Intercom Ontario, a consortium of 80 companies, including Apple Canada, Bell and IBM, invested $100 million building interactive technology into every new home in the Stonehaven West development. It has become the country's first truly wired village.

The future is sport utility vehicles.

I think you are seeing a case of more disposable income heading to cottage country.

> —Pamela Alexander
> Re/Max Canada

And someplace to drive them—upscale recreational properties. It could be Whistler or it could be Muskoka, but it has to be good.

The market for recreational properties as a whole will mirror that for traditional residential real estate, and therefore decline in value over the next two decades. But a vibrant market will exist for the best stuff and, in fact, it has already started to develop.

According to Re/Max, in the first half of 1997, for example, sales of cottages in Ontario jumped by 10%, and prices were higher by up to 20% for the Three Lakes—Muskoka, Joseph and Rosseau. Waterfront places sold in a huge range, from $100,000 to $2 million.

And it's happening elsewhere, for example, in British Columbia where waterfront property in Kelowna has about doubled in the 1990s to $250,000 and a chalet in Whistler can easily cost $600,000.

Why the rebirth of this market? Because the Boomers who have done well have done *very* well. Astute investing in financial markets has given some people massive capital gains. Others are cashing out of top-end urban real estate and looking for a lifestyle change. Still others are part of the wave of early retirees—people in their mid-fifties who are in near-perfect physical shape and want to take up an outdoors lifestyle.

But the key here is to buy the best and to always think of resale. That means a house

• that has year-round use, i.e., fully winterized;

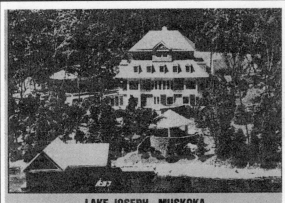
Yes, recreational properties have a future, but only the best ones in the best locations with the best neighbours. Oceanfront in Nova Scotia, Muskoka in Ontario, Whistler in B.C.

- on the waterfront or seconds from the ski lift;

- on a paved year-round road;

- with lots of privacy;

- whose value is helped by a "star factor"; having the cottage next to Goldie Hawn's, for example, guarantees buyer interest.

But also be aware even the good stuff can suffer in an economic downturn, because recreational real estate is by its very nature discretionary. When times get tough, that market suffers. Prices decline faster here than in the city.

The future is a trophy.

These buyers are downsizing, but don't want to give up their toys or their big dining room set, so they want large rooms to entertain in and big closets to store their stuff.

—*David Presnell*
U.S. homebuilder

Will a trend to trophy houses now so evident in the States sweep through Canada? The similarity of Canadian and American demographics suggests it's a real possibility. Besides, the idea of Baby Boom empty nesters pampering themselves with 7,000 square feet of granite kitchen counters, crown mouldings, libraries, marble floors, soaring ceilings and huge windows that look out on maintenance-free grounds and stone driveways is consistent with the final years of the Me Generation.

Financially prudent? No way. But when have the Boomers ever been prudent? Instead, they have moved herdlike through life buying just about everything when it reached its most expensive point—gold, real estate, mutual funds. So why not expect a certain proportion of the marketplace to go hopelessly upscale, regardless of the fact that there may be absolutely nobody around to buy properties like this when the Boomers are ready to be carried out?

In the States, Boomer demographics are driving this segment of the housing market. By 2010 the number of empty-nest families will rise by 18%, to 46 million. The number of childless couples will grow by

LE DOMAINE VALMONT
MONTEBELLO - QUÉBEC

COUNTRY MANOR built in 1947, cut stone, copper roof. 21 rooms, 10 bedrooms, 7 fireplaces. South exposure. This lifestyle comprises 100 acres of privacy, a chapel (cut stone, copper roof), a farm, and a golf driving range. UNIQUE IN CANADA. Viewing fee $100. $1,500,000. (CDN.)

It's quite possible trophy houses will become as popular in Canada as they are in the United States. And there will always be a market for the unique, stunning and irreplaceable—even when, because it's in Quebec, it goes for far, far below replacement cost. When that province's political climate improves, the buyer will be richly rewarded.

seven million, and all that growth will take place among those older than 45. People in this age bracket are in their peak earning years, and the huge expenses of college education are often behind them. They suffered the slings, arrows and outrageous costs of child-rearing. Now, it's payback time.

As a spokesman for the National Association of Homebuilders told a *Wall Street Journal* reporter: "They don't want a smaller home. They don't want to move to any lesser quality neighborhoods. They are very conscious of what they have. They want to tell the world that they have arrived."

Some of the features being demanded include main-floor bedrooms with sitting rooms, top-of-the-line kitchens and bathrooms, his-and-hers Jacuzzis and an entertainment "great room," replacing formal living and dining areas.

Outside Chicago, Painters Lake is a 20-acre enclave of trophy houses selling for between $700,000 and $2 million (U.S.). Outside Houston is another trophy showcase on a golf course with homes of up to 6,000 square feet going for $500,000.

Says a partner in the Daylar Group, which is developing another golf-course–trophy-home community, "The empty-nester market grows, regardless of whatever else happens in real estate."

The future is apartments.

Collapsing mortgage rates have suddenly made the economics of multiple-unit residential buildings make sense. And in jurisdictions where rent controls do not exist or are destined to be removed (like Ontario), this kind of investment is attracting a lot of attention.

In fact, very quietly, a miniboom in all kinds of multiple-unit buildings started in 1996 and was in full bore by 1997. Duplexes, triplexes, six-plexes and especially two- and three-storey walk-ups were being pursued by investors who figured this might be an even better deal than sticking money into RRSPs. In many cases they will be right.

You can buy an apartment building with 10% down and be in positive cash flow practically from day one, even with buildings where rents are below market levels. An example in west Toronto is a three-storey building built in 1953, renovated in 1989 and given a fire-code retrofit in 1995. It sits on three-quarters of an acre and has 21 units generating income of $90,156, net of taxes, insurance, utilities, repairs, advertising and staff.

It sold for $900,000, which means, with a downpayment of $135,000, the $765,000 mortgage (at 7%) carries for $5,358 a month, or $64,296 a year. The positive cash flow is more than $25,000 a year—not a bad income stream from the $135,000 invested.

Besides, a property like this gives you income and tax options. In the future the owner can just continue to collect rent, which is taxable as earned income (allowing him or her to make RRSP contributions). Down the road the building can be sold, with the profit being taxed as a capital gain. Or, if the equity increases with time, the property can simply be remortgaged, and the owner gets to take capital out free of any tax.

The key to successful multi-unit investing is to pick good properties with upside potential in good locations that will be easy to rent and will attract demand from tenants. Always consider such an investment a long-term one because it is considerably more difficult to sell a 48-unit building than a single residence. Your objective should be cash flow, not necessarily capital appreciation, although it's nice when that happens. And unless you like fixing toilets and dealing with late rent cheques, hire a property manager. It'll be the best 7% you ever spent.

Source: *The Toronto Star*

As the prince, so the castle . . .

If you ever buy a house and find it's a dog to sell, think of Robert Campeau. You'll feel better. Honest.

Campeau, along with junk bonds and BMWs, kind of embodied the 1980s. With borrowed billions, the former Sudbury homebuilder who transformed the Toronto waterfront waltzed into the U.S. market and seized control of that country's largest retail empire.

But, done in by soaring interest rates, weakening financial markets, bad deals and a recession, the Campeau Corporation was losing $2 billion a year by 1990. Robert was turfed from the company he'd founded.

Meanwhile, in 1981, he'd bought a double lot for $1 million on the Bridle Path, Toronto's incredible millionaires' row, and built a 28,000 square foot mansion. It was blessed by a Catholic cardinal, visited by prime ministers and featured everything from silk-covered walls to antique marble fireplaces. If you ever wanted a visual of the Eighties, this was it. Wretched excess in North York.

But after his financial woes started, Campeau went to Europe and put the house up for sale in 1994. Asking price: $15 million. Agents had to pay $100 each time they showed it.

The French chateau-style mansion finally sold in July 1997, after languishing for three years. The selling price: $6.17 million.

"It's a great price," listing broker Harvey Kalles said. And it was. The land is now worth $5 million and the replacement cost of the house is $4 million. But all that means nothing when you can't find a buyer.

Remember what Bob Campeau learned: The day you buy real estate is the day you start thinking resale.

PART 4

Chapter 8

——•

In the Second Half
of Your Life . . .

No matter what kind of residential real estate you
own, after you turn 40, use the equity you have
built up in it. Turn it into a tool to create wealth.

A fter all, you did it. You got there. This was what all the sacrifice was about—you paid off your mortgage. Now you're sitting on a bundle of cash in your house. If you own the average
Canadian house, that means about $160,000. If you live in Toronto,
about $220,000. If it's Vancouver, more than $400,000.

And if real estate values are not going up on a monthly basis, then
the return on all that capital is 0%. If real estate values are happily
increasing, then your return is that price hike, minus inflation. And to
equal the return you can get investing in quality mutual funds these
days, real estate would have to be scorching 1980s-style hot in your
area. Of course in many major markets, real estate is going nowhere. In
the late Nineties, southwestern Ontario and Halifax are flat. Montreal
is stone cold. Saskatchewan is hot. B.C. is everything at once. Toronto
is torrid and so is Calgary. Whistler and Muskoka are smoking.
Manitoba and the Maritimes are hard times.

But in all these places, no matter what the market, homeowners who
have paid off all or most of their mortgage have one thing in common.
They have equity. And equity can be a tool to build a dynamic financial
future—or, if not put to work, a wealth trap.

That's because equity sitting in a home is largely dead money. It
often represents the forced savings of a couple over the span of two or
three decades. Typically it is the largest single chunk of money a
Canadian has. And if you agree with my long-term cautions about the

future of residential real estate—especially the traditional, multi-bedroom, nuclear-family kind—this could be a very dangerous place indeed to have the bulk of your net worth.

It's time more people woke up and used The Strategy, now, while conditions are ideal—low mortgage rates, favourable financial markets, willing bankers, an improved real estate market and a growth economy. These things are going to be with us for a few years, and now is the time to build financial assets as fast as possible, so you won't be a victim of the coming retirement crisis.

Act now, while most people believe real estate has a future and while money is so plentiful and cheap. Believe me, it is not always going to be this way.

As a homeowner, here are three major options for getting at your equity:

- Sell and downsize or rent.
- Borrow against the equity in your home.
- Transfer your equity into your RRSP.

Note, I do not include getting a reverse mortgage in this list; that is usually a bad, bad idea.

However, it does appeal to a number of people. Unfortunately many of them are seniors who are less than fully informed about the consequences of taking a reverse mortgage. And the recent entry of one of the Big Six banks into the reverse-mortgage business has given it a respectability it does not deserve.

Today a stunning 80% of homeowners over 65 own mortgage-free properties. A large number of them are living below the poverty line with inadequate incomes. Others are trying to get by on the 3% or 4% their GICs are yielding, while sitting on $100,000 or $200,000 in their homes, which gives them nothing.

So when they hear about a reverse mortgage, their ears perk up in interest, because they are offered a tax-free stream of money, usually paid in the form of a monthly annuity. For house-rich, cash-poor seniors, it sounds like a great deal. And the older you are (and nearer The End), the greater the monthly payments.

But getting a term reverse mortgage could end up destroying the value of your estate, since it is, just as the name suggests, the reverse of a regular mortgage. That means interest keeps building on the amount of money you are advanced against the equity. The longer the mortgage is in place, the greater the interest bill that has to be paid when the mortgage expires. If that happens while you are still alive, you will probably have to sell the house to pay it off. Typically, because mortgage interest builds so quickly, you may have to give 100% of the sale proceeds of your house to the lender to cover a loan you took against just 30% of the equity you owned.

Or, when you die, your estate has to pay the mortgage principal (the money you received) plus the accrued interest, and that could wipe out anything you wanted to leave to family. In fact, if the real estate market heads south before the mortgage ends, you or your estate could be in even worse shape. Much better that you sell to free up equity or take a loan against it.

Are there any times a reverse mortgage does make sense?

Yes. If you or your parents cannot bear the thought of moving out of the house and have too little income to qualify for an equity loan and leaving money behind is not a priority and you are well into retirement— at least 75 years old—then it could be the appropriate thing to do. Or check out the innovative features offered by the CHIP program—the Canadian Home Income Plan.

But only take a term reverse mortgage if

- you take a life annuity, not a term one, for you don't want a surprise when you're 85

- the annuity is payable until the death of the last surviving spouse

- the lender will guarantee you'll never owe more than the value of your house

- you are given a cooling-off period to change your mind

- you make sure everything goes to, and is approved by, your lawyer before signing, and especially if

- you hate your children, because you are truly spending their inheritance.

Strategy One: sell while the selling's good

As noted, the residential real estate market will probably remain healthy as the millennium approaches. Lots of people will delude themselves into thinking this is something permanent. Others will always believe that assets you can touch, like houses, are inherently safer than paper assets or, these days, electronic ones. And there's the appeal of the capital-gains tax-free status of your principal residence.

So while mortgage rates are down and consumer confidence is up, your chances of selling for a good price are about the best they've been in the entire decade.

What a great opportunity to bail out of the kind of real estate that has no future and downsize into something that does—using the extra money to invest in financial assets. But just as buying takes care and planning, so does selling.

Here are the fundamentals.

Pick the right agent.

This is crucial. The right agent will be intimately familiar with the neighbourhood. Ideally, he or she has sold your house before. The right agent should be able to drive down your street and tell you what each place has sold for in the past few years and what's right or wrong with the property. Barring that, the agent should certainly be from a local office and know conditions in the neighbourhood.

This person has also got to have a plan. Find out what it is and insist on open houses for agents and for the public. Newspaper, cable TV and Internet advertising should be included as well as the MLS notice. The ideal agent will already have buyers interested in your place, especially in a hot market where inventory of the most desirable homes is tight.

Don't be shy about interviewing several agents, asking them about their experience, knowledge, marketing abilities and the price you should ask. But don't necessarily pick the agent who promises you the highest bucks. In fact, that's probably the last one you want.

Pick the right commission.

Yes, real estate commissions are negotiable. And while in most jurisdictions they are normally 5% or 6%, some discounters will go down to 3%. Obviously the lower the commission, the more money you get to keep on closing day.

But never forget this: a good agent will earn his or her commission by selling the house in a reasonable time for the best possible price and to a qualified buyer. Your agent is going to help you set the price, prepare the house, market it, pay for the ads, host open houses, prepare feature sheets, screen buyers, handle delicate negotiations, coordinate things between your bank and your lawyer and hold your hand. He or she has to deal with complex issues, be available at the drop of a hat and work nights and weekends. Then, of course, the commission has to be split between your agent, the buyer's agent and their companies.

Is this worth 6%? You bet it is.

Pick the right price.

The worst mistake you can make—in any market—is to price the property too high. It will get stale fast and probably end up selling for below market value.

No, much better to price the property *below* what you're hoping to get, particularly when things are hot and buyers abound. The idea is to attract multiple bids. And when you are a seller, multiple bids are as close to heaven as you can get.

Before you list the house your agent should arrive with "comparables"—listings of similar homes in the area that are on the market or have sold recently. That will tell you what ball park you're playing in, because it doesn't matter how much money you've put into your house, its worth is dictated by location and competing houses more than condition or upgrades.

Here's what a "comparable" looks like—a listing that includes the selling price, the day it sold and the day the deal closed. This house in a fashionable Toronto neighbourhood was listed for $1.4 million and sold within $20,000 of the asking price in early 1997.

Source: Toronto Real Estate Board

Pick the right plan.

When the market is cooking, why not turn up the sizzle on your property? Pricing it low to attract multiple bids is one way of doing it. Another is to post a specific time you will entertain offers, maybe three or four days after the house becomes available for viewing. That can create an air of excitement or, in some cases, almost an auction mentality among bidders. Rest assured their agents, if they know it will be a competition, will be encouraging them to come in off the top with their best offers.

And during the viewing period, you can help create excitement by having your agent schedule viewings close together or at virtually the same time. That will send a clear signal to potential bidders that they are not alone in thinking about making an offer. I have seen some listings come on the market with literally 15 or 20 groups of buyers and their agents lined up on the front lawn.

Part of your plan should be to have your property in the best possible condition. That means a tidy yard (pick up those dog droppings!), an open entranceway, neutral colours and furniture placed to make the home look as spacious as possible. It's even a good idea to get rid of a lot of your furniture, putting it in storage for a month. You'll be amazed at how much bigger your house looks with half the stuff in it.

Don't be cheap when it comes to sprucing the place up. Pay for the carpets to be cleaned and the walls to be painted. Hire a student to clean the windows. Repair broken doorknobs, steps, screens and the obvious things that buyers notice. In fact, go through the house as if you were a buyer, being extremely critical.

Remember: a house cannot be too clean. Expect buyers to open doors you have forgotten about, look inside shower stalls, kitchen drawers and even the inside of your oven.

Another part of your plan is to make it as easy as possible for the purchaser. Have an up-to-date survey ready. Be flexible about the closing date. Inquire beforehand about the portability of your mortgage or the cost of prepaying it, to ensure there are no delays after a deal is reached.

Have utility bills on hand so the buyer can see what it will cost to heat the place. Have the details of the mortgage ready if it is an assumable and attractive one.

Work with your agent in creating an exciting feature sheet, listing all the great things about the house, street and neighbourhood. Use a few colour pictures. If it's winter, include some summer shots. Your agent probably has access to a digital camera, which means that a great feature sheet with loads of pictures can be created simply on a home PC with a colour printer.

```
    $649,000 dp 10%/AMAP    43 STRATHGOWAN    CRES       NORTH YORK C10 MA2484
map    7 BC 2  nr STRATHEDEN/STRATHGOW  site f       wtr        tx 7123.00  1996
    66.90x160    FEET   lt S-133'; W-44.59       P/LT 101-11 PLN4458 zon
vend's WILLIAM ADAIR SIMONTON                        occ VAC poss 30-60/TBA
type DET    style S/S    ext B    htg HWG  gar DAT  dr D #rms  8+1 bed 4   kit 1
wr 2x4 1x3          bsmt P fp M cac N fam A pool N uffi N swrs Y crcd N h/c  90
M LR  21.98 x 14.47 O.S.F.P.    BRDLM                BEAUTIFULLY SITUATED ON
M DR  12.73 x 11.75 HRDWD FL                         QUIET CRES. FAMILY SIZED
M KIT 16.73 x 10.99 W/O YARD    EAT-IN               BRICK RESIDENCE. SECLUDED
U MBR 20.47 x 14.24 O/L'S GDN   WALK-IN CL 4 PIECE   TREED GARDEN. PRIVACY PLUS
U 2BR 13.75 x 12.99 CLOSET                           NEW SURVEY.SPEAK TO AGENTS
U 3BR 13.75 x  9.51 CLOSET                           BEFORE TYPING OFFER.*LUNCH
L 4BR 13.75 x  9.51 CLOSET                           AT O.H. AGENT MUST BE PRES
L FAM 22.97 x 13.98 O.S.F.P.   W/O YARD   W VIEW     ENT AT SHOWINGS. SHWGS STA
B REC 22.74 x 14.47                                  RT MARCH 7 11:00 AM.
extras:   OFFERS MARCH 10TH 10:00 AM BY VENDORS DIRECTION. INCL:(WASHER,DRYER,
DW, SOLD "AS IS") EXISTING ELF, BRDLM W/L, RECENT GAS BURNER & EQUIP,SOME PLANT
S IN GARDEN EXCLUDED 2 AIR COND.UNITS,SECURITY SYS,ELEC.GAR.OPENER.  *-$10.50
mtg TREAT AS CLEAR                                  ad A   o/h    DLA    1 CA
                                                    sd             11:00 to 1:00
```

An example of a vendor attempting to create an auction atmosphere and multiple bids. Offers are only entertained at a specific time three days after the property is open for showings. If you really wanted this house, you'd show up with your best offer, at asking price or over.

Source: Toronto Real Estate Board

It's also a good idea to have receipts on hand for recent renovations. And how about the home-inspection report you got when you bought the place? Or better still, hire a home inspector to do a current report. That will not only impress potential buyers, but may also remove the home-inspection condition from their offer.

Pick the right listing.
The listing agreement will spell out the commission you will pay, so there is no dispute upon closing. It can also contain a description of the marketing plan the agent is offering, including the number of times it will be advertised and where, along with open houses.

The agreement will also spell out how long the agent has the right to have the listing. In a slow market, 90 days is common. In a hot one, never go past 60. That will keep the agent more motivated to achieve a sale.

You may also be offered an exclusive listing, as opposed to an MLS listing. This means your agent is the only person who can find buyers for your house, and when he or she does, the commission is not split with the buyer's agent. So naturally why would other agents want to send their buyers over? The only advantage to you is a slightly lower commission. The big disadvantage is that without MLS exposure, the number of people who will know about your house is dramatically reduced.

So, only consider this arrangement if an agent comes to you saying he or she has buyers for your home.

Pick the right offer.

When the market's good and you've been successful in attracting multiple offers, don't blow your chances of selling the house by picking the wrong offer. And the one offering the highest price may not be the best.

There are many considerations, including the size of the deposit, the time until closing and conditions. There may be clauses making the offer conditional on selling another house (forget it, this is no offer) to securing financing (also bad—the buyer should have preapproval) to a satisfactory home inspection (normal).

How about the appliances, drapes and other chattels? Is the buyer asking for more than you're willing to throw in?

Remember, once you have an offer, you are in a position of power. You can accept, creating a binding deal. Or you can sign it back, writing in exactly what you want. With multiple offers, carefully select the one that looks the most promising, and sign it back, allowing a very short response period—just a few hours. That way, if the offer falls through, you may be in a position to accept another one that has not yet expired.

Don't be greedy.

Some people try to save paying the commission by selling privately. But it's usually a false saving, because a professional agent knows how to find the best buyers and achieve the highest selling price. Besides, private sales are a pain and always much more complicated than people think.

Chances are that sign in your front lawn is going to attract more nosy neighbours than buyers. In fact, many buyers are turned off by a private sale, because it's usually the hallmark of novice or unprofessional vendors. It can also signal that you are out for the biggest bucks possible, and who wants to deal with sellers like that?

And don't delay.

As far as I can see, conditions for Canadian residential real estate will remain favourable until the millennium. Inflation is virtually nonexistent, so no need to jack up interest rates by much. Corporate profits are galloping, jobs are being created, and by the end of 1998 there should be about 700,000 more people working than there were at the beginning of 1997. This is a very powerful combination for real estate, and boomlike conditions will be evident in most of the country.

But not in Quebec. In fact, the possibility of another referendum on Quebec independence is about the only thing we've all really got to worry about. A yes vote would dampen enthusiasm for big-ticket items like houses, and it would also do what it's always done before—bump short-term interest rates higher, including the cost of mortgages.

Of course, predicting the course of the economy is a lot easier than tracing the thought patterns of Quebec separatists, so nobody knows what will happen. But I sense that, as the Canadian economy moves into high gear, as people make money on their houses, and as jobs reappear, even the spectre of another go-round with the Bloc Québécois and the Parti Québécois will be less scary than in the past.

So, the best prediction is this: it's a great time to sell your house. A last-chance exit. This miniboom I first identified in fall 1995 will run for some time yet. You have the best opportunity in an entire decade of getting more money for an asset that faces an uncertain future.

This is the time to unload traditional residential real estate, to fine-tune your portfolio by buying the kind of home that does have a future, or to simply move to cash.

That cash, of course, must find its way into a diversified portfolio of stocks, mutual funds and other financial assets. And the sooner, the better.

Strategy Two: keep the house, spend the equity

Selling your house is only one way of getting your equity. For many people there's a better way, one that's faster, easier and more effective because it allows you to build your wealth while reducing your income taxes.

Imagine if one day you could simply dip into the equity in your home by borrowing against it, whether it's paid for completely or not. Imagine pulling out $50,000 or $100,000, at today's cheap interest rates, to invest in assets giving you a 10% or 12% yield. Now imagine if all the interest on that loan could simply be written off income tax you already have to pay on income you already earn.

Well, it's possible. It's called a home equity loan, and it's waiting for you at the corner bank or trust company.

This could be your leg up on a decent retirement. Borrowing against money you already have in your house could vault you years, even decades, ahead in the race to create wealth.

This strategy essentially converts equity in your home—money that has earned you 0% for most of the 1990s—into cash, which can be invested in financial assets like stocks, mutual funds and strip bonds.

- A home equity loan is not a mortgage, but rather a secured line of credit. Your home is the asset that backs the loan, in other words, the bank's security.

- The rate of interest on the loan is variable, floating up and down with the prime. But as I have argued in this book, the chance of rates rising substantially over the next few years is between nil and zero.

- Because the money you get from the home equity loan is used to buy financial assets, Revenue Canada considers it to be an investment loan, so the interest is tax-deductible.

- Therefore, this is good debt, unlike mortgage debt, which is not tax-deductible. You are able to use this money to buy assets that build your wealth, and at the same time deduct the interest from your taxable income. Wealth up, taxes down.

- As I write this, the prime rate is 4.75%, and several lenders will give you a home equity loan at the same rate. This is money you can then invest to earn 10%, 12% or more. So obviously you come out well ahead. But because the interest can then be deducted from income, it gets even better. If you are in the 54% tax bracket, then half the cost of the loan comes right off the income taxes you remit.

- This would be the same as actually borrowing the money at 54% less than the posted rate. On a 4.75% loan that would constitute a reduction of 2.5%, putting the effective loan rate at 2.25%.

  Now tell me, where else could you find $100,000 at 2.25% to invest to earn a double-digit rate of return? Take a look around—it could be living with you right in that house!

- Unlike what you do with a traditional mortgage, you never want to pay your home equity loan off, because while it's in place you're able to deduct the interest. So your monthly payments to the bank are not "blended," but "interest-only." With a blended payment, you return part of the principal to the borrower along with the month's interest. But with a home equity loan, it's all interest, which means you get to write it all off.

- Yes, there are fees involved in setting this home equity loan up, but they are not too stiff. Because this is an exploding aspect of banking (as I write, some of the banks have only started doing this, while others are realizing how much potential it has), it's going to be very competitive. Many lenders will actually be waiving all their fees over the next few years as they tap into the hundreds of billions of dollars in home equity now languishing in the homes of millions of Canadians. Here was the fee situation in the autumn of 1997:

Lender	Fees for:	Price	How to Apply
Bank of Montreal	Legals and appraisal	$399 package	Normal credit
Scotiabank	Legals and appraisal	$395 $175	Special form
Toronto Dominion	Refinance Collateral loan	$99 $350	Normal credit
Royal	Disbursements extra	$299	Normal credit
Bank of Commerce	Legals and appraisal	$650	Normal credit
Canada Trust	Legals and appraisal	$395 package	Special form

How do you deduct the interest payments made on your home equity loan?

You simply fill out Schedule 4 of the income tax return, indicating the total payment made during the year on your loan, and then write in the amount on page two of your tax return, right here on friendly line 221.

Carrying charges and interest expenses (Schedule 4)	221
Exploration and development expenses (Schedule 4)	224
Other employment expenses	229
Other deductions	

Source: Revenue Canada

That is a deduction from your taxable income. So a $5,000 entry there will reduce the final amount of tax you pay by $2,700 if you are in the 54% tax bracket, or $2,000 if you're in the 40% range.

The ability to deduct this interest can seriously improve your financial situation. Consider a couple earning $140,000 and living in a paid-for house in Toronto worth $325,000. They pay $21,726 in taxes on the first $64,000 of income and 52.9% tax on the rest, for a total tax bill of $61,930.

If they took out a $200,000 home equity loan at 5%, it would cost $10,000 a year in tax-deductible interest, which would save them $5,290 in taxes, reducing the total bill to $56,640. And if the $200,000 was placed in a diversified holding of mutual funds giving a yield of 12%, they'd be building their wealth by $24,000 a year. (And most of that would not be taxable until the funds were sold and the capital gains crystallized—presumably after retirement and at a lower tax rate.)

This means the couple is further ahead to borrow and invest rather than sitting on a pile of nonperforming money in their equity. And, probably, so would you.

The cost of home equity loans varies widely among lenders, but it is becoming a very competitive marketplace. Shopping around pays off handsomely.

- A home equity loan is not like a mortgage. You can arrange to borrow a certain amount in total, but you don't need to take it in a lump sum. Typically the money would flow into your bank account after you wrote a cheque to purchase financial assets.

Conversely you can pay down the line of credit at any time, without penalty. But why would you want to do that, when the loan carries tax-deductible interest?

How much can you borrow?

A surprisingly large amount. Lenders like Canada Trust will give you up to 75% of the appraised value of your home—or more than $122,000 on the average Canadian home worth $162,721. If you

---

LOW COST OPTION

Homeowner Mortgage Checklist

To help your application go quickly and smoothly, please provide us with copies of the following information:

☐ income verification (e.g., letter confirming your salary or three years tax returns and financial statements)

☐ current homeowners fire insurance policy

☐ existing registered mortgage (if not with Canada Trust)

☐ copy of deed of title (if no existing mortgage)

Your name(s) _____

Your address _____

_____

_____

Your phone no. (home) _____ (work) _____

Date _____ Canada Trust _____

Taking out a home equity line of credit at Canada Trust: here are the documents this company requires. Make sure you have them for speedy approval at this lender or others.

invested that $122,000 for six years at 12%, it would become $244,000. Six years later it would double again at that rate of return, to $488,000.

> *So if today you are 12 years away from retirement and you own the average Canadian house, by borrowing against it you stand a good chance of*

having half a million dollars at retirement. As an added bonus, between now and then, if you're in the 50% tax range, you will save about $36,000 in income tax.

Can you afford *not* to do this?

- An even more aggressive way of building your wealth is to borrow against those financial assets that you bought by borrowing against your equity.

Here's an example of a young couple with a combined income of $48,000 living in Nova Scotia in a paid-for $160,000 house. They are clients of a financial adviser there who had me in to give a seminar. I talked about The Strategy during that seminar, and they went and did it. They borrowed $87,500 against the house, paying interest of $450 a month and putting the money into mutual funds. The interest is tax-deductible, and their net worth is growing at about $10,000 a year.

In addition they have pledged $25,000 of the mutual funds as collateral for a loan of $50,000, which will also be invested in mutual funds. The $300 a month in interest is also tax-deductible, but the couple doesn't even make the payments because it's simply deducted from the investment account. Now, instead of having a $160,000 house sitting there earning nothing, they have $137,500 in financial assets earning more than $16,000 a year, while being able to write $7,800 off their taxable income. And of that $7,800, they only actually paid $4,200. The mutual funds paid the rest, but they get the tax deduction.

In fact, using a systematic withdrawal plan, you can borrow against the equity in your home to invest for growth and get a break on your taxes without actually spending a dime.

Here's how it works.

Take out a home equity loan for, say, $100,000. Write a cheque for that amount and give it to your financial adviser (you have one, right? If not, see the next chapter). Your adviser can invest that money for you in a quality mutual fund and set up the systematic withdrawal plan (called a "swip" to insiders).

That means each month an amount of money equal to the interest charge on your equity loan is taken out of your mutual fund account and sent to the bank or trust company where you got the loan. And because the mutual fund units you purchased are growing, the overall account can easily afford to pay the interest charge.

So, you have secured and invested $100,000, and it came from your house, not your bank account.

Then the mutual fund makes all the loan payments for you. Remember, you have no money of your own invested and you have no monthly payments to make. But every April, when you sit down to do your taxes, you get to deduct all the money the mutual fund sent to the bank from your taxable income. You just write it all down on line 221 and end up paying less to the federal and provincial governments.

This is where the true power of using home equity lies. You can build wealth and reduce your tax burden simply by deciding one day you will end the insanity of having wealth trapped inside an asset that could be facing a very uncertain future. Open the doors and windows. Let it out. Your very retirement security could depend on doing it. And on doing it now, when money is inexpensive and financial assets have been performing well and should continue to for at least a decade. What a time of opportunity we live in!

Four real-life examples

Let me show you by example what you could have expected if you'd employed The Strategy and combined it with a systematic withdrawal plan.

In the following examples I show you the amount invested in several mutual funds from the home equity loan and the year that investment was made. The "monthly payment" is the amount of money sent to the bank by the mutual fund to pay the interest. This is the amount you claim against income for tax purposes. The "amount withdrawn" is the total received as income since the investment was made, and the "remaining value in 1997" is just that—the amount of money you would have in your mutual fund account.

EXAMPLE ONE: DYNAMIC PARTNERS FUND				
Amount invested	Year	Monthly payment	Amount withdrawn since start	Remaining value in 1997
$100,000	1989	$833	$81,634	$128,590

I used this mutual fund because it has been an average performer—not at the top of the pack, just a solid workhorse giving ho-hum returns. But still, you can see that since 1989 the fund gave $81,634 in income on a $100,000 initial investment and, even after that, has $128,000 left in the account.

EXAMPLE TWO: FIDELITY GROWTH AMERICA

Amount invested	Year	Monthly payment	Amount withdrawn since start	Remaining value in in 1997
$50,000	1990	$415	$32,000	$148,000

Here is a mutual fund that's a little more aggressive, investing in the stocks of American companies. Note that, despite paying the interest charges for you on the $50,000 borrowed, it ended up virtually tripling the initial investment. Fifty thousand dollars left in your home equity between 1990 and 1997 would not have tripled. In fact, it probably would have declined. And it wouldn't have reduced your taxable income by $32,000. In the top tax bracket, that's a saving of more than $17,000.

EXAMPLE THREE: TRIMARK FUND

Amount invested	Year	Monthly payment	Amount withdrawn since start	Remaining value in 1997
$100,000	1981	$833	$155,000	$584,000

Trimark has been a solid performer, and here is an example of the greatest tool you can use with a mutual fund—long-term investing. We took income out of this account to pay the interest on the home equity loan, but we did not touch the principal. Over 16 years it increased 500%.

EXAMPLE FOUR: TEMPLETON GROWTH

Amount invested	Year	Monthly payment	Amount withdrawn since start	Remaining value in 1997
$100,000	1976	$833	$204,000	$1,994,000

Here is a powerful example of long-term investing and investing for growth. Templeton Growth has achieved spectacular returns and richly rewarded people who are patient and plan for the future. Once again, it is inconceivable to imagine a piece of residential real estate worth $100,000 20 years ago rising in value to $2 million today. And along the way, the money invested here has yielded $204,000 in tax-deductible interest. To someone in the top tax bracket, more money has been saved in missed income tax payments than was initially invested!

A word or two about taxes

The money invested in a mutual fund will typically yield you capital gains, which are taxable. But the good news is they are taxed at a reduced rate to interest and are only taxable when they are crystal-lized—in other words, when you sell your mutual fund units for more than you paid.

Mutual fund companies trigger some capital gains on a yearly basis, when they pay money into your account. This is taxable. And the money you take out on a monthly basis to pay the interest on a home equity loan is taxable, as well, but at a very low rate. This is because some of the money you remove is money you invested in the first place, and you've already paid tax on it (you built up your real estate equity in after-tax dollars). The rest is in the form of capital gains.

Unlike interest income, which is 100% subject to tax at your personal rate, you are required to pay tax on only 75% of the capital gains you earn. So where you will lose $458 of every $1,000 in GIC income to tax, you lose just $342 in capital gains to tax, effectively lessening your tax load by 12%.

Clearly, where you have a choice, always choose capital gains over interest.

More and more people are learning this

Thank goodness. There is some hope, after all. In increasing numbers, Canadians are waking up to the fact that interest rates are going to stay low, financial markets will continue to rise (though not in a straight line), real estate equity is dead wealth, and the greatest risk we all face is running out of money.

The amount of wealth being shifted out of cash, term deposits and bank accounts is growing daily, just as is the amount we are investing in financial assets. In mid-1997 total mutual fund assets passed the quarter-billion-dollar mark for the first time. That's an impressive

CANADIANS SHIFT OUT OF DEPOSITS

Cash, deposits and short-term paper (% of financial assets)

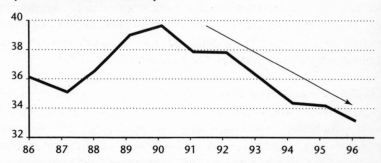

More and more Canadians are finally starting to get it. Interest rates are not going to jump higher, so money put in dead-end assets like GICs and Canada Savings Bonds has to be shifted into assets with a future, like stocks and mutual funds.

Source: Nesbitt Burns

CANADIAN HOUSEHOLD NET FINANCIAL ASSETS GROWING

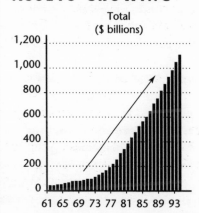

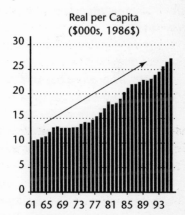

Rising financial markets are boosting household assets. Canadians have more than $250 billion invested in mutual funds, but almost three times that in fixed-rate assets.

Source: Nesbitt Burns

number, but it has to swell dramatically if we are to lessen the destructive effects of the retirement crisis that is at hand as the Baby Boomers head into the critical decade prior to retirement.

Millions of those people could be increasing their wealth daily if they just understood that the old rules no longer apply. Buying and paying off residential real estate is not a goal on its own. It's a tool to use, now that deflation is replacing inflation and as an aging population and changing real estate needs threaten the equity most people are mistakenly clinging to.

The future is not a happy one for many of them. But that doesn't need to be the case. If this is you—saving your money instead of investing it, sitting on most of your net worth in your house, afraid to put money into something that might go down in value, fearful of trusting anyone to give you guidance and advice—then you must change.

Still, you are, of course, master of your own destiny. No one can force you to invest.

But if you do, you will succeed.

Strategy Three: put your equity in your RRSP

Let's face it. More people will need an income stream from an RRSP as they get older than they will need ownership of a house. And the existing RRSP rules allow you to put your mortgage inside your RRSP and end up making mortgage payments to yourself. That's pretty cool. And it's something more people should be doing, especially conservative investors.

In my *1998 RRSP Guide*, I say:

> **Working with a self-directed RRSP and the equity you've built up in your house, there is a way to actually transfer that equity into your tax-sheltered retirement plan—even if doing so means you exceed the allowed RRSP contribution levels.**

This is a bit tricky, and you need to follow the rules closely. In addition, this strategy only works if you already have an amount of cash (or cashable investments) in your RRSP equal to the mortgage currently on your home or the one you plan to place on it to get the equity out.

It is also going to cost you a few thousand to set up and a few hundred a year in fees. But if you feel like I do—that the future belongs to liquid assets, not to real assets like housing—then this is a dramatic way for you to turn your house into a retirement plan.

How an RRSP mortgage works

Your RRSP is allowed to hold a mortgage on any Canadian real estate you own—either residential or commercial—or on property owned by an immediate relative.

That means you can take money in your RRSP and lend it as a mortgage. Then you must make regular payments back into your RRSP, just as you would with a bank mortgage.

One of the neat things about this is you will end up paying far more back into your RRSP than you ever took out. *In fact, this is the only way you can contribute more to your RRSP than is allowed under the regular contribution rules.* Because of the way mortgages are amortized, payments in the early years are almost all interest. Only in the final years of a mortgage do you actually begin paying back the principal. So over the course of a typical 25-year amortization, you will end up putting about three times more money into your RRSP than you took out.

In the meantime you can use the payments made into your RRSP to invest in growth mutual funds, preferably based on the performance of international equities, to get solid double-digit returns.

> *The idea here is completely opposite to a conventional mortgage—which you want to pay off as fast as possible. The goal with an RRSP mortgage is to make it last as long as you can and to be as costly as possible, so you can maximize the transfer of wealth into the retirement plan.*

There are several ways of doing this.

- First, go with the **longest amortization** period possible. The longer it takes you to pay it off, the more interest accrues and the greater the amount of money going into the RRSP.

- Second, the government stipulates that the rate of interest your RRSP mortgage is set at must be "comparable" to market rates. So shop around, find the **highest possible rate** being offered commercially and use that as your RRSP mortgage rate.

- Third, always make your RRSP mortgage an **open** one, allowing you to pay it off at any time (which you have no intention of doing). Open mortgages cost a premium rate, which means your interest is greater.

  For example, as I write this, a one-year closed mortgage is at 5.2%, but by choosing the open option, the rate is boosted considerably, to 5.85%. That's a nice high rate, considering that a one-year GIC is yielding just 3%.

- Fourth, you can make the mortgage a **second** one, which boosts the interest rate even higher. (But this will also cost you more in mortgage insurance—all RRSP mortgages have to be insured by CMHC or GE Capital, the only two insurers currently available.)

- Finally, stay away from all the techniques that people normally use to accelerate repayment of the mortgages. In other words, you want a **monthly-pay** mortgage, instead of a weekly one that cuts repayment time and saves a lot in interest. You don't want to pay less into your RRSP. You want to pay as much as possible!

An RRSP mortgage has the same flexibility and the same constraints as a bank mortgage. You can choose any length of term commercially available, and if you default on your payments, your RRSP ends up taking ownership of your home—which you don't want.

That's because RRSPs are allowed to *finance* real estate, but not to *own* it. Your plan would be required to sell the home within a year at market value.

There are certainly expensive setup costs and moderate maintenance costs involved, and as mentioned, this has to be done through a self-directed retirement plan. But it's still worth it.

To set the thing up you'll pay an appraisal fee (typically $150 to $200), legal fees ($500 or more) and a one-time setup fee (anywhere from $100 to $300, depending on the financial institution).

Also, all RRSP mortgages have to be insured, and the cost for that is generally about 1.5% of the mortgage amount, or $1,500 on a $100,000 loan. With a bank mortgage, you're better off paying this in cash than adding it to the mortgage principal, because by tacking it on, it also gets amortized and ends up costing you three times what you borrowed.

But in this instance, because the goal is to get money into your RRSP, you gladly add it to the outstanding debt.

MORTGAGE INSURANCE PREMIUMS

% of the portion of property's value being mortgaged	Premium as % of mortgage's entire balance
65%	0.5%
75	0.75
80	1.25
85	2.0
85+	2.5

Once in place, the RRSP mortgage will have some ongoing costs. The annual fee for the self-directed plan is typically $150, and then there is a mortgage administration fee that is anywhere from $100 to $300 annually. Revenue Canada stipulates that you can't administer your own RRSP mortgage. It must be done by a third-party agent, typically a trust company.

Not all financial institutions will allow you to have an RRSP mortgage within a self-directed plan. Others will only allow such a mortgage on your principal residence. Still others are completely flexible—so shop around.

You need to have enough cash or cashable assets in your RRSP to equal the mortgage you are transferring to your plan. If your RRSP assets are locked into GICs, for example, it won't work. And once the RRSP mortgage is set up, it's locked in until the time of renewal, when you have some options.

Using an RRSP mortgage to get equity out of your home

In most cases where people already have existing mortgages on their homes and less than $50,000 cash in their RRSP, it does not make sense to try to set up an RRSP mortgage. The initial and ongoing costs are too high to compete with the return your money could get elsewhere.

But there are some circumstances under which this strategy allows you to get equity out of real estate and at the same time exceed the RRSP contribution levels.

Is this you? It is if

• you own your home, mortgage-free, which means you have a significant amount of equity

• you have a whack of cash or cashable assets (Canada Savings Bonds, strip bonds, mutual funds, etc.) in your RRSP

• you have a good cash flow you'd like to divert into your RRSP.

Suppose you have $150,000 equity in your home, an equal amount in RRSP assets—and you want to take advantage of setting up an RRSP mortgage.

1. Get a home equity loan for $150,000. You can do this easily through financial institutions like CIBC, Bank of Montreal, ScotiaBank or Canada Trust; or most full-service financial advisers will set it all up for you, sometimes even free of charge.

2. Invest that money in, say, equity-based mutual funds to earn at least 10%. Now your home equity loan is deemed to be an investment loan for tax purposes.

3. As such, the interest on the equity loan is tax-deductible. So if you are in the 54% tax bracket, when it comes time to do your income tax, deduct 54% of the interest you paid all year. Your taxable income will drop as a result, which is a nice extra.

4. Now set up an RRSP mortgage, which means your retirement plan would buy out the bank or trust company mortgage (this costs you nothing, since you're just paying down your line of credit). You can insure this through GE Capital or, if you have waited up to a year after taking the equity loan, CMHC will insure the mortgage (CMHC has a rule against insuring equity loans, but after a period of time in existence it becomes a normal mortgage).

   GE Capital (known as Gemico), a very aggressive new player on the Canadian financial landscape, has no such silly rule and will insure your equity take-out mortgage without question.

Okay, let's review where we're at right now. You have taken $150,000 out of the equity in your home and it is now earning you at least 10% (instead of 0%). At the same time, you have created a tax deduction and reduced your income tax load. And now your RRSP holds a $150,000 mortgage, instead of the assets that used to be there. In essence, we have removed the $150,000 from your RRSP, tax-free, using this strategy.

5. Now every month you cut a cheque to your RRSP in the form of a mortgage payment. At the current five-year rate of 7% (as I write this) that cheque would be for $1,050. And so each year you would be contributing $12,607 to your RRSP. Not only is that close to the

current maximum limit of $13,500, but it doesn't matter what your income level is. To make the maximum $13,500 payment, you'd have to be earning more than $75,000. But with an RRSP mortgage you could be contributing $12,607 in this case while making just $60,000—which would normally qualify you for a maximum contribution of only $10,800.

6. In five years, you'd be able to contribute $63,037 into your RRSP, and of course during that time, if all the money were put into growth-oriented mutual funds averaging 10% (and you should do much better than that), your RRSP would have about $93,000 returned to it.

The bottom line is increased wealth. Five years after having $150,000 equity in your home and $150,000 in your RRSP (which had grown to just over $200,000), for a total of $350,000, you would now have a $150,000 mortgage in your RRSP, $93,000 in new RRSP assets and more than $200,000 in outside investments (assuming the $150,000 grew by 12–13% after capital-gains tax)—for a total of almost $450,000.

If you had not arranged the equity loan and then the RRSP mortgage, the $150,000 in your RRSP would certainly have continued to grow, but the equity in your home likely would not have grown and perhaps even shrunk. And you would not have had the mortgage interest to help reduce your taxable income.

With such things possible, isn't it amazing most people continue to sit on all that money in their homes?

Holding a mortgage inside your RRSP is not for everyone, but it could be for you. The strategy above allows you to enjoy both the growth of mutual funds and also the security of holding a fixed-income asset (your mortgage). It slowly and steadily transfers equity into your RRSP and out of your house, while giving you some serious tax advantages.

There are other strategies that harness the power of RRSPs when it comes to real estate, whether you are a buyer or a homeowner. I suggest you refer to my annual *RRSP Guide* for the latest ones.

Chapter 9

How to Find an Adviser You Can Trust

A t a time when the Canadian economy is booming in an environment of low interest rates, negligible inflation and roaring financial markets, how can it be that so many people are doing so poorly in their personal financial affairs?

The answer is clear. It's because they entrust their money entirely to rank amateurs with no formal training who devote, on average, about two hours a year to the job and refuse to consider any research or investment information that isn't free.

Who are these rank amateurs? That's right—they're you. People trying to do their own financial planning. Big, big mistake.

Need evidence?

- About half the people in the country **will not have $250,000 in net worth** on the day they retire. That's according to a Gallup poll, and it's shocking evidence of the unpreparedness of Canadians for what lies ahead.

- **Record numbers of people have been going bankrupt** just when interest rates and unemployment have been declining, the country is doing record amounts of trade, and corporate profits are at an all-time high.

- Canadians continue to have far too much of their net worth locked up in one type of asset that has been declining in value for most of the decade—**residential real estate**. That makes us some of the least diversified investors on the planet. Most people think real estate moves in cycles and all the equity they have lost in their homes will return. Sure, along with Elvis and your waistline.

- **About two-thirds of Canadians have never made an RRSP contribution**, despite the fact this is the continent's best tax shelter. And most taxpayers have no idea that with one phone call they can open an RRSP with no cash and transfer into it things they already own, earning a rebate cheque from the government.

- Dan Richards, of Toronto-based Marketing Solutions, does public surveys showing that **Canadians know next to nothing about investing**. For example, most people think Canada Savings Bonds provide an excellent long-term return, when they actually wither as an investment. And only a quarter of the people with bond or mortgage mutual funds know those funds will fall when interest rates rise. Worse still, only 14% of people can identify the best-performing investment class since the Second World War. Stocks.

- **Crazed investors sold hundreds of millions of dollars' worth of mutual funds** in the last three trading days before the Quebec referendum of October 30, 1995—just after the TSE 300 had been clobbered and those funds reduced in value. The day after the referendum, most of those people bought the funds back—at higher prices. Traditional Canadian investment strategy: sell low and buy high.

- **People clamour to buy investments when they are at their highest value and dump them when they fall.** Remember the folks lined up on Yonge Street in Toronto to buy gold at $1,000 an ounce? Today the metal is worth half that, and no lineups. How about the people who bought houses at $1 million each on a nice street north of Toronto in 1989? Today half that street's for sale at $500,000 a house. And recall how many investors bailed out of their stocks after Black Monday 1987? They missed one of the greatest run-ups in stock market history. You can rest assured that in the next major market correction, history will repeat itself.

- Surveys also show us that **Canadians, on average, hold their mutual funds for about 18 months, a period of time so short it just about guarantees they will lose money**. This is especially true for people who invest in the no-load funds. Some are so obsessed with saving a few dollars that they trade off solid investment advice for no commission.

- **Millions of Canadians keep billions in low-yield guaranteed investment certificates** when they could be earning more of a return with less risk in other securities. Why? Because they've never heard of strip bonds or mortgage-backed securities.

I could go on for pages, but I hope this is enough for you to get my point: you, as an average Canadian, are the last person you should trust with something as important as personal financial planning, tax and investment strategies. And yet most do, which is sad. That's one reason a giant retirement crisis is going to descend on this country. It's why millions of Boomers will end up being both old and poor.

I've written before about my experiences giving financial seminars across Canada. Various companies hire me to conduct these, from the largest of Toronto-based national investment houses owned by the great banks to individual financial planners in rural Nova Scotia and the Lower Mainland of British Columbia.

Invariably the same pattern emerges. A few hundred people show up, many of them armed with notebooks and tape recorders. They madly scribble information for an hour and a half and try to run for the door at the end of the evening before any representative of the hosting company can convince them to come in for a free consultation. At first I just thought they were being cheap—only taking what was offered for nothing. Then I realized most of them are just scared, **worried about their own financial futures but also convinced a financial planner will cost them a lot in commission and maybe lose their money in an investment they don't understand.**

The irony is that those people who do listen and then take up the offer of professional money management, almost always go on to improve their wealth. By sharing the burden, they gain a lot.

Yes, there are rip-off artists, but . . .

For the record, there have been a lot of people ripped off by unscrupulous financial advisers. Some advisers turn out to be nothing but churners, excessively buying and selling investments just to maximize commissions, at the expense of the client's portfolio. Others are just cheats, and over the past few months some spectacular cases have made the front page.

Some of the "top producers" at rapidly growing financial-services companies get to be top producers not by making wise investments but rather by racing through legions of clients.

Others are more motivated by the goodies flowing from mutual fund companies than the best interests of investors. Ontario is one jurisdiction that is taking some action to curb that, backed by the Investment Funds Institute of Canada. Looks good on them both.

So you are right to approach this exercise with caution and care—but not with cynicism or scepticism. The simple truth is almost everyone is better off with a personal financial adviser than trying to get all your financial information at the corner bank (where you will be offered only the bank's own limited products), from free seminars, the media or even books like this one.

Here are my answers to the questions I'm most often asked about finding an adviser you can trust:

How do I know if a planner is qualified? Are there regulations?

People who sell you financial securities have to be licenced. But the industry as a whole is unregulated, which means finding a good adviser is going to take some work on your part. The Canadian Association of Financial Planners has about 1,600 members, but that accounts for just 20% or so of all those who call themselves planners. There are currently no national standards, but there are a few designations you should be aware of.

A "registered financial planner," or RFP, is a designation given by the Canadian Association of Financial Planners; a "chartered financial planner," or CFP, designates someone who's completed the correspondence course of the Canadian Institute of Financial Planning; and a "chartered financial consultant," or CHFC, is an approval from the Life Underwriters of Canada.

To further confuse things, the Canadian Association of Financial Planners and the Life Underwriters have teamed up to create the Financial Planners Standards Council of Canada, which will be promoting yet another designation—the "certified financial planner," or, also, CFP. It looks like this last one may turn out to be the industry norm, since that term is already recognized in the United States and a few other countries.

The bottom line: make sure what training and education a planner has, along with experience and references.

What is this going to cost me?

Most people think a financial planner will cost them a huge amount of money. Usually that's not the case. In fact, most planners work for you free.

The right way to think about planners is the same way you think about travel agents: you can get your ticket to Montreal and pay Air Canada $500, or your travel agent can arrange it for you, and it still costs $500.

That's because Air Canada will do a lot more business each year with your agent than with you, and so the airline is happy to pay the agent a commission—in effect, lowering the cost of the ticket.

So, your financial planner is paid a commission by the mutual fund company or bond issuer when you add that investment to your portfolio. Of course, you can hire an adviser who is fee-only and does not actually arrange for any investments to be made. That will cost you up to $2,000 for a complete financial plan and an hourly consultation fee ranging from $50 to $250, with most in the $100 area.

You will often see "expert" opinion in the media warning you away from commission-paid advisers and into the arms of fee-paid ones. Ignore it. For the vast majority of people who have less than $1 million in liquid assets, an adviser remunerated through commissions is just fine.

What can you expect from a person like that? For starters, a free first consultation that will last an hour or ninety minutes, followed by an analysis of your existing assets and a draft financial plan making recommendations. All that typically costs you nothing—so what possible excuse could you have for not getting such a valuable second opinion on how you're doing?

EIGHT COMMON INVESTOR MISTAKES AN ADVISER CAN HELP YOU AVOID

- Waiting for the "best" time to invest, or never investing
- Buying at a high price; selling at a low one
- Buying yesterday's hot investment
- Choosing investments not suited to individual goals or time horizons
- Failing to diversify; "putting all your eggs in one basket"
- Reacting to short-term events rather than long-term trends
- Basing investment decisions on fees and sales charges
- Basing investment decisions on emotions rather than facts

Source: Mutual Fund Forum

Where do I start?

- *Ask others*—friends, family members, co-workers, the boss— whom they use as advisers. Word-of-mouth references are good because you can get a feel for an adviser's track record from somebody you know.

- *Respond to ads* published in the financial section of your local newspaper or in the *Financial Post*—especially during RRSP season, when lots are offering particular investments.

- *Attend a few financial seminars.* Most are free and, again, during RRSP season there's a flurry to choose from. A great deal of information can be had in a short period of time, and the financial planners hosting them invariably offer anyone who attends a free consultation in their office or your home. This gives you an opportunity to meet and assess that person.

  A word of caution: not all seminars are what they appear. Some are come-ons for expensive and needless courses on no-money-down real estate or sure-thing business opportunities. So, if you go, leave your chequebook at home.

  Just listen and you can quickly determine if this is a shameless sales pitch—with one or two specific investment products being hyped— or the introduction to a service that might be useful and an adviser who sounds promising.

What questions should I ask?

When you have that first meeting, the adviser will ask you for a lot of information on your income, assets, taxes, family situation and goals.

In return you should ask your adviser how he or she expects to be paid, his or her areas of personal expertise, and track record and credentials. Be tough. Be frank. Be candid. Ask where the adviser puts his or her own money and why, and what the results have been.

Here is a list of questions American investors are urged to ask of a potential planner, published in the *Wall Street Journal*. It's a good one to start with.

THINGS YOU SHOULD ASK ADVISERS DURING INTERVIEWS

- What is your area of expertise?
- What is your approach to saving and investing?
- Will you provide an individualized financial plan?
- What kinds of communications can I expect from you on an ongoing basis (account statements, newsletters, etc.)?
- How often will you review my portfolio?

- How are you compensated for the service you provide?
- How are fees calculated?
- On average how much can I expect to pay for your service?
- What do I receive in return for that fee?
- What, if anything, do you expect of me during our relationship?

Should I ask for references?

Absolutely. In fact, this is the most important thing you should ask for. *A good adviser has nothing to hide.* In fact, a good adviser should have a lot to be proud of and will want to share his or her clients' success with you.

So ask for a list of 10 or 12 people they have worked with. Then call them and ask for a candid appraisal of the planner's effectiveness. Has the adviser reduced their tax bill? Increased their net worth? Diversified their investments? What overall rate of return are they getting on their portfolios? How often do they hear from the adviser? Are they kept fully informed? Are they concerned about excessive trading in their accounts? Are they related to the adviser (it does happen!)?

What level of service should I expect?

Several meetings at first to approve an investment and tax strategy, then regular updates, perhaps quarterly. Your portfolio should be reviewed several times a year or as changing conditions dictate.

You should get a regular account statement—monthly is best—and that statement should break down all transactions, giving you rates of return and securities held along with weightings by asset class (for example, 41% mutual funds, 32% fixed income, 27% equities).

Many good advisers provide clients with newsletters, access to investment research or client-appreciation nights where investment professionals come to speak. Advisers with some of the larger investment firms are backed by substantial research departments along with access to new stock and bond offerings.

Examples of these include:

- Midland Walwyn

- Nesbitt Burns

- RBC Dominion Securities

- Richardson Greenshields

- ScotiaMcLeod

- TD Evergreen

- Yorkton Securities

The most important thing to expect is a comfortable working relationship with somebody you trust.

How can I tell if it's not working?

A telltale sign you're working with the wrong person is churning. That's when the adviser is buying and selling a lot of mutual fund units or stocks for no good reason other than to earn more in commission. Check your regular statement and look for any evidence of unnecessary trades.

What's the difference between a planner, a broker and a counsellor?

As I've mentioned, anybody can call themselves a **financial planner**—there are no national standards or regulations. But that does not mean you should look elsewhere. Far from it. Using a planner you get along with can be the most cost-effective way of building wealth.

Many planners work for companies that offer a full range of financial products, including strip bonds, stocks, mutual funds, GICs and more. Examples of these are:

- Financial Concept Group

- Investment Planning Counsel of Canada

- The Financial Planning Group

- DPM Financial Planning

- Partners in Planning

- Money Concepts

- Regal Capital

- Berkshire Investment Group

- Networth Financial

- Reimer Financial Services

- Gordon Financial

- Money Watch Consultants

- Capital Management Group

- Fortune Financial

- Investors Group, which is the largest in terms of assets managed and has recently moved far beyond its own range of mutual funds to offer clients dozens more.

The planners with these companies usually earn their living through commissions paid by the mutual fund and other companies. Ask, and most will be happy to tell you exactly who pays them and how much.

A **broker** is licensed to sell any financial product and must have completed the Canadian Securities Course. He or she will work for a brokerage company regulated by the Investment Dealers Association of Canada. A broker will also earn money through commissions on every transaction in your account.

An investment **counsellor** is paid through fees that can take the form of an annual payment or a percentage of the total portfolio under management. Usually counsellors are the preserve of the rich—those with more than $500,000 in investible assets. They, by the way, account for only 1.6% of the population. Pity.

How do I know if an adviser is full-service?

Ask. Some planners only sell mutual funds, so obviously they will not be able to give your portfolio the balance and diversity it should have. Everybody needs a little fixed-income holdings, for example, and you also want an adviser who will look at your total financial picture— real estate, insurance, estate, tax and investment plans.

Remember, the people at the bank or trust company will only offer you the products that institution itself sells (with the exception of Toronto Dominion, which is slowly offering more and more competitors' mutual funds, now forcing a couple of its competitors to follow suit—a good move).

What about the discount brokers?

These are no-frills operations that allow you to buy stocks, bonds or funds at a vastly cheaper commission than a full-service broker or planner charges. Examples are the T-D's impressive Green Line operation and the Royal Bank's Action Direct.

The discount brokers are innovative and on the cutting edge in terms of the latest investor technology. Canada Trust, Action Direct and Green Line all offer the option of real-time trading via personal computer and modem—an experience that surely gets the adrenalin coursing.

The downside is the same as with no-load mutual funds, which is no-help. The people on the other end of the phone or the modem line are merely order takers, not experienced investment advisers.

The discounters also don't publish research, send out newsletters with in-depth information or call you with new "initial public offerings" (IPOs). But if you know what you want to buy and are determined to save some dollars on commission—accepting the risk of a bad decision—then go for it.

Should I go with a small company or a big one?

There is no right answer to this question, because it is the individual adviser that really matters. The advantage of a small office or firm is that you stand a better chance of getting personal service from an experienced individual.

But the advantage of a large firm is its access to research and, of course, a full range of investment options. I have dealt with scores of advisers, brokers and their support staff across the country, and my personal recommendation is to find a small office of a big company. That way you can establish a close relationship with the people working there and still enjoy the benefits accorded the clients of the busiest downtown megaoperation.

And always remember this: a good financial adviser is more interested in a long-term relationship with you than in making quick commissions. As your wealth grows, so does the adviser's compensation. Therefore, because you use your adviser over a 15- or 20-year period, your financial well-being is his or her main concern. Put yourself in your adviser's chair and you quickly realize this is the prudent way to build a business.

So if you're getting churned, you're getting burned. Move on.

Should I give my adviser all my money?

Probably not—at least not at first. You need to build a relationship and also see your adviser at work before you hand over a cheque representing your life savings. But by the same token, don't hand over $5,000 and expect to see dramatic results in a few weeks.

Once you feel comfortable with the advice you're getting, it does make sense to consolidate your portfolio with one person. That way you can achieve diversity, organize the best tax-planning strategies and ensure the right mix of mutual funds, bonds, real estate and equities for your stage of life and risk tolerance.

Where do I go from here?

Why not come out to a financial seminar and meet some planners? Make up your own mind.

You can access my current seminar schedule through my Internet web site. Here's how to reach me:

• By phone: (416) 489-2188

• By fax: (416) 489-2189

• By e-mail: garth@garth.ca

• On the World Wide Web: http://www.garth.ca

• By lettermail:

Garth Turner
Suite 310, 1670 Bayview Ave.,
Toronto, Ont. M4G 3C2

---•

Chapter 10

The Turner Report

This monthly update of The Strategy can be sent to you for $49 a year.
Are you going to be different from the crowd? I hope so.

The amount Canadians are borrowing through credit cards, lines of credit, loans and mortgages has never been higher. Household debt is at an unprecedented level. The economy is booming, but savings are at a 24-year low. That rate actually plunged from 10.2% in 1992 to a scant 1.7% in 1997. Said the Royal Bank: "Once contractual reasons to save (pensions, life insurance) and tax incentives (RRSPs) are removed, households are seen to be engaging in *negative* discretionary savings." Incredible. Frightening.

The number of bankruptcies set a record in 1996. Then another one in 1997. The amount we've been saving for retirement has been falling steadily since 1979. Last year we contributed just 20% of the money to our RRSPs that the rules allowed.

Most people don't have an RRSP or a company pension. The public pension plan is being changed, making us contribute more to it and get less in return. Middle-class seniors will have at least half their income taxed away after changes in the year 2001 as the Seniors' Benefit comes in.

Does this sound like a recipe for retirement disaster?

You bet it does. But if you follow at least some of the strategies in this book, you should be better off than most—prepared at least for what now appears to be inevitable: the economic bankrupting of the country by the "What, me worry?" attitude of the grey-templed Baby Boomers.

But as I have also shown, for those people who realize where we are right now in the economic cycle, who see the fundamental shift from real assets to financial assets, who properly use the equity in their homes and understand the actions of the worried Boomers over the next decade and a half, this is a time of unbridled opportunity.

> *BMW sales set a record in Canada last year. Some models of Mercedes are sold out until 1999. Obviously a growing number of people have wealth creation figured out.*

- You can borrow $50,000 or $100,000 from your paid-up real estate at an effective rate of less than 4%. It just takes a phone call.

- You can invest to earn double-digit rates of return in any one of hundreds of quality mutual funds.

- You can double and triple your money without risk in government bonds.

- You can use the government's own RRSP rules to sell yourself assets you already own, and get a tax break for doing it.

- You can invest in a mutual fund, have it pay the interest on money borrowed to make the investment and then write that interest off your taxable income.

- You can invest in oil and gas interests that give you cash income and a capital gain, and it's all tax-deductible.

- You can use an RRSP to leverage up the down payment on a first home with money from Ottawa.

- And you can get wise and reputable financial advice free of charge.

With these things possible, why are most middle-class Canadians slipping behind financially?

It can only be because they're not aware of what a powerful time we live in for increasing personal assets. Money is cheap. Financial markets are soaring. Inflation is down. And the surge into mutual funds, equities and government securities by millions of people after the year 2000, now just months away, will make those who see it coming, and take action, secure and comfortable.

Will you be one of them?

I hope so. I hope this book helps guide you. I enjoyed writing it and will issue a new chapter every month in *The Turner Report*.

An affordable newsletter of tax and investment strategies

The Turner Report is a newsletter that builds on the information in *The Strategy*, and you can receive it ten times a year. Its intention is to present current strategies for reducing your tax exposure, and investment opportunities that make sense.

It covers mutual funds, strip bonds, real estate, precious metals, stocks, oil and gas and all the aspects of personal finance you need to know. *The Turner Report* does not suffer the long lead times books demand, nor is it to be another Bay Street publication written by committee. And it has nothing to sell.

Instead, it's the living extension of *The Strategy, 2015: After the Boom* (my financial guide for Baby Boomers) and my *1998 RRSP Guide*. It is as timely and inexpensive as I can possibly make it and it is also interactive—answering your questions in detail. In fact, *I have assembled the finest financial planners from across Canada to respond to every letter*.

> *The cost is less than $5 an issue. And I will send you the first issue as a gift for subscribing. If you are not satisfied, send it back for a full refund. You'll risk nothing.*

Currently there are many good investment newsletters, ones devoted to choosing stocks, selecting mutual funds, and purchasing gold and silver or commercial real estate. If I thought any one of them was adequate for aggressive middle-class Canadians, 30 to 65, who are determined to succeed, then I would simply recommend it, instead of writing my own.

But to date I have found none that combines tax and investment strategies in the big-picture context of where the economy is headed or what the impact of demographics will be. Nobody seems to be talking about what people want to hear: how you can get ahead at a time when salaries are frozen, jobs are not secure and taxes are rising.

There are ways. Powerful ones. And now more than ever the difference between financial independence and dependence has come down to one thing and one thing only: **knowledge**.

Clip or photocopy this coupon, and mail it to me at Suite 310, 1670 Bayview Ave., Toronto M4G 3C2

Subscribe now, and get your first issue FREE

A special offer for new subscribers: The first issue will be sent to you without charge. Your subscription will start with the next issue. If you are not pleased, return it for a full refund.

❑ By Lettermail: $49 a year
❑ By Fax: $59 a year
❑ By E-mail: $40 a year

Name: _____

Address: _____ Apt.: _____

City: _____ Prov.: _____ Code: _____

Phone: Home ( ) _____ Business ( ) _____

E-mail: _____ Fax: ( ) _____

❑ Enclosed is: My cheque payable to *The Turner Report*

❑ Bill my **VISA** # ____ / ____ / ____ / ____

❑ Bill my **MasterCard** # ____ / ____ / ____ / ____

Mail to: The Turner Report   Expiry ____ / ____
            310—1670 Bayview Ave.,
            Toronto M4G 3C2
fax: (416) 489-2189
e-mail: garth@garth.ca   Prices valid in Canada only.

PART 5

Amortization Tables

K nowing how much mortgage you can afford is essential when you buy real estate. Here, towards the end of the 1990s, we are incredibly fortunate, blessed with the lowest mortgage rates since the 1950s.

> *Mortgage money is plentiful. Lenders are the most flexible ever. Repayment terms are generous. Options abound, and new mortgage products are constantly being created. You should shop around intensely before signing up and feel free to pit one lender against another to get the best possible rate.*

But the rate alone isn't everything. With a non-tax-deductible mortgage, you also want features that allow you a quick payback. As I detailed in Chapter 6 in the section "How to find the right mortgage," ideally that will mean a weekly-pay mortgage. But as I also wrote, not all weekly mortgages are equal, or even what they appear to be.

The weekly mortgage that will pay down your loan the fastest has a payment equal to one-quarter of a traditional monthly-pay mortgage. Don't accept any substitute. You can use these tables to make sure you're being offered the right thing.

Now, pages of numbers can be mind numbing, but despair not. It is incredibly simple to use these tables.

The factor
The numbers printed here are called "factors," and by multiplying the amount of money borrowed by the factor, you get the payment—

whether it's once a month ("monthly"), twice a month ("semimonthly"), every two weeks ("biweekly") or every seven days ("weekly"). The more often you pay, the lesser the payment.

Amortization

The other variable affecting the amount of the payment is called "amortization." That word comes from the French *mort*, which means death. So amortization is how quickly you put this mortgage out of its misery—the total length of time it will take to pay it off.

The longer the amortization, the lower the payment. But because the mortgage lives longer, the total amount of interest you pay is greater. A traditional 25-year amortization means you will repay about three times what you borrowed, which is not a cool idea. So by cutting the amortization period, you end up making bigger payments but save tons in interest.

A weekly-pay mortgage is a good idea because you can have the benefits of a longer amortization period but, because you make the equivalent of an extra monthly payment a year and do it a little bit each week, the effective amortization period is sliced and you save a lot of money.

So, how do these tables work? You need to know the following:

- How much do you need to borrow?

- What rate have you been offered?

- How long do you want to spend paying back the mortgage?

- How frequently will you be paying?

- What can you afford?

Of course, you can choose various options to get a mortgage payment that's affordable to you. For example, to make the payment cheap you can take a longer amortization and a monthly payment. But to pay it off the fastest, you choose the shortest amortization and the most frequent payment you can afford. It's common for cash-strapped first-time buyers to start out with long amortizations and low payments, while people renewing their mortgages switch to fast-track, higher-payment schemes. Then, of course, when you pay the place off (or a good chunk of it), you should remortgage through a home equity loan or line of credit to get that great tax-deductible loan to invest in financial assets.

How to use these tables:

Just take the amount you want to borrow—say, $100,000—and wipe off the zeros. Ask yourself, how many thousands do I want to borrow? Here it's 100 thousands. Now find the chart with the interest rate you've been offered by the lender. Say it's 6%, and you're going to calculate the payment based on a 25-year amortization.

Now multiply the number of thousands you want to borrow—say, 100—times the factor on the chart for 6% at 25 years amortization (6.39807). That gives you $639 as a monthly payment; a weekly payment would be one thirtieth of that, multiplied by seven, or about $148.

Here's the formula:

$$\text{Mortgage amount in thousands} \times \text{factor} = \text{payment}$$

The payment this formula gives you is called a "blended" one. That means it blends the interest and the repayment of the principal amount borrowed. There are more complicated formulas for breaking down the two components and for giving you the number of years left to pay off the loan using various payment frequencies, but in all my years as a real estate investor, I've never used them, so I'm not going to complicate things here. If you have such questions, just ask your lender to answer them. The bank has all kinds of software to let it respond instantly.

Blended vs. interest-only

It's important to note that the blended payment is the kind you make when paying off a non-tax-deductible mortgage. When you take out a home equity loan or line of credit against your paid-for home, the payments will be different—they will be "interest-only," not blended.

Why?

Because a home equity loan is good debt, as opposed to a mortgage, which is bad debt. Bad debt you want to get rid of, while good debt you'd like to keep forever, because the interest can be applied against your income, reducing your taxes (when the money is used for investment purposes, which does not include buying a new Volvo).

So don't use these tables to determine an interest-only payment. Instead, use the following formula to arrive at the monthly payment:

$$\text{loan amount} \times \text{interest rate} = \frac{\text{annual payment}}{12}$$

A $100,000 home equity loan at 6% would cost you $6,000 a year, or $500 a month. This would be 100% interest, no repayment of the loan.

So when you come to do your annual income-tax return, you can write in $5,000 on line 221 and use it to reduce your taxable income. If you live in British Columbia, for example, and earn $80,000, then 54.2% of this amount of money comes right off your income taxes— saving you $3,252. And if the $100,000 you borrowed was wisely invested to earn 12%, your net worth would have risen by $12,000 in a year, and the after-tax cost of having that loan would be only $2,652.

This is The Strategy. Use it today. It works.

My thanks to the Canadian Imperial Bank of Commerce for the tables printed here.

3.000% Blended-payment factor for a loan of $1000
Amortization Periods 1 to 35 years

YRS AMORT	MONTHLY	SEMIMONTHLY	BIWEEKLY	WEEKLY
1	84.68524	42.31635	39.05774	19.52329
2	42.97299	21.47317	19.81881	9.90657
3	29.07302	14.52749	13.40772	6.70194
4	22.12612	11.05620	10.20358	5.10033
5	17.96044	8.97465	8.28223	4.13993
6	15.18537	7.58797	7.00227	3.50014
7	13.20493	6.59837	6.08882	3.04354
8	11.72113	5.85693	5.40444	2.70145
9	10.56844	5.28094	4.87276	2.43169
10	9.64750	4.82076	4.44799	2.22236
11	8.89512	4.44480	4.10095	2.04989
12	8.26915	4.13201	3.81222	1.90557
13	7.74042	3.86781	3.56834	1.78366
14	7.28809	3.64179	3.35970	1.67937
15	6.89688	3.44630	3.17924	1.58917
16	6.55533	3.27563	3.02169	1.51042
17	6.25467	3.12539	2.88301	1.44109
18	5.98808	2.99218	2.76003	1.37962
19	5.75019	2.87331	2.65029	1.32477
20	5.53668	2.76662	2.55180	1.27554
21	5.34407	2.67038	2.46295	1.23112
22	5.16951	2.58315	2.38242	1.19087
23	5.01065	2.50377	2.30914	1.15424
24	4.86551	2.43125	2.24218	1.12077
25	4.73245	2.36476	2.18080	1.09009
26	4.61008	2.30361	2.12434	1.06187
27	4.49720	2.24721	2.07226	1.03583
28	4.39280	2.19504	2.02409	1.01176
29	4.29600	2.14667	1.97943	0.98943
30	4.20603	2.10171	1.93792	0.96868
31	4.12223	2.05984	1.89925	0.94936
32	4.04402	2.02076	1.86317	0.93132
33	3.97090	1.98422	1.82943	0.91445
34	3.90240	1.94999	1.79782	0.89865
35	3.83814	1.91788	1.76817	0.88383

3.125% Blended-payment factor for a loan of $1000
Amortization Periods 1 to 35 years

MONTHLY	SEMIMONTHLY	BIWEEKLY	WEEKLY	YRS AMORT
84.74147	42.34336	39.08252	19.53545	1
43.02760	21.49990	19.84338	9.91874	2
29.12744	14.55431	13.43237	6.71419	3
22.18070	11.08318	10.22840	5.11268	4
18.01532	9.00184	8.30725	4.15239	5
15.24063	7.61539	7.02749	3.51270	6
13.26061	6.62602	6.11426	3.05622	7
11.77726	5.88482	5.43010	2.71424	8
10.62501	5.30907	4.89865	2.44860	9
9.70455	4.84914	4.47410	2.23638	10
8.95264	4.47343	4.12729	2.06303	11
8.32716	4.16089	3.83879	1.91882	12
7.79891	3.89694	3.59514	1.79703	13
7.34707	3.67116	3.38672	1.69286	14
6.95635	3.47593	3.20650	1.60277	15
6.61529	3.30551	3.04918	1.52414	16
6.31512	3.15552	2.91072	1.45493	17
6.04903	3.02256	2.78798	1.39357	18
5.81163	2.90394	2.67847	1.33884	19
5.59861	2.79750	2.58020	1.28972	20
5.40649	2.70150	2.49158	1.24542	21
5.23242	2.61452	2.41128	1.20528	22
5.07405	2.53538	2.33822	1.16876	23
4.92940	2.46311	2.27149	1.13541	24
4.79683	2.39686	2.21033	1.10484	25
4.67494	2.33596	2.15409	1.07673	26
4.56254	2.27980	2.10224	1.05081	27
4.45862	2.22787	2.05429	1.02684	28
4.36229	2.17974	2.00985	1.00463	29
4.27280	2.13502	1.96856	0.98399	30
4.18947	2.09338	1.93011	0.96477	31
4.11174	2.05454	1.89424	0.94684	32
4.03908	2.01824	1.86072	0.93008	33
3.97105	1.98424	1.82933	0.91439	34
3.90725	1.95236	1.79989	0.89968	35

3.250% Blended-payment factor for a loan of $1000 — Amortization Periods 1 to 35 years

YRS AMORT	MONTHLY	SEMIMONTHLY	BIWEEKLY	WEEKLY
1	84.79769	42.37037	39.10730	19.54761
2	43.08223	21.52665	19.86795	9.93091
3	29.18189	14.58115	13.45705	6.72644
4	22.23533	11.11020	10.25325	5.12504
5	18.07028	9.02907	8.33229	4.16486
6	15.29599	7.64286	7.05276	3.52529
7	13.31640	6.65373	6.13975	3.06893
8	11.83351	5.91278	5.45582	2.72707
9	10.68175	5.33729	4.92460	2.46154
10	9.76177	4.87761	4.50029	2.24945
11	9.01037	4.50216	4.15372	2.07622
12	8.38538	4.18987	3.86545	1.93213
13	7.85764	3.92618	3.62204	1.81046
14	7.40631	3.70067	3.41387	1.70641
15	7.01610	3.50570	3.23388	1.61644
16	6.67555	3.33553	3.07680	1.53792
17	6.37589	3.18581	2.93858	1.46884
18	6.11031	3.05310	2.81607	1.40760
19	5.87342	2.93474	2.70680	1.35298
20	5.66091	2.82855	2.60877	1.30398
21	5.46930	2.73282	2.52039	1.25980
22	5.29574	2.64609	2.44032	1.21978
23	5.13787	2.56721	2.36750	1.18338
24	4.99373	2.49519	2.30100	1.15014
25	4.86166	2.42920	2.24007	1.11969
26	4.74027	2.36854	2.18407	1.09170
27	4.62837	2.31263	2.13244	1.06589
28	4.52495	2.26095	2.08473	1.04204
29	4.42912	2.21307	2.04051	1.01994
30	4.34011	2.16860	1.99945	0.99941
31	4.25728	2.12721	1.96123	0.98031
32	4.18003	2.08861	1.92558	0.96249
33	4.10786	2.05255	1.89228	0.94585
34	4.04031	2.01880	1.86111	0.93027
35	3.97699	1.98716	1.83189	0.91566

3.375% Blended-payment factor for a loan of $1000 — Amortization Periods 1 to 35 years

MONTHLY	SEMIMONTHLY	BIWEEKLY	WEEKLY	YRS AMORT
84.85390	42.39737	39.13208	19.55976	1
43.13687	21.55339	19.89253	9.94308	2
29.23638	14.60800	13.48173	6.73870	3
22.29002	11.13724	10.27812	5.13741	4
18.12532	9.05634	8.35737	4.17735	5
15.35144	7.67037	7.07807	3.53790	6
13.37232	6.68150	6.16529	3.08166	7
11.88991	5.94081	5.48160	2.73992	8
10.73865	5.36558	4.95063	2.47452	9
9.81918	4.90617	4.52656	2.26255	10
9.06829	4.53098	4.18023	2.08945	11
8.44383	4.21897	3.89222	1.94548	12
7.91661	3.95555	3.64905	1.82394	13
7.46581	3.73030	3.44113	1.72001	14
7.07613	3.53560	3.26139	1.63017	15
6.73611	3.36571	3.10456	1.55178	16
6.43698	3.21625	2.96658	1.48282	17
6.17193	3.08381	2.84432	1.42171	18
5.93556	2.96571	2.73530	1.36721	19
5.72359	2.85980	2.63751	1.31833	20
5.53251	2.76432	2.54937	1.27428	21
5.35947	2.67787	2.46955	1.23438	22
5.20212	2.59925	2.39697	1.19810	23
5.05850	2.52749	2.33071	1.16498	24
4.92695	2.46176	2.27002	1.13465	25
4.80608	2.40137	2.21426	1.10677	26
4.69470	2.34571	2.16287	1.08109	27
4.59179	2.29429	2.11539	1.05736	28
4.49647	2.24667	2.07141	1.03537	29
4.40797	2.20245	2.03058	1.01496	30
4.32564	2.16131	1.99259	0.99598	31
4.24889	2.12296	1.95718	0.97828	32
4.17722	2.08715	1.92411	0.96174	33
4.11016	2.05365	1.89317	0.94628	34
4.04734	2.02226	1.86417	0.93179	35

3.500% — Blended-payment factor for a loan of $1000
Amortization Periods 1 to 35 years

YRS AMORT	MONTHLY	SEMIMONTHLY	BIWEEKLY	WEEKLY
1	84.91011	42.42437	39.15685	19.57191
2	43.19152	21.58015	19.91712	9.95525
3	29.29090	14.63486	13.50644	6.75097
4	22.34477	11.16431	10.30301	5.14979
5	18.18044	9.08365	8.38249	4.18985
6	15.40700	7.69793	7.10342	3.55053
7	13.42835	6.70932	6.19089	3.09441
8	11.94645	5.96891	5.50744	2.75281
9	10.79570	5.39395	4.97672	2.48753
10	9.87676	4.93481	4.55291	2.27570
11	9.12641	4.55991	4.20684	2.10272
12	8.50249	4.24817	3.91908	1.95889
13	7.97582	3.98503	3.67617	1.83748
14	7.52556	3.76006	3.46850	1.73368
15	7.13643	3.56564	3.28902	1.64396
16	6.79696	3.39602	3.13245	1.56570
17	6.49838	3.24684	2.99473	1.49687
18	6.23388	3.11468	2.87272	1.43588
19	5.99806	2.99686	2.76395	1.38152
20	5.78663	2.89122	2.66642	1.33277
21	5.59610	2.79602	2.57853	1.28884
22	5.42360	2.70984	2.49896	1.24907
23	5.26680	2.63150	2.42663	1.21291
24	5.12371	2.56001	2.36062	1.17992
25	4.99270	2.49455	2.30018	1.14971
26	4.87237	2.43442	2.24467	1.12196
27	4.76152	2.37904	2.19352	1.09640
28	4.65913	2.32788	2.14629	1.07279
29	4.56434	2.28052	2.10255	1.05093
30	4.47636	2.23656	2.06196	1.03064
31	4.39455	2.19569	2.02421	1.01177
32	4.31832	2.15760	1.98904	0.99419
33	4.24716	2.12204	1.95620	0.97777
34	4.18061	2.08880	1.92549	0.96243
35	4.11829	2.05766	1.89673	0.94805

3.625% — Blended-payment factor for a loan of $1000
Amortization Periods 1 to 35 years

MONTHLY	SEMIMONTHLY	BIWEEKLY	WEEKLY	YRS AMORT
84.96631	42.45136	39.18162	19.58406	1
43.24618	21.60691	19.94171	9.96742	2
29.34546	14.66175	13.53115	6.76325	3
22.39958	11.19141	10.32793	5.16219	4
18.23563	9.11099	8.40764	4.20237	5
15.46265	7.72554	7.12881	3.56318	6
13.48450	6.73720	6.21654	3.10720	7
12.00312	5.99707	5.53335	2.76572	8
10.85291	5.42240	5.00289	2.50058	9
9.93452	4.96354	4.57934	2.28888	10
9.18473	4.58893	4.23354	2.11604	11
8.56137	4.27748	3.94604	1.97234	12
8.03526	4.01463	3.70340	1.85106	13
7.58557	3.78995	3.49600	1.74740	14
7.19701	3.59581	3.31678	1.65782	15
6.85811	3.42649	3.16047	1.57969	16
6.56010	3.27759	3.02302	1.51099	17
6.29616	3.14572	2.90127	1.45014	18
6.06091	3.02819	2.79276	1.39590	19
5.85004	2.92283	2.69550	1.34729	20
5.66007	2.82792	2.60787	1.30349	21
5.48814	2.74202	2.52856	1.26384	22
5.33189	2.66395	2.45648	1.22782	23
5.18936	2.59274	2.39073	1.19495	24
5.05891	2.52756	2.33055	1.16487	25
4.93912	2.46771	2.27529	1.13725	26
4.82882	2.41260	2.22440	1.11182	27
4.72698	2.36172	2.17741	1.08833	28
4.63272	2.31463	2.13392	1.06659	29
4.54529	2.27094	2.09358	1.04643	30
4.46401	2.23033	2.05608	1.02769	31
4.38831	2.19251	2.02115	1.01023	32
4.31767	2.15722	1.98855	0.99393	33
4.25165	2.12423	1.95809	0.97871	34
4.18984	2.09335	1.92956	0.96445	35

3.750%

Blended-payment factor for a loan of $1000
Amortization Periods 1 to 35 years

YRS AMORT	MONTHLY	SEMIMONTHLY	BIWEEKLY	WEEKLY
1	85.02250	42.47835	39.20639	19.59621
2	43.30086	21.63367	19.96631	9.97960
3	29.40005	14.68865	13.55589	6.77553
4	22.45444	11.21853	10.35287	5.17459
5	18.29090	9.13837	8.43282	4.21491
6	15.51840	7.75319	7.15425	3.57585
7	13.54077	6.76514	6.24224	3.12001
8	12.05993	6.02530	5.55932	2.77867
9	10.91028	5.45092	5.02913	2.51367
10	9.99246	4.99236	4.60585	2.30211
11	9.24324	4.61804	4.26032	2.12940
12	8.62046	4.30690	3.97310	1.98584
13	8.09494	4.04434	3.73074	1.86470
14	7.64584	3.81996	3.52361	1.76118
15	7.25786	3.62612	3.34467	1.67174
16	6.91955	3.45709	3.18863	1.59375
17	6.62212	3.30850	3.05144	1.52518
18	6.35877	3.17692	2.92998	1.46447
19	6.12410	3.05968	2.82174	1.41037
20	5.91382	2.95462	2.72474	1.36188
21	5.72443	2.86000	2.63738	1.31822
22	5.55307	2.77439	2.55834	1.27871
23	5.39740	2.69661	2.48653	1.24282
24	5.25545	2.62569	2.42104	1.21009
25	5.12556	2.56080	2.36112	1.18014
26	5.00634	2.50123	2.30612	1.15265
27	4.89660	2.44641	2.25549	1.12734
28	4.79532	2.39580	2.20876	1.10399
29	4.70162	2.34899	2.16553	1.08238
30	4.61474	2.30558	2.12544	1.06234
31	4.53400	2.26525	2.08819	1.04372
32	4.45885	2.22770	2.05351	1.02639
33	4.38875	2.19268	2.02116	1.01022
34	4.32326	2.15996	1.99094	0.99512
35	4.26199	2.12934	1.96267	0.98098

3.875%

Blended-payment factor for a loan of $1000
Amortization Periods 1 to 35 years

MONTHLY	SEMIMONTHLY	BIWEEKLY	WEEKLY	YRS AMORT
85.07868	42.50533	39.23115	19.60835	1
43.35556	21.66045	19.99091	9.99178	2
29.45468	14.71556	13.58063	6.78782	3
22.50935	11.24568	10.37784	5.18701	4
18.34624	9.16579	8.45804	4.22746	5
15.57424	7.78089	7.17973	3.58854	6
13.59715	6.79314	6.26799	3.13284	7
12.11688	6.05359	5.58535	2.79165	8
10.96781	5.47952	5.05544	2.52679	9
10.05058	5.02127	4.63244	2.31537	10
9.30195	4.64726	4.28720	2.14281	11
8.67977	4.33642	4.00026	1.99939	12
8.15486	4.07417	3.75818	1.87840	13
7.70636	3.85010	3.55133	1.77501	14
7.31899	3.65657	3.37267	1.68572	15
6.98128	3.48785	3.21692	1.60787	16
6.68446	3.33956	3.08001	1.53944	17
6.42171	3.20829	2.95883	1.47887	18
6.18765	3.09135	2.85087	1.42491	19
5.97796	2.98659	2.75415	1.37657	20
5.78917	2.89227	2.66706	1.33304	21
5.61841	2.80696	2.58829	1.29367	22
5.46333	2.72948	2.51676	1.25792	23
5.32196	2.65885	2.45154	1.22532	24
5.19266	2.59425	2.39189	1.19551	25
5.07402	2.53498	2.33716	1.16815	26
4.96486	2.48045	2.28680	1.14298	27
4.86415	2.43013	2.24034	1.11976	28
4.77102	2.38360	2.19737	1.09828	29
4.68470	2.34048	2.15754	1.07837	30
4.60453	2.30043	2.12055	1.05988	31
4.52993	2.26316	2.08612	1.04268	32
4.46039	2.22841	2.05403	1.02664	33
4.39545	2.19597	2.02406	1.01166	34
4.33471	2.16562	1.99603	0.99765	35

4.000% Blended-payment factor for a loan of $1000
Amortization Periods 1 to 35 years

YRS AMORT	MONTHLY	SEMIMONTHLY	BIWEEKLY	WEEKLY
1	85.13486	42.53231	39.25590	19.62050
2	43.41027	21.68722	20.01552	10.00396
3	29.50934	14.74249	13.60539	6.80011
4	22.56432	11.27285	10.40283	5.19944
5	18.40166	9.19324	8.48329	4.24003
6	15.63018	7.80864	7.20525	3.60126
7	13.65365	6.82119	6.29379	3.14570
8	12.17396	6.08196	5.61144	2.80465
9	11.02549	5.50820	5.08182	2.53995
10	10.10887	5.05026	4.65911	2.32867
11	9.36086	4.67657	4.31416	2.15626
12	8.73930	4.36605	4.02752	2.01299
13	8.21501	4.10412	3.78572	1.89214
14	7.76714	3.88036	3.57917	1.78890
15	7.38039	3.68715	3.40080	1.69976
16	7.04330	3.51874	3.24534	1.62205
17	6.74710	3.37077	3.10872	1.55377
18	6.48498	3.23981	2.98782	1.49334
19	6.25153	3.12319	2.88015	1.43953
20	6.04246	3.01874	2.78372	1.39133
21	5.85428	2.92473	2.69692	1.34795
22	5.68414	2.83972	2.61843	1.30872
23	5.52967	2.76255	2.54718	1.27310
24	5.38890	2.69223	2.48224	1.24065
25	5.26020	2.62793	2.42287	1.21097
26	5.14216	2.56896	2.36841	1.18376
27	5.03359	2.51472	2.31832	1.15872
28	4.93347	2.46470	2.27213	1.13563
29	4.84093	2.41847	2.22943	1.11429
30	4.75519	2.37563	2.18987	1.09452
31	4.67559	2.33587	2.15314	1.07616
32	4.60156	2.29888	2.11898	1.05909
33	4.53258	2.26442	2.08715	1.04318
34	4.46820	2.23225	2.05744	1.02833
35	4.40802	2.20219	2.02966	1.01445

4.125% Blended-payment factor for a loan of $1000
Amortization Periods 1 to 35 years

MONTHLY	SEMIMONTHLY	BIWEEKLY	WEEKLY	YRS AMORT
85.19103	42.55928	39.28065	19.63264	1
43.46499	21.71401	20.04013	10.01614	2
29.56403	14.76944	13.63017	6.81242	3
22.61935	11.30005	10.42784	5.21188	4
18.45716	9.22073	8.50857	4.25262	5
15.68622	7.83644	7.23082	3.61399	6
13.71027	6.84930	6.31965	3.15859	7
12.23118	6.11039	5.63759	2.81769	8
11.08333	5.53695	5.10827	2.55314	9
10.16734	5.07934	4.68586	2.34202	10
9.41996	4.70598	4.34121	2.16976	11
8.79904	4.39578	4.05487	2.02664	12
8.27539	4.13418	3.81338	1.90594	13
7.82816	3.91075	3.60712	1.80285	14
7.44206	3.71786	3.42906	1.71386	15
7.10561	3.54978	3.27389	1.63630	16
6.81006	3.40213	3.13757	1.56817	17
6.54857	3.27150	3.01697	1.50789	18
6.31576	3.15519	2.90959	1.45423	19
6.10733	3.05107	2.81345	1.40618	20
5.91978	2.95737	2.72694	1.36294	21
5.75026	2.87268	2.64875	1.32386	22
5.59641	2.79583	2.57778	1.28839	23
5.45627	2.72581	2.51313	1.25607	24
5.32818	2.66183	2.45404	1.22654	25
5.21075	2.60316	2.39987	1.19946	26
5.10279	2.54923	2.35006	1.17457	27
5.00328	2.49951	2.30415	1.15162	28
4.91133	2.45357	2.26172	1.13042	29
4.82618	2.41104	2.22243	1.11078	30
4.74717	2.37157	2.18598	1.09256	31
4.67372	2.33487	2.15208	1.07562	32
4.60531	2.30070	2.12051	1.05984	33
4.54150	2.26882	2.09107	1.04512	34
4.48189	2.23904	2.06355	1.03137	35

4.250% Blended-payment factor for a loan of $1000
Amortization Periods 1 to 35 years

YRS AMORT	MONTHLY	SEMIMONTHLY	BIWEEKLY	WEEKLY
1	85.24719	42.58625	39.30540	19.64477
2	43.51972	21.74080	20.06475	10.02833
3	29.61876	14.79641	13.65496	6.82473
4	22.67443	11.32728	10.45288	5.22433
5	18.51273	9.24826	8.53389	4.26522
6	15.74235	7.86428	7.25643	3.62675
7	13.76700	6.87747	6.34556	3.17150
8	12.28854	6.13889	5.66380	2.83076
9	11.14133	5.56578	5.13479	2.56636
10	10.22598	5.10851	4.71269	2.35540
11	9.47926	4.73548	4.36835	2.18329
12	8.85900	4.42562	4.08232	2.04033
13	8.33601	4.16435	3.84113	1.91979
14	7.88944	3.94126	3.63519	1.81686
15	7.50400	3.74871	3.45743	1.72802
16	7.16821	3.58097	3.30257	1.65062
17	6.87331	3.43365	3.16656	1.58264
18	6.61248	3.30334	3.04626	1.52252
19	6.38033	3.18737	2.93919	1.46900
20	6.17255	3.08357	2.84335	1.42110
21	5.98565	2.99020	2.75714	1.37801
22	5.81677	2.90584	2.67924	1.33908
23	5.66356	2.82930	2.60857	1.30376
24	5.52406	2.75961	2.54422	1.27159
25	5.39660	2.69594	2.48542	1.24221
26	5.27980	2.63759	2.43153	1.21528
27	5.17246	2.58396	2.38201	1.19052
28	5.07356	2.53456	2.33638	1.16772
29	4.98222	2.48893	2.29423	1.14665
30	4.89768	2.44669	2.25523	1.12716
31	4.81927	2.40752	2.21904	1.10907
32	4.74641	2.37112	2.18542	1.09227
33	4.67859	2.33725	2.15413	1.07663
34	4.61536	2.30566	2.12495	1.06204
35	4.55632	2.27616	2.09770	1.04842

4.375% Blended-payment factor for a loan of $1000
Amortization Periods 1 to 35 years

MONTHLY	SEMIMONTHLY	BIWEEKLY	WEEKLY	YRS AMORT
85.30334	42.61321	39.33014	19.65691	1
43.57447	21.76759	20.08937	10.04052	2
29.67353	14.82339	13.67977	6.83704	3
22.72956	11.35453	10.47794	5.23680	4
18.56838	9.27582	8.55923	4.27784	5
15.79858	7.89217	7.28208	3.63953	6
13.82385	6.90569	6.37152	3.18444	7
12.34603	6.16745	5.69008	2.84386	8
11.19948	5.59469	5.16138	2.57962	9
10.28480	5.13776	4.73960	2.36882	10
9.53875	4.76508	4.39558	2.19688	11
8.91917	4.45556	4.10986	2.05408	12
8.39686	4.19464	3.86900	1.93370	13
7.95097	3.97190	3.66337	1.83092	14
7.56620	3.77969	3.48593	1.74224	15
7.23110	3.61229	3.33138	1.66500	16
6.93688	3.46531	3.19569	1.59718	17
6.67672	3.33535	3.07570	1.53721	18
6.44524	3.21971	2.96894	1.48385	19
6.23812	3.11625	2.87341	1.43611	20
6.05189	3.02321	2.78751	1.39317	21
5.88367	2.93918	2.70991	1.35439	22
5.73112	2.86297	2.63954	1.31922	23
5.59226	2.79361	2.57549	1.28721	24
5.46545	2.73026	2.51699	1.25797	25
5.34929	2.67223	2.46340	1.23119	26
5.24258	2.61893	2.41417	1.20658	27
5.14431	2.56984	2.36883	1.18392	28
5.05359	2.52452	2.32697	1.16300	29
4.96967	2.48259	2.28824	1.14365	30
4.89187	2.44373	2.25235	1.12571	31
4.81962	2.40764	2.21900	1.10904	32
4.75240	2.37406	2.18798	1.09354	33
4.68976	2.34276	2.15907	1.07909	34
4.63130	2.31356	2.13209	1.06560	35

4.500% Blended-payment factor for a loan of $1000
Amortization Periods 1 to 35 years

YRS AMORT	MONTHLY	SEMIMONTHLY	BIWEEKLY	WEEKLY
1	85.35948	42.64017	39.35488	19.66904
2	43.62923	21.79439	20.11400	10.05271
3	29.72833	14.85038	13.70459	6.84937
4	22.78475	11.38181	10.50303	5.24927
5	18.62410	9.30342	8.58462	4.29048
6	15.85490	7.92010	7.30777	3.65233
7	13.88081	6.93397	6.39753	3.19740
8	12.40366	6.19608	5.71641	2.85699
9	11.25778	5.62367	5.18804	2.59291
10	10.34379	5.16710	4.76659	2.38228
11	9.59844	4.79477	4.42289	2.21050
12	8.97955	4.48561	4.13750	2.06787
13	8.45794	4.22505	3.89696	1.94765
14	8.01275	4.00266	3.69166	1.84504
15	7.62868	3.81080	3.51455	1.75652
16	7.29427	3.64375	3.36032	1.67944
17	7.00074	3.49713	3.22495	1.61179
18	6.74128	3.36751	3.10529	1.55198
19	6.51048	3.25222	2.99884	1.49878
20	6.30405	3.14910	2.90363	1.45910
21	6.11849	3.05641	2.81804	1.40842
22	5.95095	2.97272	2.74076	1.36979
23	5.79907	2.89685	2.67070	1.33478
24	5.66088	2.82782	2.60695	1.30292
25	5.53473	2.76480	2.54875	1.27383
26	5.41922	2.70010	2.49546	1.24720
27	5.31316	2.65412	2.44653	1.22274
28	5.21553	2.60535	2.40149	1.20023
29	5.12545	2.56035	2.35992	1.17946
30	5.04216	2.51874	2.32149	1.16025
31	4.96498	2.48019	2.28588	1.14245
32	4.89334	2.44440	2.25282	1.12593
33	4.82673	2.41113	2.22207	1.11056
34	4.76469	2.38014	2.19344	1.09625
35	4.70683	2.35123	2.16673	1.08291

Blended-payment factor for a loan of $1000 4.625%
Amortization Periods 1 to 35 years

MONTHLY	SEMIMONTHLY	BIWEEKLY	WEEKLY	YRS AMORT
85.41562	42.66713	39.37961	19.68117	1
43.68401	21.82120	20.13864	10.06490	2
29.78316	14.87740	13.72942	6.86170	3
22.84000	11.40912	10.52814	5.26176	4
18.67990	9.33105	8.61003	4.30313	5
15.91132	7.94808	7.33351	3.66515	6
13.93789	6.96231	6.42359	3.21039	7
12.46142	6.22477	5.74281	2.87014	8
11.31624	5.65273	5.21477	2.60624	9
10.40296	5.19652	4.79365	2.39578	10
9.65832	4.82456	4.45029	2.22417	11
9.04015	4.51577	4.16524	2.08171	12
8.51925	4.25557	3.92504	1.96166	13
8.07477	4.03354	3.72007	1.85922	14
7.69142	3.84205	3.54328	1.77087	15
7.35773	3.67536	3.38939	1.69395	16
7.06491	3.52909	3.25435	1.62646	17
6.80615	3.39983	3.13501	1.56682	18
6.57606	3.28490	3.02889	1.51378	19
6.37033	3.18213	2.93400	1.46636	20
6.18547	3.08979	2.84874	1.42374	21
6.01862	3.00644	2.77178	1.38528	22
5.86742	2.93092	2.70203	1.35042	23
5.72991	2.86223	2.63860	1.31872	24
5.60443	2.79955	2.58071	1.28979	25
5.48959	2.74218	2.52773	1.26331	26
5.38419	2.68953	2.47910	1.23901	27
5.28722	2.64109	2.43436	1.21665	28
5.19778	2.59642	2.39309	1.19602	29
5.11513	2.55513	2.35495	1.17696	30
5.03589	2.51689	2.31963	1.15931	31
4.96757	2.48142	2.28686	1.14293	32
4.90158	2.44845	2.25640	1.12771	33
4.84015	2.41777	2.22805	1.11354	34
4.78289	2.38917	2.20162	1.10033	35

4.750% Blended-payment factor for a loan of $1000
Amortization Periods 1 to 35 years

YRS AMORT	MONTHLY	SEMIMONTHLY	BIWEEKLY	WEEKLY
1	85.47174	42.69408	39.40434	19.69330
2	43.73880	21.84801	20.16327	10.07710
3	29.83803	14.90442	13.75427	6.87404
4	22.89530	11.43645	10.55328	5.27426
5	18.73577	9.35872	8.63548	4.31580
6	15.96784	7.97611	7.35928	3.67799
7	13.99509	6.99070	6.44971	3.22340
8	12.51932	6.25354	5.76926	2.88333
9	11.37485	5.68186	5.24157	2.61960
10	10.46230	5.22603	4.82080	2.40931
11	9.71839	4.85444	4.47778	2.23788
12	9.10095	4.54602	4.19307	2.09559
13	8.58079	4.28620	3.95321	1.97572
14	8.13705	4.06455	3.74859	1.87345
15	7.75443	3.87342	3.57214	1.78527
16	7.42147	3.70710	3.41859	1.70853
17	7.12938	3.56120	3.28389	1.64121
18	6.87134	3.43231	3.16489	1.58173
19	6.64197	3.31774	3.05910	1.52886
20	6.43696	3.21533	2.96454	1.48160
21	6.25281	3.12335	2.87960	1.43915
22	6.08666	3.04035	2.80297	1.40085
23	5.93616	2.96518	2.73354	1.36616
24	5.79935	2.89684	2.67043	1.33461
25	5.67456	2.83450	2.61286	1.30584
26	5.56039	2.77748	2.56019	1.27952
27	5.45567	2.72517	2.51188	1.25537
28	5.35936	2.67706	2.46744	1.23316
29	5.27059	2.63272	2.42648	1.21269
30	5.18858	2.59175	2.38864	1.19378
31	5.11268	2.55384	2.35361	1.17628
32	5.04230	2.51869	2.32113	1.16004
33	4.97694	2.48604	2.29096	1.14497
34	4.91613	2.45566	2.26290	1.13094
35	4.85948	2.42736	2.23675	1.11787

4.875% Blended-payment factor for a loan of $1000
Amortization Periods 1 to 35 years

MONTHLY	SEMIMONTHLY	BIWEEKLY	WEEKLY	YRS AMORT
85.52786	42.72102	39.42906	19.70543	1
43.79360	21.87483	20.18792	10.08930	2
29.89293	14.93147	13.77913	6.88638	3
22.95065	11.46381	10.57843	5.28677	4
18.79172	9.38643	8.66096	4.32848	5
16.02444	8.00418	7.38510	3.69085	6
14.05230	7.01915	6.47587	3.23644	7
12.57735	6.28236	5.79578	2.89655	8
11.43362	5.71107	5.26844	2.63300	9
10.52181	5.25563	4.84802	2.42289	10
9.77865	4.88442	4.50535	2.25163	11
9.16197	4.57639	4.22100	2.10952	12
8.64256	4.31694	3.98149	1.98983	13
8.19957	4.09567	3.77722	1.88774	14
7.81770	3.90493	3.60112	1.79973	15
7.48549	3.73899	3.44792	1.72316	16
7.19414	3.59346	3.31356	1.65601	17
6.93685	3.46494	3.19490	1.59671	18
6.70822	3.35074	3.08945	1.54401	19
6.50393	3.24870	2.99523	1.49693	20
6.32051	3.15708	2.91063	1.45464	21
6.15508	3.07445	2.83433	1.41651	22
6.00530	2.99964	2.76523	1.38198	23
5.86919	2.93165	2.70245	1.35060	24
5.74510	2.86967	2.64520	1.32199	25
5.63163	2.81299	2.59285	1.29583	26
5.52759	2.76102	2.54485	1.27184	27
5.43196	2.71325	2.50073	1.24979	28
5.34385	2.66925	2.46007	1.22947	29
5.26251	2.62861	2.42254	1.21071	30
5.18726	2.59103	2.38781	1.19335	31
5.11753	2.55620	2.35563	1.17727	32
5.05280	2.52387	2.32576	1.16234	33
4.99262	2.49380	2.29798	1.14846	34
4.93659	2.46582	2.27211	1.13553	35

5.000% Blended-payment factor for a loan of $1000 — Amortization Periods 1 to 35 years

YRS AMORT	MONTHLY	SEMIMONTHLY	BIWEEKLY	WEEKLY
1	85.58397	42.74796	39.45378	19.71755
2	43.84842	21.90165	20.21257	10.10150
3	29.94787	14.95853	13.80401	6.89874
4	23.00606	11.49120	10.60361	5.29930
5	18.84774	9.41417	8.68648	4.34118
6	16.08115	8.03230	7.41096	3.70373
7	14.10982	7.04765	6.50209	3.24950
8	12.63551	6.31125	5.82235	2.90980
9	11.49254	5.74036	5.29537	2.64643
10	10.58149	5.28530	4.87531	2.43650
11	9.83910	4.91449	4.53301	2.26543
12	9.22319	4.60685	4.24902	2.12350
13	8.70455	4.34780	4.00987	2.00399
14	8.26234	4.12692	3.80596	1.90208
15	7.88124	3.93656	3.63022	1.81425
16	7.54979	3.77101	3.47737	1.73786
17	7.25920	3.62587	3.34337	1.67089
18	7.00267	3.49773	3.22506	1.61176
19	6.77479	3.38391	3.11996	1.55924
20	6.57125	3.28224	3.02608	1.51232
21	6.38856	3.19100	2.94182	1.47021
22	6.22387	3.10874	2.86586	1.43225
23	6.07482	3.03428	2.79710	1.39789
24	5.93943	2.96666	2.73464	1.36667
25	5.81605	2.90503	2.67773	1.33823
26	5.70329	2.84871	2.62570	1.31223
27	5.59994	2.79709	2.57802	1.28840
28	5.50500	2.74967	2.53422	1.26651
29	5.41758	2.70600	2.49388	1.24635
30	5.33691	2.66571	2.45665	1.22774
31	5.26232	2.62845	2.42223	1.21054
32	5.19324	2.59395	2.39035	1.19461
33	5.12916	2.56194	2.36077	1.17983
34	5.06961	2.53220	2.33329	1.16609
35	5.01421	2.50452	2.30771	1.15331

5.125% Blended-payment factor for a loan of $1000 — Amortization Periods 1 to 35 years

MONTHLY	SEMIMONTHLY	BIWEEKLY	WEEKLY	YRS AMORT
85.64008	42.77490	39.47850	19.72967	1
43.90325	21.92848	20.23722	10.11370	2
30.00284	14.98560	13.82890	6.91110	3
23.06152	11.51861	10.62882	5.31183	4
18.90383	9.44195	8.71203	4.35390	5
16.13794	8.06047	7.43687	3.71663	6
14.16735	7.07621	6.52835	3.26259	7
12.69381	6.34021	5.84899	2.92307	8
11.55161	5.76972	5.32238	2.65990	9
10.64135	5.31507	4.90269	2.45015	10
9.89975	4.94465	4.56076	2.27927	11
9.28462	4.63742	4.27713	2.13753	12
8.76678	4.37877	4.03836	2.01820	13
8.32535	4.15828	3.83481	1.91647	14
7.94503	3.96833	3.65944	1.82883	15
7.61436	3.80317	3.50695	1.75262	16
7.32456	3.65842	3.37331	1.68583	17
7.06880	3.53067	3.25535	1.62689	18
6.84169	3.41724	3.15061	1.57454	19
6.63891	3.31596	3.05709	1.52780	20
6.45698	3.22509	2.97317	1.48587	21
6.29304	3.14320	2.89755	1.44807	22
6.14472	3.06912	2.82914	1.41388	23
6.01006	3.00186	2.76702	1.38284	24
5.88741	2.94060	2.71044	1.35456	25
5.77537	2.88464	2.65875	1.32873	26
5.67273	2.83338	2.61139	1.30506	27
5.57849	2.78630	2.56791	1.28333	28
5.49176	2.74298	2.52789	1.26333	29
5.41177	2.70303	2.49097	1.24488	30
5.33785	2.66611	2.45686	1.22784	31
5.26944	2.63194	2.42529	1.21206	32
5.20600	2.60026	2.39601	1.19742	33
5.14710	2.57084	2.36882	1.18384	34
5.09233	2.54348	2.34354	1.17120	35

5.250% — Blended-payment factor for a loan of $1000, Amortization Periods 1 to 35 years

5.375% — Blended-payment factor for a loan of $1000, Amortization Periods 1 to 35 years

YRS AMORT	MONTHLY	SEMIMONTHLY	BIWEEKLY	WEEKLY	MONTHLY	SEMIMONTHLY	BIWEEKLY	WEEKLY	YRS AMORT
1	85.69617	42.80183	39.50321	19.74179	85.75226	42.82875	39.52791	19.75390	1
2	43.95809	21.95532	20.26188	10.12591	44.01295	21.98216	20.28654	10.13811	2
3	30.05784	15.01270	13.85381	6.92346	30.11288	15.03980	13.87873	6.93584	3
4	23.11704	11.54604	10.65405	5.32438	23.17261	11.57350	10.67930	5.33693	4
5	18.96000	9.46977	8.73761	4.36663	19.01625	9.49762	8.76322	4.37938	5
6	16.19483	8.08868	7.46281	3.72955	16.25182	8.11693	7.48880	3.74250	6
7	14.22500	7.10482	6.55467	3.27571	14.28277	7.13349	6.58104	3.28885	7
8	12.75224	6.36924	5.87568	2.93638	12.81080	6.39832	5.90244	2.94972	8
9	11.61084	5.79915	5.34945	2.67340	11.67022	5.82866	5.37659	2.68693	9
10	10.70138	5.34491	4.93014	2.46385	10.76157	5.37484	4.95767	2.47757	10
11	9.96058	4.97491	4.58859	2.29315	10.02160	5.00526	4.61650	2.30708	11
12	9.34626	4.66809	4.30534	2.15160	9.40811	4.69886	4.33364	2.16572	12
13	8.82922	4.40985	4.06694	2.03246	8.89190	4.44104	4.09563	2.04677	13
14	8.38860	4.18977	3.86377	1.93092	8.45210	4.22138	3.89284	1.94543	14
15	8.00909	4.00022	3.68877	1.84347	8.07341	4.03224	3.71822	1.85816	15
16	7.67922	3.83546	3.53665	1.76745	7.74435	3.86790	3.56648	1.78233	16
17	7.39021	3.69112	3.40338	1.70084	7.45615	3.72396	3.43358	1.71592	17
18	7.13524	3.56377	3.28579	1.64208	7.20198	3.59701	3.31637	1.65734	18
19	6.90891	3.45072	3.18141	1.58991	6.97645	3.48437	3.21236	1.60536	19
20	6.70691	3.34983	3.08825	1.54336	6.77524	3.38388	3.11956	1.55898	20
21	6.52575	3.25935	3.00469	1.50160	6.59487	3.29379	3.03636	1.51741	21
22	6.36257	3.17785	2.92942	1.46398	6.43246	3.21268	2.96145	1.47997	22
23	6.21501	3.10415	2.86135	1.42997	6.28567	3.13936	2.89374	1.44613	23
24	6.08109	3.03726	2.79958	1.39909	6.15251	3.07286	2.83231	1.41544	24
25	5.95918	2.97637	2.74334	1.37099	6.03135	3.01234	2.77642	1.38750	25
26	5.84786	2.92077	2.69198	1.34532	5.92077	2.95711	2.72540	1.36201	26
27	5.74595	2.86987	2.64496	1.32182	5.81959	2.90658	2.67871	1.33868	27
28	5.65242	2.82316	2.60180	1.30025	5.72677	2.86022	2.63589	1.31727	28
29	5.56638	2.78019	2.56210	1.28041	5.64145	2.81761	2.59652	1.29760	29
30	5.48708	2.74058	2.52551	1.26213	5.56285	2.77835	2.56024	1.27947	30
31	5.41385	2.70400	2.49171	1.24524	5.49031	2.74212	2.52676	1.26274	31
32	5.34611	2.67017	2.46044	1.22961	5.42324	2.70862	2.49581	1.24727	32
33	5.28333	2.63881	2.43147	1.21513	5.36113	2.67760	2.46714	1.23294	33
34	5.22508	2.60972	2.40458	1.20169	5.30353	2.64884	2.44055	1.21965	34
35	5.17094	2.58268	2.37959	1.18920	5.25004	2.62212	2.41586	1.20731	35

5.500%

Blended-payment factor for a loan of $1000
Amortization Periods 1 to 35 years

YRS AMORT	MONTHLY	SEMIMONTHLY	BIWEEKLY	WEEKLY
1	85.80834	42.85567	39.55262	19.76602
2	44.06782	22.00900	20.31121	10.15032
3	30.16795	15.06693	13.90367	6.94822
4	23.22824	11.60099	10.70458	5.34950
5	19.07257	9.52550	8.78886	4.39215
6	16.30890	8.14523	7.51483	3.75546
7	14.34064	7.16222	6.60746	3.30201
8	12.86950	6.42748	5.92925	2.96308
9	11.72974	5.85824	5.40380	2.70049
10	10.82194	5.40485	4.98527	2.49134
11	10.08281	5.03571	4.64450	2.32104
12	9.47017	4.72973	4.36204	2.17989
13	8.95479	4.47234	4.12442	2.06114
14	8.51583	4.25310	3.92202	1.95999
15	8.13798	4.06439	3.74779	1.87292
16	7.80976	3.90046	3.59644	1.79728
17	7.52238	3.75694	3.46392	1.73106
18	7.26904	3.63041	3.34708	1.67267
19	7.04432	3.51818	3.24345	1.62088
20	6.84391	3.41809	3.15102	1.57469
21	6.66433	3.32840	3.06819	1.53330
22	6.50272	3.24768	2.99364	1.49604
23	6.35670	3.17476	2.92629	1.46238
24	6.22432	3.10864	2.86522	1.43187
25	6.10391	3.04851	2.80967	1.40411
26	5.99409	2.99366	2.75900	1.37878
27	5.89364	2.94349	2.71266	1.35562
28	5.80156	2.89750	2.67017	1.33439
29	5.71696	2.85525	2.63113	1.31488
30	5.63906	2.81634	2.59518	1.29692
31	5.56722	2.78046	2.56202	1.28034
32	5.50083	2.74731	2.53138	1.26503
33	5.43940	2.71662	2.50302	1.25086
34	5.38246	2.68819	2.47674	1.23773
35	5.32962	2.66180	2.45234	1.22553

5.625%

Blended-payment factor for a loan of $1000
Amortization Periods 1 to 35 years

MONTHLY	SEMIMONTHLY	BIWEEKLY	WEEKLY	YRS AMORT
85.86441	42.88259	39.57731	19.77813	1
44.12270	22.03585	20.33589	10.16253	2
30.22306	15.09407	13.92862	6.96060	3
23.28392	11.62850	10.72988	5.36208	4
19.12896	9.55343	8.81454	4.40493	5
16.36607	8.17358	7.54090	3.76844	6
14.39863	7.19099	6.63393	3.31520	7
12.92833	6.45669	5.95612	2.97648	8
11.78942	5.88790	5.43108	2.71409	9
10.88248	5.43495	5.01296	2.50514	10
10.14421	5.06624	4.67259	2.33505	11
9.53243	4.76070	4.39053	2.19410	12
9.01791	4.50375	4.15331	2.07555	13
8.57981	4.28495	3.95131	1.97460	14
8.20281	4.09667	3.77747	1.88773	15
7.87544	3.93317	3.62651	1.81229	16
7.58890	3.79007	3.49438	1.74626	17
7.33639	3.66396	3.37793	1.68807	18
7.11250	3.55214	3.27468	1.63647	19
6.91291	3.45246	3.18263	1.59047	20
6.73414	3.36318	3.10018	1.54926	21
6.57333	3.28287	3.02600	1.51220	22
6.42811	3.21034	2.95901	1.47872	23
6.29651	3.14461	2.89830	1.44838	24
6.17687	3.08487	2.84311	1.42080	25
6.06781	3.03040	2.79279	1.39565	26
5.96811	2.98061	2.74679	1.37267	27
5.87677	2.93499	2.70464	1.35160	28
5.79289	2.89310	2.66594	1.33226	29
5.71571	2.85455	2.63032	1.31446	30
5.64457	2.81902	2.59748	1.29805	31
5.57888	2.78621	2.56716	1.28290	32
5.51812	2.75587	2.53912	1.26888	33
5.46185	2.72777	2.51314	1.25590	34
5.40966	2.70171	2.48904	1.24386	35

5.750% Blended-payment factor for a loan of $1000 — Amortization Periods 1 to 35 years

YRS AMORT	MONTHLY	SEMIMONTHLY	BIWEEKLY	WEEKLY
1	85.92048	42.90950	39.60201	19.79024
2	44.17760	22.06271	20.36057	10.17475
3	30.27820	15.12122	13.95358	6.97300
4	23.33965	11.65604	10.75520	5.37468
5	19.18542	9.58138	8.84025	4.41772
6	16.42333	8.20197	7.56701	3.78145
7	14.45673	7.21983	6.66045	3.32841
8	12.98728	6.48597	5.98305	2.98990
9	11.84925	5.91763	5.45842	2.72773
10	10.94318	5.46513	5.04071	2.51899
11	10.20579	5.09687	4.70076	2.34910
12	9.59489	4.79178	4.41911	2.20835
13	9.08126	4.53527	4.18230	2.09001
14	8.64403	4.31691	3.98070	1.98927
15	8.26790	4.12907	3.80727	1.90260
16	7.94138	3.96600	3.65671	1.82736
17	7.65571	3.82333	3.52498	1.76153
18	7.40405	3.69765	3.40892	1.70354
19	7.18100	3.58626	3.30606	1.65213
20	6.98224	3.48700	3.21439	1.60632
21	6.80430	3.39813	3.13232	1.56531
22	6.64430	3.31823	3.05852	1.52843
23	6.49988	3.24610	2.99190	1.49514
24	6.36907	3.18078	2.93156	1.46498
25	6.25022	3.12142	2.87673	1.43758
26	6.14193	3.06734	2.82676	1.41261
27	6.04299	3.01793	2.78111	1.38980
28	5.95239	2.97268	2.73931	1.36891
29	5.86925	2.93116	2.70094	1.34974
30	5.79280	2.89298	2.66565	1.33210
31	5.72236	2.85780	2.63315	1.31586
32	5.65737	2.82534	2.60315	1.30087
33	5.59730	2.79534	2.57541	1.28701
34	5.54170	2.76758	2.54975	1.27418
35	5.49017	2.74184	2.52595	1.26229

5.875% Blended-payment factor for a loan of $1000 — Amortization Periods 1 to 35 years

MONTHLY	SEMIMONTHLY	BIWEEKLY	WEEKLY	YRS AMORT
85.97653	42.93641	39.62669	19.80235	1
44.23251	22.08957	20.38525	10.18697	2
30.33337	15.14839	13.97856	6.98540	3
23.39544	11.68361	10.78054	5.38728	4
19.24196	9.60937	8.86599	4.43054	5
16.48069	8.23041	7.59316	3.79447	6
14.51495	7.24872	6.68702	3.34165	7
13.04638	6.51532	6.01004	3.00335	8
11.90923	5.94743	5.48583	2.74139	9
11.00406	5.49539	5.06855	2.53287	10
10.26757	5.12759	4.72901	2.36319	11
9.65756	4.82295	4.44778	2.22266	12
9.14482	4.56689	4.21138	2.10452	13
8.70848	4.34899	4.01020	2.00399	14
8.33324	4.16159	3.83719	1.91753	15
8.00760	3.99897	3.68703	1.84249	16
7.72280	3.85674	3.55571	1.77687	17
7.47200	3.73149	3.44005	1.71907	18
7.24981	3.62053	3.33758	1.66786	19
7.05190	3.52170	3.24630	1.62225	20
6.87479	3.43325	3.16462	1.58143	21
6.71562	3.35376	3.09120	1.54474	22
6.57201	3.28204	3.02496	1.51164	23
6.44201	3.21712	2.96498	1.48167	24
6.32395	3.15816	2.91052	1.45445	25
6.21644	3.10447	2.86091	1.42966	26
6.11827	3.05545	2.81562	1.40703	27
6.02843	3.01058	2.77416	1.38631	28
5.94603	2.96943	2.73613	1.36731	29
5.87031	2.93161	2.70118	1.34984	30
5.80059	2.89680	2.66900	1.33376	31
5.73630	2.86469	2.63933	1.31893	32
5.67691	2.83503	2.61191	1.30523	33
5.62199	2.80760	2.58656	1.29256	34
5.57112	2.78220	2.56307	1.28082	35

6.000% Blended-payment factor for a loan of $1000
Amortization Periods 1 to 35 years

YRS AMORT	MONTHLY	SEMIMONTHLY	BIWEEKLY	WEEKLY
1	86.03258	42.96331	39.65138	19.81445
2	44.28743	22.11644	20.40994	10.19918
3	30.38858	15.17557	14.00355	6.99781
4	23.45128	11.71120	10.80591	5.39989
5	19.29857	9.63740	8.89177	4.44336
6	16.53814	8.25889	7.61936	3.80752
7	14.57327	7.27766	6.71364	3.35492
8	13.10560	6.54473	6.03709	3.01683
9	11.96936	5.97731	5.51331	2.75509
10	11.06510	5.52574	5.09645	2.54678
11	10.32952	5.15840	4.75735	2.37733
12	9.72043	4.85423	4.47655	2.23700
13	9.20860	4.59863	4.24057	2.11908
14	8.77317	4.38118	4.03981	2.01876
15	8.39883	4.19424	3.86721	1.93251
16	8.07409	4.03207	3.71748	1.85769
17	7.79018	3.89029	3.58656	1.79226
18	7.54025	3.76548	3.47131	1.73467
19	7.31893	3.65496	3.36924	1.68366
20	7.12188	3.55656	3.27836	1.63825
21	6.94562	3.46853	3.19707	1.59763
22	6.78729	3.38946	3.12403	1.56113
23	6.64451	3.31816	3.05817	1.52822
24	6.51532	3.25365	2.99858	1.49844
25	6.39807	3.19509	2.94448	1.47140
26	6.29134	3.14180	2.89524	1.44680
27	6.19395	3.09316	2.85030	1.42434
28	6.10487	3.04868	2.80919	1.40380
29	6.02322	3.00790	2.77151	1.38497
30	5.94823	2.97045	2.73690	1.36768
31	5.87924	2.93600	2.70506	1.35176
32	5.81566	2.90425	2.67571	1.33709
33	5.75697	2.87494	2.64861	1.32356
34	5.70272	2.84785	2.62357	1.31104
35	5.65252	2.82278	2.60039	1.29946

6.125% Blended-payment factor for a loan of $1000
Amortization Periods 1 to 35 years

MONTHLY	SEMIMONTHLY	BIWEEKLY	WEEKLY	YRS AMORT
86.08862	42.99021	39.67606	19.82655	1
44.34237	22.14332	20.43463	10.21141	2
30.44382	15.20278	14.02856	7.01022	3
23.50717	11.73881	10.83131	5.41252	4
19.35526	9.66546	8.91757	4.45621	5
16.59568	8.28741	7.64559	3.82058	6
14.63171	7.30666	6.74031	3.36820	7
13.16495	6.57420	6.06420	3.03034	8
12.02964	6.00726	5.54086	2.76883	9
11.12631	5.55616	5.12444	2.56074	10
10.39166	5.18930	4.78577	2.39150	11
9.78350	4.88560	4.50540	2.25140	12
9.27260	4.63047	4.26986	2.13370	13
8.83810	4.41349	4.06953	2.03359	14
8.46467	4.22702	3.89736	1.94755	15
8.14084	4.06531	3.74804	1.87294	16
7.85783	3.92398	3.61754	1.80772	17
7.60880	3.79962	3.50270	1.75034	18
7.38836	3.68954	3.40104	1.69954	19
7.19219	3.59157	3.31057	1.65433	20
7.01679	3.50398	3.22967	1.61390	21
6.85930	3.42534	3.15703	1.57760	22
6.71736	3.35446	3.09155	1.54488	23
6.58900	3.29036	3.03233	1.51529	24
6.47256	3.23221	2.97861	1.48844	25
6.36663	3.17931	2.92974	1.46402	26
6.27002	3.13107	2.88516	1.44175	27
6.18172	3.08697	2.84441	1.42138	28
6.10082	3.04658	2.80708	1.40273	29
6.02658	3.00950	2.77281	1.38560	30
5.95831	2.97541	2.74130	1.36986	31
5.89544	2.94401	2.71228	1.35535	32
5.83745	2.91506	2.68550	1.34198	33
5.78389	2.88831	2.66077	1.32962	34
5.73435	2.86357	2.63790	1.31819	35

6.250% — Blended-payment factor for a loan of $1000, Amortization Periods 1 to 35 years

YRS AMORT	MONTHLY	SEMIMONTHLY	BIWEEKLY	WEEKLY
1	86.14465	43.01710	39.70073	19.83865
2	44.39731	22.17020	20.45933	10.22363
3	30.49909	15.22999	14.05358	7.02264
4	23.56311	11.76645	10.85672	5.42516
5	19.41201	9.69356	8.94341	4.46907
6	16.65332	8.31598	7.67187	3.83367
7	14.69026	7.33571	6.76703	3.38152
8	13.22443	6.60374	6.09136	3.04388
9	12.09006	6.03728	5.56847	2.78259
10	11.18768	5.58667	5.15250	2.57473
11	10.45399	5.22029	4.81427	2.40572
12	9.84678	4.91708	4.53435	2.26584
13	9.33682	4.66243	4.29925	2.14835
14	8.90326	4.44592	4.09935	2.04847
15	8.53076	4.25991	3.92761	1.96265
16	8.20786	4.09867	3.77872	1.88825
17	7.92577	3.95780	3.64865	1.82325
18	7.67764	3.83390	3.53423	1.76607
19	7.45810	3.72427	3.43298	1.71548
20	7.26281	3.62675	3.34291	1.67047
21	7.08829	3.53960	3.26242	1.63025
22	6.93166	3.46139	3.19017	1.59415
23	6.79057	3.39093	3.12509	1.56162
24	6.66304	3.32725	3.06626	1.53222
25	6.54742	3.26951	3.01291	1.50557
26	6.44230	3.21702	2.96441	1.48133
27	6.34648	3.16917	2.92020	1.45924
28	6.25896	3.12547	2.87981	1.43905
29	6.17883	3.08545	2.84283	1.42057
30	6.10533	3.04875	2.80890	1.40362
31	6.03779	3.01503	2.77773	1.38805
32	5.97564	2.98399	2.74904	1.37371
33	5.91835	2.95538	2.72259	1.36049
34	5.86548	2.92898	2.69817	1.34829
35	5.81661	2.90458	2.67561	1.33701

6.375% — Blended-payment factor for a loan of $1000, Amortization Periods 1 to 35 years

MONTHLY	SEMIMONTHLY	BIWEEKLY	WEEKLY	YRS AMORT
86.20068	43.04399	39.72540	19.85075	1
44.45228	22.19708	20.48403	10.23585	2
30.55439	15.25722	14.07861	7.03507	3
23.61911	11.79412	10.88216	5.43781	4
19.46884	9.72169	8.96928	4.48194	5
16.71105	8.34460	7.69818	3.84678	6
14.74892	7.36482	6.79379	3.39485	7
13.28404	6.63334	6.11858	3.05745	8
12.15064	6.06738	5.59615	2.79639	9
11.24922	5.61726	5.18063	2.58876	10
10.51650	5.25137	4.84286	2.41997	11
9.91025	4.94865	4.56338	2.28032	12
9.40126	4.69449	4.32873	2.16306	13
8.96865	4.47846	4.12928	2.06340	14
8.59711	4.29293	3.95798	1.97780	15
8.27514	4.13216	3.80953	1.90362	16
7.99398	3.99176	3.67988	1.83883	17
7.74678	3.86832	3.56589	1.78187	18
7.52814	3.75915	3.46506	1.73149	19
7.33375	3.66208	3.37541	1.68669	20
7.16011	3.57537	3.29532	1.64667	21
7.00436	3.49760	3.22348	1.61077	22
6.86412	3.42757	3.15879	1.57844	23
6.73744	3.36431	3.10034	1.54924	24
6.62265	3.30699	3.04738	1.52277	25
6.51834	3.25491	2.99926	1.49873	26
6.42333	3.20747	2.95541	1.47682	27
6.33658	3.16415	2.91538	1.45681	28
6.25722	3.12452	2.87876	1.43851	29
6.18448	3.08820	2.84518	1.42173	30
6.11768	3.05484	2.81434	1.40633	31
6.05625	3.02417	2.78598	1.39215	32
5.99967	2.99591	2.75986	1.37910	33
5.94748	2.96985	2.73576	1.36706	34
5.89929	2.94579	2.71351	1.35594	35

6.500% Blended-payment factor for a loan of $1000 — Amortization Periods 1 to 35 years

YRS AMORT	MONTHLY	SEMIMONTHLY	BIWEEKLY	WEEKLY
1	86.25669	43.07087	39.75007	19.86284
2	44.50725	22.22397	20.50874	10.24808
3	30.60973	15.28447	14.10366	7.04750
4	23.67516	11.82181	10.90762	5.45047
5	19.52575	9.74986	8.99519	4.49483
6	16.76887	8.37326	7.72454	3.85990
7	14.80769	7.39398	6.82061	3.40821
8	13.34378	6.66300	6.14587	3.07105
9	12.21136	6.09754	5.62389	2.81022
10	11.31093	5.64793	5.20884	2.60282
11	10.57919	5.28255	4.87153	2.43427
12	9.97393	4.98032	4.59251	2.29485
13	9.46591	4.72665	4.35831	2.17782
14	9.03427	4.51112	4.15931	2.07838
15	8.66369	4.32607	3.98846	1.99301
16	8.34269	4.16579	3.84045	1.91905
17	8.06247	4.02586	3.71124	1.85448
18	7.81620	3.90289	3.59767	1.79773
19	7.59848	3.79418	3.49727	1.74756
20	7.40500	3.69757	3.40804	1.70298
21	7.23226	3.61131	3.32837	1.66316
22	7.07739	3.53398	3.25693	1.62747
23	6.93802	3.46439	3.19264	1.59534
24	6.81219	3.40156	3.13459	1.56633
25	6.69824	3.34466	3.08202	1.54006
26	6.59476	3.29298	3.03427	1.51620
27	6.50055	3.24594	2.99080	1.49448
28	6.41460	3.20302	2.95113	1.47466
29	6.33601	3.16378	2.91486	1.45654
30	6.26402	3.12784	2.88163	1.43993
31	6.19797	3.09485	2.85114	1.42470
32	6.13726	3.06454	2.82311	1.41069
33	6.08139	3.03664	2.79731	1.39780
34	6.02989	3.01093	2.77353	1.38592
35	5.98237	2.98720	2.75159	1.37495

6.625% Blended-payment factor for a loan of $1000 — Amortization Periods 1 to 35 years

MONTHLY	SEMIMONTHLY	BIWEEKLY	WEEKLY	YRS AMORT
86.31270	43.09775	39.77473	19.87494	1
44.56224	22.25087	20.53346	10.26031	2
30.66510	15.31173	14.12872	7.05995	3
23.73127	11.84952	10.93310	5.46314	4
19.58272	9.77806	9.02112	4.50774	5
16.82678	8.40196	7.75094	3.87305	6
14.86657	7.42319	6.84748	3.42160	7
13.40365	6.69273	6.17320	3.08467	8
12.27223	6.12778	5.65170	2.82408	9
11.37280	5.67868	5.23712	2.61692	10
10.64207	5.31381	4.90028	2.44861	11
10.03780	5.01209	4.62173	2.30942	12
9.53078	4.75892	4.38799	2.19262	13
9.10013	4.54389	4.18945	2.09342	14
8.73053	4.35934	4.01905	2.00827	15
8.41049	4.19954	3.87149	1.93453	16
8.13123	4.06009	3.74272	1.87019	17
7.88591	3.93760	3.62959	1.81366	18
7.66913	3.82936	3.52962	1.76371	19
7.47657	3.73321	3.44082	1.71933	20
7.30473	3.64741	3.36156	1.67973	21
7.15075	3.57052	3.29054	1.64424	22
7.01227	3.50137	3.22665	1.61232	23
6.88730	3.43897	3.16900	1.58351	24
6.77419	3.38250	3.11681	1.55743	25
6.67154	3.33124	3.06945	1.53377	26
6.57815	3.28461	3.02635	1.51223	27
6.49299	3.24209	2.98705	1.49259	28
6.41518	3.20324	2.95114	1.47465	29
6.34396	3.16767	2.91826	1.45822	30
6.27865	3.13506	2.88811	1.44315	31
6.21867	3.10511	2.86042	1.42932	32
6.16350	3.07757	2.83495	1.41659	33
6.11270	3.05220	2.81149	1.40487	34
6.06586	3.02881	2.78985	1.39405	35

6.750%
Blended-payment factor for a loan of $1000
Amortization Periods 1 to 35 years

YRS AMORT	MONTHLY	SEMIMONTHLY	BIWEEKLY	WEEKLY
1	86.36870	43.12462	39.79939	19.88703
2	44.61724	22.27777	20.55817	10.27254
3	30.72051	15.33901	14.15380	7.07239
4	23.78743	11.87726	10.95861	5.47582
5	19.63977	9.80630	9.04709	4.52066
6	16.88478	8.43071	7.77738	3.88621
7	14.92556	7.45246	6.87439	3.43501
8	13.46365	6.72251	6.20060	3.09833
9	12.33324	6.15809	5.67958	2.83798
10	11.43484	5.70951	5.26547	2.63106
11	10.70512	5.34516	4.92911	2.46299
12	10.10187	5.04395	4.65103	2.32404
13	9.59587	4.79130	4.41777	2.20748
14	9.16622	4.57677	4.21969	2.10850
15	8.79761	4.39272	4.04975	2.02358
16	8.47855	4.23341	3.90264	1.95008
17	8.20027	4.09446	3.77432	1.88596
18	7.95590	3.97245	3.66164	1.82966
19	7.74007	3.86468	3.56211	1.77992
20	7.54844	3.76900	3.47373	1.73576
21	7.37752	3.68366	3.39490	1.69637
22	7.22445	3.60723	3.32429	1.66109
23	7.08685	3.53852	3.26082	1.62937
24	6.96275	3.47656	3.20356	1.60076
25	6.85050	3.42051	3.15177	1.57488
26	6.74868	3.36967	3.10479	1.55141
27	6.65611	3.32345	3.06207	1.53006
28	6.57176	3.28133	3.02314	1.51061
29	6.49473	3.24288	2.98759	1.49285
30	6.42428	3.20770	2.95507	1.47659
31	6.35971	3.17546	2.92526	1.46170
32	6.30046	3.14588	2.89791	1.44803
33	6.24601	3.11869	2.87276	1.43547
34	6.19590	3.09367	2.84962	1.42390
35	6.14973	3.07061	2.82830	1.41325

6.875%
Blended-payment factor for a loan of $1000
Amortization Periods 1 to 35 years

MONTHLY	SEMIMONTHLY	BIWEEKLY	WEEKLY	YRS AMORT
86.42469	43.15149	39.82404	19.89911	1
44.67225	22.30467	20.58290	10.28478	2
30.77595	15.36630	14.17889	7.08485	3
23.84364	11.90503	10.98414	5.48851	4
19.69688	9.83457	9.07309	4.53360	5
16.94287	8.45950	7.80385	3.89940	6
14.98466	7.48178	6.90136	3.44844	7
13.52378	6.75237	6.22805	3.11201	8
12.39440	6.18847	5.70752	2.85191	9
11.49704	5.74042	5.29390	2.64524	10
10.76836	5.37660	4.95802	2.47740	11
10.16614	5.07591	4.68043	2.33870	12
9.66116	4.82378	4.44764	2.22238	13
9.23253	4.60976	4.25003	2.12364	14
8.86493	4.42622	4.08056	2.03896	15
8.54687	4.26742	3.93391	1.96568	16
8.26957	4.12896	3.80605	1.90179	17
8.02618	4.00744	3.69382	1.84571	18
7.81131	3.90015	3.59473	1.79620	19
7.62062	3.80495	3.50679	1.75226	20
7.45063	3.72007	3.42838	1.71308	21
7.29847	3.64410	3.35819	1.67801	22
7.16176	3.57584	3.29513	1.64650	23
7.03855	3.51432	3.23828	1.61809	24
6.92715	3.45870	3.18689	1.59241	25
6.82618	3.40829	3.14030	1.56913	26
6.73444	3.36248	3.09796	1.54798	27
6.65089	3.32076	3.05940	1.52871	28
6.57466	3.28270	3.02421	1.51113	29
6.50497	3.24790	2.99204	1.49505	30
6.44116	3.21604	2.96258	1.48033	31
6.38264	3.18683	2.93557	1.46683	32
6.32890	3.15999	2.91075	1.45443	33
6.27949	3.13532	2.88793	1.44303	34
6.23399	3.11261	2.86691	1.43253	35

7.000%

Blended-payment factor for a loan of $1000
Amortization Periods 1 to 35 years

YRS AMORT	MONTHLY	SEMIMONTHLY	BIWEEKLY	WEEKLY
1	86.48067	43.17836	39.84869	19.91120
2	44.72728	22.33158	20.60763	10.29701
3	30.83142	15.39361	14.20399	7.09731
4	23.89990	11.93282	11.00969	5.50122
5	19.75407	9.86288	9.09912	4.54656
6	17.00105	8.48834	7.83037	3.91260
7	15.04387	7.51115	6.92837	3.46190
8	13.58403	6.78228	6.25556	3.12572
9	12.45571	6.21893	5.73553	2.86587
10	11.55940	5.77142	5.32240	2.65945
11	10.83177	5.40812	4.98702	2.49186
12	10.23061	5.10797	4.70991	2.35340
13	9.72667	4.85636	4.47760	2.23732
14	9.29907	4.64287	4.28048	2.13883
15	8.93249	4.45985	4.11148	2.05438
16	8.61545	4.30155	3.96530	1.98134
17	8.33914	4.16360	3.83790	1.91768
18	8.09674	4.04257	3.72612	1.86183
19	7.88283	3.93577	3.62748	1.81254
20	7.69311	3.84104	3.53998	1.76882
21	7.52405	3.75663	3.46200	1.72986
22	7.37281	3.68112	3.39224	1.69500
23	7.23701	3.61332	3.32960	1.66370
24	7.11468	3.55224	3.27316	1.63550
25	7.00416	3.49706	3.22216	1.61002
26	6.90404	3.44707	3.17596	1.58693
27	6.81312	3.40168	3.13401	1.56597
28	6.73039	3.36037	3.09582	1.54689
29	6.65495	3.32270	3.06100	1.52949
30	6.58603	3.28830	3.02919	1.51359
31	6.52298	3.25681	3.00007	1.49905
32	6.46519	3.22796	2.97339	1.48572
33	6.41217	3.20149	2.94891	1.47348
34	6.36345	3.17716	2.92640	1.46224
35	6.31863	3.15479	2.90570	1.45189

7.125%

Blended-payment factor for a loan of $1000
Amortization Periods 1 to 35 years

MONTHLY	SEMIMONTHLY	BIWEEKLY	WEEKLY	YRS AMORT
86.53665	43.20522	39.87334	19.92328	1
44.78232	22.35850	20.63236	10.30925	2
30.88692	15.42094	14.22911	7.10978	3
23.95621	11.96064	11.03527	5.51393	4
19.81134	9.89122	9.12518	4.55953	5
17.05932	8.51722	7.85693	3.92583	6
15.10318	7.54058	6.95544	3.47538	7
13.64441	6.81226	6.28313	3.13946	8
12.51716	6.24945	5.76360	2.87986	9
11.62192	5.80249	5.35098	2.67369	10
10.89537	5.43974	5.01609	2.50636	11
10.29527	5.14013	4.73948	2.36815	12
9.79239	4.88905	4.50766	2.25232	13
9.36584	4.67609	4.31103	2.15407	14
9.00030	4.49359	4.14250	2.06986	15
8.68428	4.33581	3.99680	1.99706	16
8.40898	4.19836	3.86987	1.93364	17
8.16758	4.07783	3.75855	1.87801	18
7.95465	3.97153	3.66036	1.82895	19
7.76589	3.87728	3.57330	1.78545	20
7.59779	3.79335	3.49577	1.74671	21
7.44748	3.71831	3.42644	1.71207	22
7.31259	3.65096	3.36421	1.68098	23
7.19115	3.59033	3.30818	1.65298	24
7.08150	3.53559	3.25759	1.62770	25
6.98224	3.48603	3.21179	1.60482	26
6.89216	3.44105	3.17022	1.58404	27
6.81024	3.40015	3.13241	1.56515	28
6.73560	3.36289	3.09795	1.54794	29
6.66746	3.32887	3.06650	1.53222	30
6.60516	3.29776	3.03773	1.51785	31
6.54811	3.26928	3.01139	1.50468	32
6.49580	3.24316	2.98723	1.49261	33
6.44777	3.21919	2.96505	1.48153	34
6.40363	3.19715	2.94466	1.47134	35

7.250% — Blended-payment factor for a loan of $1000, Amortization Periods 1 to 35 years

YRS AMORT	MONTHLY	SEMIMONTHLY	BIWEEKLY	WEEKLY
1	86.59262	43.23207	39.89797	19.93536
2	44.83737	22.38542	20.65710	10.32149
3	30.94246	15.44827	14.25424	7.12225
4	24.01258	11.98848	11.06087	5.52666
5	19.86867	9.91960	9.15127	4.57251
6	17.11769	8.54615	7.88353	3.93907
7	15.16261	7.57006	6.98255	3.48889
8	13.70492	6.84229	6.31076	3.15322
9	12.57876	6.28005	5.79174	2.89389
10	11.68461	5.83364	5.37963	2.68798
11	10.95914	5.47144	5.04525	2.52090
12	10.36012	5.17238	4.76914	2.38294
13	9.85831	4.92184	4.53782	2.26736
14	9.43283	4.70942	4.34168	2.16936
15	9.06834	4.52744	4.17364	2.08540
16	8.75336	4.37019	4.02842	2.01283
17	8.47909	4.23325	3.90196	1.94965
18	8.23869	4.11323	3.79111	1.89426
19	8.02676	4.00743	3.69337	1.84543
20	7.83897	3.91367	3.60677	1.80215
21	7.67183	3.83022	3.52967	1.76363
22	7.52246	3.75565	3.46077	1.72920
23	7.38849	3.68876	3.39897	1.69833
24	7.26795	3.62859	3.34336	1.67054
25	7.15919	3.57428	3.29318	1.64546
26	7.06078	3.52515	3.24777	1.62277
27	6.97155	3.48060	3.20658	1.60220
28	6.89045	3.44011	3.16915	1.58349
29	6.81660	3.40325	3.13506	1.56646
30	6.74924	3.36962	3.10397	1.55092
31	6.68770	3.33889	3.07555	1.53673
32	6.63139	3.31078	3.04955	1.52373
33	6.57979	3.28502	3.02572	1.51183
34	6.53246	3.26139	3.00386	1.50090
35	6.48899	3.23968	2.98378	1.49087

7.375% — Blended-payment factor for a loan of $1000, Amortization Periods 1 to 35 years

MONTHLY	SEMIMONTHLY	BIWEEKLY	WEEKLY	YRS AMORT
86.64858	43.25892	39.92261	19.94744	1
44.89244	22.41235	20.68184	10.33374	2
30.99803	15.47563	14.27938	7.13473	3
24.06900	12.01634	11.08649	5.53939	4
19.92607	9.94800	9.17739	4.58551	5
17.17614	8.57511	7.91017	3.95234	6
15.22215	7.59959	7.00970	3.50242	7
13.76555	6.87239	6.33844	3.16702	8
12.64050	6.31071	5.81994	2.90795	9
11.74746	5.86487	5.40835	2.70230	10
11.02309	5.50323	5.07448	2.53548	11
10.42517	5.20472	4.79888	2.39777	12
9.92445	4.95474	4.56807	2.28245	13
9.50004	4.74285	4.37243	2.18469	14
9.13662	4.56142	4.20488	2.10098	15
8.82269	4.40469	4.06015	2.02866	16
8.54946	4.26828	3.93417	1.96572	17
8.31008	4.14877	3.82378	1.91056	18
8.09915	4.04347	3.72651	1.86196	19
7.91235	3.95021	3.64036	1.81892	20
7.74617	3.86724	3.56372	1.78062	21
7.59775	3.79314	3.49525	1.74641	22
7.46471	3.72672	3.43388	1.71575	23
7.34508	3.66700	3.37869	1.68817	24
7.23720	3.61314	3.32891	1.66330	25
7.13967	3.56445	3.28390	1.64081	26
7.05128	3.52032	3.24310	1.62043	27
6.97100	3.48024	3.20605	1.60191	28
6.89796	3.44378	3.17233	1.58507	29
6.83138	3.41054	3.14160	1.56971	30
6.77060	3.38019	3.11353	1.55568	31
6.71502	3.35244	3.08787	1.54286	32
6.66414	3.32704	3.06437	1.53112	33
6.61750	3.30376	3.04282	1.52036	34
6.57471	3.28239	3.02305	1.51048	35

7.500% Blended-payment factor for a loan of $1000
Amortization Periods 1 to 35 years

YRS AMORT	MONTHLY	SEMIMONTHLY	BIWEEKLY	WEEKLY
1	86.70453	43.28577	39.94724	19.95952
2	44.94751	22.43928	20.70658	10.34598
3	31.05363	15.50300	14.30454	7.14722
4	24.12547	12.04423	11.11213	5.55214
5	19.98355	9.97645	9.20355	4.59852
6	17.23469	8.60412	7.93685	3.96562
7	15.28179	7.62918	7.03691	3.51597
8	13.82631	6.90255	6.36617	3.18084
9	12.70238	6.34145	5.84820	2.92204
10	11.81047	5.89617	5.43714	2.71665
11	11.08722	5.53511	5.10380	2.55010
12	10.49041	5.23716	4.82871	2.41265
13	9.99080	4.98774	4.59842	2.29758
14	9.56748	4.77640	4.40328	2.20008
15	9.20514	4.59551	4.23623	2.11662
16	8.89227	4.43932	4.09199	2.04455
17	8.62009	4.30343	3.96649	1.98185
18	8.38174	4.18444	3.85659	1.92693
19	8.17183	4.07965	3.75978	1.87856
20	7.98602	3.98689	3.67409	1.83575
21	7.82082	3.90441	3.59789	1.79768
22	7.67335	3.83079	3.52987	1.76369
23	7.54125	3.76484	3.46893	1.73324
24	7.42254	3.70557	3.41416	1.70587
25	7.31555	3.65216	3.36479	1.68121
26	7.21888	3.60391	3.32018	1.65892
27	7.13134	3.56020	3.27978	1.63873
28	7.05189	3.52054	3.24311	1.62041
29	6.97966	3.48448	3.20976	1.60375
30	6.91386	3.45163	3.17938	1.58857
31	6.85384	3.42166	3.15167	1.57472
32	6.79900	3.39429	3.12634	1.56207
33	6.74884	3.36924	3.10317	1.55049
34	6.70289	3.34630	3.08195	1.53989
35	6.66076	3.32527	3.06249	1.53016

7.625% Blended-payment factor for a loan of $1000
Amortization Periods 1 to 35 years

MONTHLY	SEMIMONTHLY	BIWEEKLY	WEEKLY	YRS AMORT
86.76047	43.31261	39.97187	19.97159	1
45.00260	22.46622	20.73134	10.35823	2
31.10926	15.53038	14.32972	7.15972	3
24.18199	12.07215	11.13780	5.56490	4
20.04110	10.00493	9.22973	4.61156	5
17.29332	8.63318	7.96357	3.97893	6
15.34154	7.65881	7.06417	3.52955	7
13.88720	6.93278	6.39397	3.19469	8
12.76441	6.37225	5.87653	2.93616	9
11.87363	5.92756	5.46600	2.73104	10
11.15152	5.56707	5.13319	2.56475	11
10.55584	5.26969	4.85863	2.42757	12
10.05735	5.02083	4.62885	2.31277	13
9.63514	4.81006	4.43423	2.21552	14
9.27389	4.62971	4.26769	2.13231	15
8.96210	4.47406	4.12394	2.06049	16
8.69097	4.33871	3.99893	1.99803	17
8.45367	4.22025	3.88951	1.94336	18
8.24478	4.11596	3.79318	1.89523	19
8.05998	4.02371	3.70795	1.85265	20
7.89576	3.94173	3.63221	1.81480	21
7.74926	3.86859	3.56463	1.78104	22
7.61810	3.80311	3.50412	1.75080	23
7.50031	3.74431	3.44977	1.72365	24
7.39422	3.69135	3.40082	1.69919	25
7.29843	3.64353	3.35662	1.67710	26
7.21174	3.60025	3.31661	1.65711	27
7.13312	3.56100	3.28032	1.63898	28
7.06169	3.52534	3.24734	1.62250	29
6.99668	3.49289	3.21732	1.60751	30
6.93742	3.46330	3.18996	1.59383	31
6.88332	3.43629	3.16497	1.58135	32
6.83387	3.41161	3.14213	1.56994	33
6.78861	3.38901	3.12122	1.55949	34
6.74716	3.36832	3.10207	1.54992	35

7.750% Blended-payment factor for a loan of $1000
Amortization Periods 1 to 35 years

YRS AMORT	MONTHLY	SEMIMONTHLY	BIWEEKLY	WEEKLY
1	86.81641	43.33944	39.99649	19.98366
2	45.05771	22.49317	20.75609	10.37048
3	31.16493	15.55778	14.35490	7.17222
4	24.23857	12.10009	11.16349	5.57767
5	20.09871	10.03344	9.25595	4.62460
6	17.35204	8.66228	7.99032	3.99225
7	15.40140	7.68850	7.09147	3.54315
8	13.94821	6.96306	6.42182	3.20857
9	12.82658	6.40313	5.90493	2.95031
10	11.93696	5.95903	5.49494	2.74547
11	11.21600	5.59912	5.16266	2.57945
12	10.62147	5.30232	4.88864	2.44254
13	10.12410	5.05403	4.65938	2.32799
14	9.70301	4.84382	4.46528	2.23101
15	9.34287	4.66404	4.29925	2.14806
16	9.03217	4.50893	4.15601	2.07649
17	8.76212	4.37412	4.03149	2.01428
18	8.52587	4.25618	3.92256	1.95985
19	8.31802	4.15242	3.82670	1.91196
20	8.13423	4.06067	3.74194	1.86961
21	7.97100	3.97919	3.66666	1.83199
22	7.82547	3.90654	3.59952	1.79845
23	7.69526	3.84154	3.53945	1.76844
24	7.57839	3.78319	3.48553	1.74150
25	7.47321	3.73069	3.43700	1.71724
26	7.37830	3.68331	3.39320	1.69536
27	7.29247	3.64046	3.35358	1.67557
28	7.21468	3.60163	3.31767	1.65763
29	7.14406	3.56637	3.28507	1.64134
30	7.07983	3.53431	3.25541	1.62652
31	7.02133	3.50510	3.22840	1.61302
32	6.96797	3.47846	3.20375	1.60071
33	6.91923	3.45413	3.18124	1.58946
34	6.87467	3.43189	3.16065	1.57917
35	6.83387	3.41152	3.14180	1.56976

7.875% Blended-payment factor for a loan of $1000
Amortization Periods 1 to 35 years

MONTHLY	SEMIMONTHLY	BIWEEKLY	WEEKLY	YRS AMORT
86.87234	43.36627	40.02111	19.99573	1
45.11282	22.52011	20.78085	10.38273	2
31.22062	15.58519	14.38010	7.18473	3
24.29519	12.12805	11.18920	5.59045	4
20.15640	10.06198	9.28220	4.63766	5
17.41085	8.69142	8.01712	4.00559	6
15.46137	7.71825	7.11882	3.55677	7
14.00935	6.99340	6.44972	3.22247	8
12.88889	6.43408	5.93338	2.96449	9
12.00045	5.99057	5.52394	2.75993	10
11.28066	5.63125	5.19221	2.59418	11
10.68728	5.33504	4.91873	2.45754	12
10.19107	5.08733	4.69001	2.34327	13
9.77111	4.87769	4.49642	2.24655	14
9.41208	4.69847	4.33091	2.16385	15
9.10249	4.54392	4.18818	2.09254	16
8.83352	4.40965	4.06417	2.03058	17
8.59834	4.29225	3.95572	1.97640	18
8.39153	4.18901	3.86035	1.92875	19
8.20876	4.09778	3.77606	1.88663	20
8.04654	4.01679	3.70124	1.84925	21
7.90198	3.94463	3.63455	1.81593	22
7.77273	3.88011	3.57492	1.78614	23
7.65679	3.82224	3.52143	1.75941	24
7.55252	3.77018	3.47331	1.73537	25
7.45849	3.72324	3.42992	1.71369	26
7.37352	3.68083	3.39070	1.69409	27
7.29657	3.64241	3.35518	1.67635	28
7.22675	3.60756	3.32295	1.66024	29
7.16331	3.57589	3.29365	1.64561	30
7.10557	3.54707	3.26699	1.63228	31
7.05294	3.52080	3.24268	1.62014	32
7.00492	3.49682	3.22049	1.60905	33
6.96104	3.47492	3.20022	1.59893	34
6.92091	3.45489	3.18168	1.58966	35

8.000% — Blended-payment factor for a loan of $1000, Amortization Periods 1 to 35 years

YRS AMORT	MONTHLY	SEMIMONTHLY	BIWEEKLY	WEEKLY
1	86.92826	43.39310	40.04572	20.00780
2	45.16795	22.54707	20.80562	10.39499
3	31.27635	15.61262	14.40532	7.19724
4	24.35187	12.15604	11.21493	5.60325
5	20.21416	10.09056	9.30848	4.65074
6	17.46975	8.72060	8.04396	4.01895
7	15.52144	7.74804	7.14622	3.57042
8	14.07061	7.02381	6.47768	3.23640
9	12.95135	6.46509	5.96190	2.97871
10	12.06409	6.02219	5.55302	2.77442
11	11.34549	5.66347	5.22184	2.60896
12	10.75328	5.36786	4.94890	2.47259
13	10.25823	5.12073	4.72072	2.35858
14	9.83942	4.91167	4.52767	2.26213
15	9.48153	4.73302	4.36268	2.17970
16	9.17305	4.57903	4.22046	2.10864
17	8.90517	4.44531	4.09696	2.04694
18	8.67106	4.32845	3.98901	1.99300
19	8.46531	4.22574	3.89412	1.94560
20	8.28357	4.13502	3.81031	1.90372
21	8.12236	4.05454	3.73595	1.86657
22	7.97879	3.98288	3.66972	1.83348
23	7.85050	3.91883	3.61053	1.80391
24	7.73550	3.86143	3.55747	1.77740
25	7.63213	3.80983	3.50977	1.75357
26	7.53900	3.76334	3.46679	1.73209
27	7.45488	3.72135	3.42796	1.71269
28	7.37877	3.68336	3.39283	1.69514
29	7.30977	3.64891	3.36097	1.67922
30	7.24711	3.61763	3.33204	1.66477
31	7.19013	3.58919	3.30572	1.65162
32	7.13824	3.56329	3.28175	1.63964
33	7.09092	3.53967	3.25989	1.62872
34	7.04773	3.51811	3.23994	1.61875
35	7.00826	3.49841	3.22170	1.60964

8.125% — Blended-payment factor for a loan of $1000, Amortization Periods 1 to 35 years

MONTHLY	SEMIMONTHLY	BIWEEKLY	WEEKLY	YRS AMORT
86.98417	43.41992	40.07033	20.01986	1
45.22309	22.57403	20.83039	10.40724	2
31.33212	15.64006	14.43054	7.20976	3
24.40860	12.18405	11.24068	5.61605	4
20.27199	10.11917	9.33479	4.66383	5
17.52874	8.74983	8.07083	4.03234	6
15.58162	7.77789	7.17367	3.58409	7
14.13200	7.05427	6.50570	3.25036	8
13.01394	6.49617	5.99049	2.99296	9
12.12789	6.05388	5.58217	2.78895	10
11.41049	5.69578	5.25155	2.62377	11
10.81947	5.40076	4.97916	2.48768	12
10.32560	5.15423	4.75152	2.37395	13
9.90795	4.94576	4.55901	2.27776	14
9.55120	4.76768	4.39455	2.19560	15
9.24385	4.61425	4.25286	2.12480	16
8.97708	4.48109	4.12986	2.06335	17
8.74405	4.36477	4.02241	2.00967	18
8.53936	4.26260	3.92801	1.96251	19
8.35867	4.17240	3.84468	1.92087	20
8.19847	4.09243	3.77079	1.88395	21
8.05589	4.02126	3.70502	1.85109	22
7.92857	3.95771	3.64627	1.82174	23
7.81451	3.90077	3.59365	1.79545	24
7.71206	3.84963	3.54637	1.77183	25
7.61981	3.80358	3.50380	1.75056	26
7.53656	3.76203	3.46537	1.73136	27
7.46129	3.72445	3.43062	1.71400	28
7.39310	3.69041	3.39913	1.69827	29
7.33122	3.65953	3.37056	1.68399	30
7.27500	3.63147	3.34460	1.67102	31
7.22384	3.60593	3.32097	1.65921	32
7.17724	3.58266	3.29943	1.64846	33
7.13473	3.56144	3.27979	1.63864	34
7.09592	3.54207	3.26186	1.62968	35

8.250% Blended-payment factor for a loan of $1000
Amortization Periods 1 to 35 years

YRS AMORT	MONTHLY	SEMIMONTHLY	BIWEEKLY	WEEKLY
1	87.04007	43.44674	40.09493	20.03192
2	45.27824	22.60099	20.85516	10.41950
3	31.38791	15.66752	14.45578	7.22229
4	24.46538	12.21209	11.26646	5.62886
5	20.32988	10.14782	9.36113	4.67694
6	17.58782	8.77910	8.09775	4.04574
7	15.64191	7.80779	7.20116	3.59779
8	14.19351	7.08480	6.53377	3.26435
9	13.07667	6.52733	6.01914	3.00723
10	12.19185	6.08566	5.61139	2.80352
11	11.47566	5.72817	5.28133	2.63862
12	10.88585	5.43376	5.00950	2.50281
13	10.39317	5.18783	4.78242	2.38936
14	9.97669	4.97995	4.59045	2.29345
15	9.62110	4.80245	4.42653	2.21155
16	9.31488	4.64960	4.28536	2.14102
17	9.04923	4.51700	4.16287	2.07982
18	8.81730	4.40123	4.05593	2.02639
19	8.61368	4.29959	3.96203	1.97948
20	8.43404	4.20992	3.87918	1.93808
21	8.27486	4.13046	3.80576	1.90140
22	8.13328	4.05979	3.74045	1.86877
23	8.00693	3.99672	3.68215	1.83965
24	7.89382	3.94026	3.62996	1.81357
25	7.79229	3.88958	3.58311	1.79016
26	7.70093	3.84398	3.54094	1.76910
27	7.61855	3.80286	3.50291	1.75010
28	7.54411	3.76570	3.46855	1.73293
29	7.47673	3.73207	3.43744	1.71739
30	7.41565	3.70158	3.40923	1.70329
31	7.36018	3.67389	3.38361	1.69049
32	7.30975	3.64872	3.36032	1.67886
33	7.26385	3.62581	3.33911	1.66826
34	7.22202	3.60493	3.31978	1.65860
35	7.18387	3.58588	3.30215	1.64979

8.375% Blended-payment factor for a loan of $1000
Amortization Periods 1 to 35 years

MONTHLY	SEMIMONTHLY	BIWEEKLY	WEEKLY	YRS AMORT
87.09597	43.47355	40.11953	20.04398	1
45.33341	22.62796	20.87994	10.43176	2
31.44374	15.69500	14.48104	7.23482	3
24.52221	12.24015	11.29226	5.64169	4
20.38785	10.17650	9.38750	4.69006	5
17.64699	8.80841	8.12470	4.05916	6
15.70230	7.83773	7.22870	3.61151	7
14.25514	7.11539	6.56189	3.27837	8
13.13955	6.55855	6.04784	3.02154	9
12.25596	6.11751	5.64068	2.81812	10
11.54101	5.76064	5.31120	2.65351	11
10.95242	5.46685	5.03993	2.51798	12
10.46093	5.22153	4.81341	2.40481	13
10.04565	5.01424	4.62199	2.30917	14
9.69123	4.83733	4.45860	2.22755	15
9.38616	4.68506	4.31796	2.15728	16
9.12164	4.55302	4.19600	2.09635	17
8.89081	4.43781	4.08957	2.04317	18
8.68827	4.33671	3.99616	1.99651	19
8.50968	4.24757	3.91380	1.95536	20
8.35153	4.16863	3.84085	1.91891	21
8.21096	4.09846	3.77600	1.88652	22
8.08558	4.03588	3.71816	1.85762	23
7.97342	3.97990	3.66641	1.83176	24
7.87281	3.92968	3.61998	1.80856	25
7.78235	3.88453	3.57822	1.78770	26
7.70084	3.84384	3.54060	1.76891	27
7.62724	3.80710	3.50662	1.75193	28
7.56067	3.77388	3.47588	1.73657	29
7.50037	3.74378	3.44803	1.72266	30
7.44566	3.71647	3.42276	1.71004	31
7.39597	3.69166	3.39981	1.69857	32
7.35077	3.66910	3.37892	1.68813	33
7.30961	3.64856	3.35991	1.67863	34
7.27211	3.62984	3.34257	1.66997	35

8.500% Blended-payment factor for a loan of $1000
Amortization Periods 1 to 35 years

YRS AMORT	MONTHLY	SEMIMONTHLY	BIWEEKLY	WEEKLY
1	87.15186	43.50036	40.14413	20.05604
2	45.38858	22.65494	20.90473	10.44402
3	31.49959	15.72248	14.50630	7.24736
4	24.57909	12.26823	11.31808	5.65452
5	20.44589	10.20521	9.41390	4.70319
6	17.70624	8.83777	8.15170	4.07259
7	15.76280	7.86773	7.25629	3.62525
8	14.31689	7.14603	6.59008	3.29241
9	13.20256	6.58983	6.07662	3.03588
10	12.32023	6.14943	5.67004	2.83275
11	11.60652	5.79320	5.34113	2.66843
12	11.01917	5.50003	5.07044	2.53320
13	10.52890	5.25532	4.84448	2.42031
14	10.11482	5.04864	4.65362	2.32495
15	9.76158	4.87232	4.49078	2.24360
16	9.45767	4.72063	4.35067	2.17360
17	9.19428	4.58917	4.22924	2.11293
18	8.96457	4.47451	4.12332	2.06001
19	8.76312	4.37396	4.03042	2.01360
20	8.58559	4.28535	3.94854	1.97269
21	8.42848	4.20693	3.87607	1.93649
22	8.28892	4.13727	3.81169	1.90432
23	8.16452	4.07518	3.75430	1.87565
24	8.05332	4.01967	3.70298	1.85001
25	7.95364	3.96992	3.65698	1.82703
26	7.86407	3.92522	3.61564	1.80638
27	7.78342	3.88496	3.57841	1.78778
28	7.71067	3.84865	3.54482	1.77100
29	7.64491	3.81583	3.51446	1.75583
30	7.58539	3.78612	3.48697	1.74209
31	7.53144	3.75919	3.46205	1.72964
32	7.48247	3.73475	3.43943	1.71834
33	7.43797	3.71254	3.41887	1.70807
34	7.39749	3.69233	3.40016	1.69872
35	7.36063	3.67393	3.38312	1.69021

8.625% Blended-payment factor for a loan of $1000
Amortization Periods 1 to 35 years

MONTHLY	SEMIMONTHLY	BIWEEKLY	WEEKLY	YRS AMORT
87.20774	43.52716	40.16872	20.06810	1
45.44377	22.68191	20.92952	10.45629	2
31.55548	15.74999	14.53158	7.25991	3
24.63602	12.29634	11.34393	5.66737	4
20.50399	10.23396	9.44033	4.71635	5
17.76558	8.86716	8.17873	4.08605	6
15.82341	7.89778	7.28392	3.63901	7
14.37877	7.17674	6.61831	3.30648	8
13.26572	6.62119	6.10545	3.05025	9
12.38466	6.18144	5.69946	2.84742	10
11.67221	5.82584	5.37115	2.68340	11
11.08610	5.53330	5.10104	2.54845	12
10.59707	5.28921	4.87565	2.43585	13
10.18420	5.08314	4.68534	2.34077	14
9.83215	4.90743	4.52306	2.25970	15
9.52941	4.75632	4.38349	2.18997	16
9.26717	4.62544	4.26259	2.12957	17
9.03858	4.51134	4.15718	2.07691	18
8.83823	4.41134	4.06479	2.03075	19
8.66177	4.32327	3.98340	1.99009	20
8.50571	4.24537	3.91142	1.95413	21
8.36716	4.17622	3.84750	1.92219	22
8.24375	4.11462	3.79056	1.89375	23
8.13350	4.05960	3.73969	1.86833	24
8.03475	4.01031	3.69411	1.84556	25
7.94608	3.96605	3.65319	1.82512	26
7.86630	3.92623	3.61636	1.80672	27
7.79439	3.89034	3.58316	1.79013	28
7.72944	3.85792	3.55317	1.77515	29
7.67070	3.82860	3.52604	1.76159	30
7.61750	3.80205	3.50147	1.74931	31
7.56926	3.77797	3.47918	1.73818	32
7.52546	3.75611	3.45894	1.72807	33
7.48564	3.73624	3.44054	1.71888	34
7.44943	3.71816	3.42379	1.71051	35

8.750% — Blended-payment factor for a loan of $1000, Amortization Periods 1 to 35 years

YRS AMORT	MONTHLY	SEMIMONTHLY	BIWEEKLY	WEEKLY
1	87.26361	43.55396	40.19330	20.08015
2	45.49898	22.70890	20.95431	10.46855
3	31.61140	15.77750	14.55688	7.27246
4	24.69301	12.32447	11.36979	5.68023
5	20.56217	10.26274	9.46680	4.72951
6	17.82501	8.89660	8.20580	4.09953
7	15.88411	7.92789	7.31160	3.65280
8	14.44077	7.20750	6.64660	3.32057
9	13.32901	6.65261	6.13435	3.06466
10	12.44924	6.21351	5.72896	2.86213
11	11.73806	5.85856	5.40124	2.69840
12	11.15322	5.56666	5.13171	2.56375
13	10.66543	5.32320	4.90690	2.45143
14	10.25379	5.11775	4.71716	2.35664
15	9.90294	4.94264	4.55544	2.27585
16	9.60139	4.79213	4.41642	2.20639
17	9.34031	4.66182	4.29604	2.14626
18	9.11285	4.54829	4.19116	2.09386
19	8.91360	4.44885	4.09927	2.04795
20	8.73822	4.36131	4.01839	2.00754
21	8.58320	4.28394	3.94688	1.97182
22	8.44567	4.21530	3.88344	1.94012
23	8.32325	4.15420	3.82696	1.91191
24	8.21396	4.09965	3.77653	1.88671
25	8.11614	4.05083	3.73138	1.86416
26	8.02838	4.00703	3.69087	1.84392
27	7.94947	3.96764	3.65444	1.82572
28	7.87839	3.93217	3.62162	1.80932
29	7.81426	3.90016	3.59201	1.79453
30	7.75630	3.87123	3.56524	1.78115
31	7.70385	3.84505	3.54101	1.76905
32	7.65633	3.82133	3.51905	1.75808
33	7.61322	3.79982	3.49913	1.74813
34	7.57407	3.78028	3.48104	1.73909
35	7.53849	3.76252	3.46459	1.73087

8.875% — Blended-payment factor for a loan of $1000, Amortization Periods 1 to 35 years

MONTHLY	SEMIMONTHLY	BIWEEKLY	WEEKLY	YRS AMORT
87.31947	43.58075	40.21788	20.09220	1
45.55419	22.73589	20.97911	10.48082	2
31.66736	15.80503	14.58218	7.28502	3
24.75004	12.35263	11.39568	5.69309	4
20.62042	10.29156	9.49329	4.74269	5
17.88452	8.92608	8.23291	4.11303	6
15.94493	7.95804	7.33933	3.66661	7
14.50289	7.23833	6.67495	3.33469	8
13.39244	6.68411	6.16331	3.07909	9
12.51397	6.24567	5.75853	2.87687	10
11.80409	5.89137	5.43140	2.71344	11
11.22052	5.60011	5.16247	2.57909	12
10.73399	5.35729	4.93824	2.46706	13
10.32359	5.15245	4.74908	2.37256	14
9.97396	4.97796	4.58791	2.29205	15
9.67359	4.82805	4.44944	2.22287	16
9.41368	4.69832	4.32961	2.16300	17
9.18736	4.58537	4.22525	2.11087	18
8.98922	4.48648	4.13388	2.06522	19
8.81493	4.39949	4.05349	2.02506	20
8.66096	4.32265	3.98247	1.98958	21
8.52446	4.25452	3.91950	1.95812	22
8.40303	4.19392	3.86347	1.93013	23
8.29471	4.13985	3.81349	1.90516	24
8.19782	4.09149	3.76877	1.88282	25
8.11096	4.04814	3.72867	1.86278	26
8.03292	4.00919	3.69265	1.84479	27
7.96268	3.97414	3.66022	1.82858	28
7.89936	3.94253	3.63097	1.81397	29
7.84218	3.91399	3.60456	1.80078	30
7.79048	3.88819	3.58068	1.78885	31
7.74367	3.86483	3.55905	1.77804	32
7.70125	3.84366	3.53945	1.76825	33
7.66276	3.82445	3.52166	1.75936	34
7.62781	3.80701	3.50550	1.75129	35

9.000% Blended-payment factor for a loan of $1000
Amortization Periods 1 to 35 years

YRS AMORT	MONTHLY	SEMIMONTHLY	BIWEEKLY	WEEKLY
1	87.37533	43.60754	40.24246	20.10425
2	45.60942	22.76288	21.00391	10.49309
3	31.72334	15.83258	14.60751	7.29759
4	24.80712	12.38081	11.42159	5.70597
5	20.67873	10.32040	9.51981	4.75589
6	17.94413	8.95561	8.26005	4.12654
7	16.00584	7.98824	7.36710	3.68044
8	14.56514	7.26921	6.70335	3.34884
9	13.45601	6.71566	6.19233	3.09355
10	12.57886	6.27789	5.78816	2.89164
11	11.87028	5.92425	5.46165	2.72852
12	11.28800	5.63365	5.19331	2.59446
13	10.80274	5.39147	4.96967	2.48274
14	10.39359	5.18726	4.78108	2.38852
15	10.04519	5.01338	4.62049	2.30829
16	9.74603	4.86408	4.48257	2.23939
17	9.48729	4.73494	4.36328	2.17980
18	9.26212	4.62257	4.25945	2.12793
19	9.06510	4.52424	4.16860	2.08254
20	8.89189	4.43779	4.08871	2.04263
21	8.73899	4.36148	4.01818	2.00739
22	8.60352	4.29387	3.95568	1.97617
23	8.48309	4.23377	3.90012	1.94841
24	8.37573	4.18018	3.85057	1.92366
25	8.27977	4.13229	3.80629	1.90154
26	8.19381	4.08939	3.76661	1.88171
27	8.11665	4.05088	3.73098	1.86392
28	8.04725	4.01624	3.69894	1.84791
29	7.98473	3.98504	3.67006	1.83348
30	7.92833	3.95689	3.64401	1.82047
31	7.87737	3.93146	3.62047	1.80871
32	7.83128	3.90846	3.59917	1.79807
33	7.78954	3.88763	3.57988	1.78843
34	7.75171	3.86875	3.56240	1.77969
35	7.71739	3.85162	3.54653	1.77177

9.125% Blended-payment factor for a loan of $1000
Amortization Periods 1 to 35 years

MONTHLY	SEMIMONTHLY	BIWEEKLY	WEEKLY	YRS AMORT
87.43117	43.63432	40.26703	20.11629	1
45.66466	22.78988	21.02872	10.50536	2
31.77936	15.86014	14.63284	7.31016	3
24.86426	12.40902	11.44752	5.71886	4
20.73711	10.34928	9.54637	4.76910	5
18.00381	8.98517	8.28724	4.14007	6
16.06687	8.01850	7.39492	3.69430	7
14.62750	7.30015	6.73180	3.36302	8
13.51971	6.74729	6.22141	3.10804	9
12.64389	6.31019	5.81786	2.90644	10
11.93664	5.95722	5.49196	2.74363	11
11.35566	5.66728	5.22423	2.60988	12
10.87169	5.42574	5.00119	2.49845	13
10.46380	5.22217	4.81318	2.40453	14
10.11664	5.04891	4.65316	2.32459	15
9.81869	4.90022	4.51580	2.25597	16
9.56113	4.77168	4.39706	2.19665	17
9.33712	4.65988	4.29376	2.14504	18
9.14123	4.56212	4.20343	2.09991	19
8.96912	4.47622	4.12405	2.06026	20
8.81728	4.40045	4.05401	2.02527	21
8.68284	4.33335	3.99198	1.99428	22
8.56341	4.27375	3.93688	1.96676	23
8.45702	4.22065	3.88778	1.94223	24
8.36200	4.17323	3.84393	1.92032	25
8.27694	4.13078	3.80466	1.90070	26
8.20065	4.09270	3.76944	1.88311	27
8.13209	4.05848	3.73778	1.86729	28
8.07037	4.02768	3.70927	1.85305	29
8.01474	3.99992	3.68358	1.84021	30
7.96453	3.97486	3.66038	1.82862	31
7.91915	3.95221	3.63941	1.81815	32
7.87809	3.93172	3.62043	1.80867	33
7.84091	3.91317	3.60325	1.80008	34
7.80721	3.89635	3.58767	1.79230	35

9.250% Blended-payment factor for a loan of $1000
Amortization Periods 1 to 35 years

YRS AMORT	MONTHLY	SEMIMONTHLY	BIWEEKLY	WEEKLY
1	87.48701	43.66110	40.29160	20.12833
2	45.71991	22.81689	21.05353	10.51764
3	31.83541	15.88772	14.65819	7.32274
4	24.92144	12.43725	11.47347	5.73176
5	20.79556	10.37819	9.57295	4.78232
6	18.06359	9.01478	8.31446	4.15363
7	16.12799	8.04880	7.42279	3.70818
8	14.68998	7.33115	6.76030	3.37722
9	13.58355	6.77898	6.25055	3.12256
10	12.70908	6.34257	5.84763	2.92128
11	12.00316	5.99027	5.52235	2.75878
12	11.42350	5.70099	5.25523	2.62534
13	10.94083	5.46011	5.03279	2.51421
14	10.53421	5.25718	4.84538	2.42059
15	10.18830	5.08455	4.68593	2.34093
16	9.89157	4.93647	4.54913	2.27260
17	9.63521	4.80853	4.43094	2.21355
18	9.41236	4.69732	4.32818	2.16222
19	9.21760	4.60012	4.23837	2.11735
20	9.04660	4.51478	4.15950	2.07795
21	8.89583	4.43954	4.08995	2.04320
22	8.76242	4.37296	4.02840	2.01246
23	8.64400	4.31386	3.97376	1.98516
24	8.53858	4.26125	3.92511	1.96085
25	8.44450	4.21429	3.88169	1.93916
26	8.36034	4.17230	3.84284	1.91975
27	8.28491	4.13465	3.80801	1.90236
28	8.21719	4.10085	3.77674	1.88673
29	8.15628	4.07046	3.74861	1.87268
30	8.10142	4.04308	3.72326	1.86002
31	8.05194	4.01839	3.70041	1.84860
32	8.00727	3.99609	3.67976	1.83829
33	7.96689	3.97594	3.66110	1.82896
34	7.93036	3.95771	3.64421	1.82052
35	7.89728	3.94120	3.62891	1.81288

9.375% Blended-payment factor for a loan of $1000
Amortization Periods 1 to 35 years

MONTHLY	SEMIMONTHLY	BIWEEKLY	WEEKLY	YRS AMORT
87.54284	43.68787	40.31617	20.14037	1
45.77517	22.84390	21.07835	10.52991	2
31.89149	15.91531	14.68355	7.33532	3
24.97868	12.46550	11.49945	5.74467	4
20.85408	10.40714	9.59956	4.79557	5
18.12345	9.04443	8.34173	4.16720	6
16.18922	8.07916	7.45070	3.72208	7
14.75259	7.36221	6.78886	3.39145	8
13.64753	6.81074	6.27975	3.13712	9
12.77442	6.37502	5.87747	2.93615	10
12.06985	6.02341	5.55282	2.77397	11
11.49152	5.73480	5.28632	2.64084	12
11.01016	5.49457	5.06448	2.53001	13
10.60483	5.29229	4.87766	2.43669	14
10.26017	5.12030	4.71879	2.35732	15
9.96468	4.97283	4.58257	2.28927	16
9.70952	4.84549	4.46493	2.23050	17
9.48784	4.73487	4.36271	2.17944	18
9.29423	4.63824	4.27342	2.13483	19
9.12433	4.55346	4.19506	2.09569	20
8.97463	4.47875	4.12601	2.06119	21
8.84227	4.41270	4.06494	2.03068	22
8.72485	4.35410	4.01076	2.00362	23
8.62040	4.30197	3.96256	1.97954	24
8.52726	4.25549	3.91957	1.95806	25
8.44400	4.21394	3.88113	1.93886	26
8.36945	4.17674	3.84671	1.92166	27
8.30256	4.14335	3.81582	1.90623	28
8.24245	4.11336	3.78806	1.89236	29
8.18835	4.08636	3.76307	1.87988	30
8.13961	4.06204	3.74055	1.86863	31
8.09564	4.04010	3.72023	1.85848	32
8.05594	4.02028	3.70187	1.84931	33
8.02004	4.00237	3.68528	1.84102	34
7.98757	3.98616	3.67026	1.83352	35

9.500% — Blended-payment factor for a loan of $1000, Amortization Periods 1 to 35 years

YRS AMORT	MONTHLY	SEMIMONTHLY	BIWEEKLY	WEEKLY
1	87.59867	43.71464	40.34073	20.15241
2	45.83044	22.87091	21.10317	10.54219
3	31.94760	15.94291	14.70892	7.34791
4	25.03596	12.49378	11.52544	5.75759
5	20.91267	10.43612	9.62621	4.80882
6	18.18340	9.07412	8.36903	4.18079
7	16.25055	8.10957	7.47866	3.73600
8	14.81531	7.39333	6.81748	3.40570
9	13.71164	6.84257	6.30901	3.15170
10	12.83991	6.40754	5.90738	2.95106
11	12.13670	6.05662	5.58336	2.78919
12	11.55972	5.76869	5.31748	2.65637
13	11.07968	5.52913	5.09625	2.54586
14	10.67564	5.32750	4.91003	2.45283
15	10.33226	5.15614	4.75175	2.37376
16	10.03801	5.00930	4.61610	2.30600
17	9.78406	4.88257	4.49902	2.24751
18	9.56356	4.77254	4.39735	2.19672
19	9.37109	4.67649	4.30859	2.15238
20	9.20231	4.59226	4.23074	2.11349
21	9.05369	4.51809	4.16218	2.07924
22	8.92237	4.45256	4.10159	2.04897
23	8.80596	4.39447	4.04788	2.02214
24	8.70248	4.34283	4.00013	1.99828
25	8.61028	4.29681	3.95756	1.97702
26	8.52793	4.25572	3.91955	1.95803
27	8.45424	4.21894	3.88552	1.94103
28	8.38818	4.18598	3.85502	1.92579
29	8.32887	4.15638	3.82762	1.91211
30	8.27554	4.12977	3.80298	1.89980
31	8.22753	4.10581	3.78080	1.88872
32	8.18426	4.08422	3.76080	1.87873
33	8.14522	4.06473	3.74275	1.86971
34	8.10996	4.04714	3.72645	1.86157
35	8.07809	4.03124	3.71172	1.85421

9.625% — Blended-payment factor for a loan of $1000, Amortization Periods 1 to 35 years

MONTHLY	SEMIMONTHLY	BIWEEKLY	WEEKLY	YRS AMORT
87.65448	43.74141	40.36528	20.16445	1
45.88573	22.89793	21.12799	10.55447	2
32.00374	15.97053	14.73431	7.36051	3
25.09330	12.52208	11.55146	5.77052	4
20.97133	10.46513	9.65288	4.82209	5
18.24343	9.10385	8.39636	4.19440	6
16.31199	8.14002	7.50666	3.74995	7
14.87815	7.42451	6.84614	3.41999	8
13.77589	6.87446	6.33834	3.16631	9
12.90555	6.44014	5.93735	2.96600	10
12.20372	6.08991	5.61397	2.80445	11
11.62810	5.80266	5.34872	2.67195	12
11.14939	5.56378	5.12811	2.56174	13
10.74666	5.36281	4.94250	2.46902	14
10.40456	5.19209	4.78481	2.39025	15
10.11155	5.04588	4.64973	2.32277	16
9.85883	4.91976	4.53321	2.26456	17
9.63952	4.81032	4.43209	2.21405	18
9.44820	4.71485	4.34386	2.16997	19
9.28053	4.63118	4.26652	2.13134	20
9.13300	4.55755	4.19847	2.09734	21
9.00272	4.49254	4.13836	2.06732	22
8.88732	4.43496	4.08511	2.04072	23
8.78482	4.38381	4.03781	2.01708	24
8.69355	4.33826	3.99568	1.99604	25
8.61210	4.29762	3.95808	1.97725	26
8.53928	4.26128	3.92445	1.96046	27
8.47405	4.22873	3.89433	1.94541	28
8.41554	4.19953	3.86730	1.93191	29
8.36297	4.17330	3.84301	1.91977	30
8.31569	4.14970	3.82116	1.90886	31
8.27311	4.12845	3.80148	1.89903	32
8.23473	4.10930	3.78374	1.89016	33
8.20010	4.09202	3.76773	1.88217	34
8.16883	4.07642	3.75327	1.87494	35

9.750%
Blended-payment factor for a loan of $1000
Amortization Periods 1 to 35 years

YRS AMORT	MONTHLY	SEMIMONTHLY	BIWEEKLY	WEEKLY
1	87.71029	43.76817	40.38983	20.17648
2	45.94103	22.92496	21.15282	10.56676
3	32.05991	15.99816	14.75970	7.37312
4	25.15068	12.55040	11.57750	5.78346
5	21.03005	10.49417	9.67958	4.83537
6	18.30355	9.13362	8.42374	4.20802
7	16.37352	8.17053	7.53471	3.76392
8	14.94111	7.45574	6.87486	3.43429
9	13.84027	6.90641	6.36772	3.18095
10	12.97134	6.47281	5.96739	2.98097
11	12.27090	6.12328	5.64466	2.81975
12	11.69665	5.83673	5.38004	2.68756
13	11.21929	5.59852	5.16005	2.57767
14	10.81788	5.39821	4.97505	2.48525
15	10.47707	5.22814	4.81796	2.40678
16	10.18532	5.08256	4.68346	2.33959
17	9.93382	4.95706	4.56751	2.28167
18	9.71570	4.84822	4.46693	2.23143
19	9.52554	4.75332	4.37924	2.18762
20	9.35899	4.67022	4.30242	2.14925
21	9.21255	4.59714	4.23486	2.11550
22	9.08332	4.53265	4.17524	2.08572
23	8.96894	4.47557	4.12246	2.05935
24	8.86741	4.42491	4.07560	2.03594
25	8.77708	4.37984	4.03390	2.01511
26	8.69653	4.33964	3.99672	1.99653
27	8.62457	4.30373	3.96349	1.97994
28	8.56017	4.27160	3.93375	1.96508
29	8.50245	4.24279	3.90708	1.95176
30	8.45064	4.21694	3.88314	1.93980
31	8.40408	4.19371	3.86163	1.92905
32	8.36219	4.17280	3.84227	1.91938
33	8.32447	4.15398	3.82483	1.91067
34	8.29046	4.13701	3.80910	1.90281
35	8.25979	4.12170	3.79492	1.89573

9.875%
Blended-payment factor for a loan of $1000
Amortization Periods 1 to 35 years

MONTHLY	SEMIMONTHLY	BIWEEKLY	WEEKLY	YRS AMORT
87.76609	43.79492	40.41438	20.18851	1
45.99634	22.95199	21.17765	10.57904	2
32.11611	16.02581	14.78512	7.38573	3
25.20811	12.57875	11.60356	5.79642	4
21.08884	10.52325	9.70632	4.84867	5
18.36375	9.16344	8.45115	4.22167	6
16.43516	8.20108	7.56281	3.77791	7
15.00419	7.48703	6.90363	3.44863	8
13.90479	6.93843	6.39716	3.19563	9
13.03728	6.50555	5.99749	2.99598	10
12.33825	6.15673	5.67541	2.83508	11
11.76538	5.87087	5.41144	2.70322	12
11.28937	5.63335	5.19208	2.59364	13
10.88929	5.43371	5.00769	2.50153	14
10.54978	5.26430	4.85120	2.42336	15
10.25930	5.11935	4.71729	2.35646	16
10.00904	4.99447	4.60191	2.29883	17
9.79212	4.88623	4.50188	2.24886	18
9.60312	4.79192	4.41472	2.20532	19
9.43770	4.70937	4.33842	2.16721	20
9.29234	4.63684	4.27137	2.13371	21
9.16417	4.57288	4.21223	2.10417	22
9.05080	4.51631	4.15992	2.07804	23
8.95025	4.46614	4.11351	2.05485	24
8.86085	4.42153	4.07224	2.03424	25
8.78121	4.38179	4.03547	2.01587	26
8.71011	4.34631	4.00264	1.99947	27
8.64654	4.31459	3.97328	1.98480	28
8.58960	4.28618	3.94698	1.97166	29
8.53855	4.26070	3.92339	1.95988	30
8.49270	4.23783	3.90220	1.94930	31
8.45150	4.21726	3.88315	1.93978	32
8.41443	4.19876	3.86601	1.93122	33
8.38104	4.18210	3.85058	1.92351	34
8.35095	4.16709	3.83666	1.91656	35

10.000% Blended-payment factor for a loan of $1000
Amortization Periods 1 to 35 years

YRS AMORT	MONTHLY	SEMIMONTHLY	BIWEEKLY	WEEKLY
1	87.82188	43.82167	40.43892	20.20054
2	46.05166	22.97902	21.20249	10.59133
3	32.17235	16.05347	14.81054	7.39834
4	25.26560	12.60712	11.62964	5.80938
5	21.14770	10.55235	9.73308	4.86199
6	18.42404	9.19329	8.47860	4.23533
7	16.49690	8.23168	7.59094	3.79192
8	15.06739	7.51838	6.93246	3.46299
9	13.96943	6.97052	6.42667	3.21033
10	13.10337	6.53836	6.02767	3.01101
11	12.40575	6.19027	5.70624	2.85045
12	11.83427	5.90511	5.44292	2.71891
13	11.35964	5.66827	5.22419	2.60965
14	10.96090	5.46931	5.04042	2.51785
15	10.62270	5.30055	4.88453	2.43998
16	10.33350	5.15625	4.75121	2.37338
17	10.08447	5.03199	4.63640	2.31603
18	9.86876	4.92435	4.53693	2.26634
19	9.68093	4.83063	4.45031	2.22307
20	9.51664	4.74865	4.37454	2.18522
21	9.37238	4.67666	4.30798	2.15198
22	9.24526	4.61323	4.24933	2.12268
23	9.13290	4.55717	4.19748	2.09678
24	9.03333	4.50748	4.15153	2.07382
25	8.94487	4.46334	4.11069	2.05342
26	8.86612	4.42405	4.07433	2.03526
27	8.79589	4.38900	4.04190	2.01906
28	8.73314	4.35769	4.01291	2.00458
29	8.67699	4.32967	3.98697	1.99162
30	8.62668	4.30457	3.96373	1.98001
31	8.58155	4.28205	3.94287	1.96959
32	8.54103	4.26183	3.92414	1.96023
33	8.50460	4.24365	3.90730	1.95182
34	8.47182	4.22730	3.89214	1.94425
35	8.44231	4.21257	3.87849	1.93743

10.125% Blended-payment factor for a loan of $1000
Amortization Periods 1 to 35 years

MONTHLY	SEMIMONTHLY	BIWEEKLY	WEEKLY	YRS AMORT
87.87766	43.84842	40.46346	20.21257	1
46.10700	23.00606	21.22733	10.60361	2
32.22861	16.08115	14.83598	7.41096	3
25.32313	12.63551	11.65574	5.82235	4
21.20662	10.58149	9.75987	4.87531	5
18.48442	9.22319	8.50609	4.24902	6
16.55875	8.26234	7.61913	3.80596	7
15.13071	7.54979	6.96134	3.47737	8
14.03422	7.00267	6.45623	3.22506	9
13.16960	6.57125	6.05790	3.02608	10
12.47341	6.22387	5.73715	2.86586	11
11.90335	5.93943	5.47447	2.73464	12
11.43009	5.70329	5.25638	2.62570	13
11.03271	5.50500	5.07324	2.53422	14
10.69582	5.33691	4.91796	2.45665	15
10.40791	5.19324	4.78523	2.39035	16
10.16013	5.06961	4.67100	2.33329	17
9.94563	4.96258	4.57209	2.28388	18
9.75897	4.86945	4.48601	2.24088	19
9.59582	4.78804	4.41075	2.20329	20
9.45265	4.71660	4.34471	2.17030	21
9.32659	4.65370	4.28654	2.14124	22
9.21525	4.59814	4.23516	2.11557	23
9.11665	4.54895	4.18965	2.09284	24
9.02913	4.50528	4.14925	2.07266	25
8.95128	4.46643	4.11330	2.05470	26
8.88190	4.43181	4.08126	2.03870	27
8.81997	4.40091	4.05266	2.02441	28
8.76460	4.37328	4.02708	2.01163	29
8.71504	4.34855	4.00417	2.00019	30
8.67062	4.32639	3.98364	1.98994	31
8.63076	4.30650	3.96522	1.98073	32
8.59497	4.28864	3.94867	1.97247	33
8.56281	4.27259	3.93379	1.96503	34
8.53387	4.25815	3.92041	1.95835	35

10.250% Blended-payment factor for a loan of $1000 — Amortization Periods 1 to 35 years

YRS AMORT	MONTHLY	SEMIMONTHLY	BIWEEKLY	WEEKLY
1	87.93344	43.87516	40.48799	20.22459
2	46.16235	23.03311	21.25218	10.61591
3	32.28491	16.10884	14.86143	7.42359
4	25.38071	12.66393	11.68187	5.83534
5	21.26562	10.61067	9.78669	4.88866
6	18.54487	9.25313	8.53362	4.26272
7	16.62069	8.29304	7.64736	3.82001
8	15.19414	7.58125	6.99026	3.49178
9	14.09913	7.03488	6.48585	3.23982
10	13.23598	6.60421	6.08821	3.04119
11	12.54124	6.25756	5.76812	2.88130
12	11.97259	5.97383	5.50610	2.75041
13	11.50073	5.73839	5.28866	2.64180
14	11.10471	5.54079	5.10614	2.55062
15	10.76915	5.37336	4.95148	2.47337
16	10.48252	5.23035	4.81935	2.40736
17	10.23601	5.10734	4.70569	2.35059
18	10.02272	5.00092	4.60734	2.30146
19	9.83725	4.90838	4.52180	2.25873
20	9.67523	4.82754	4.44707	2.22141
21	9.53316	4.75665	4.38153	2.18867
22	9.40815	4.69428	4.32385	2.15985
23	9.29783	4.63923	4.27294	2.13442
24	9.20021	4.59052	4.22788	2.11192
25	9.11362	4.54732	4.18791	2.09195
26	9.03667	4.50892	4.15238	2.07420
27	8.96814	4.47473	4.12073	2.05839
28	8.90703	4.44424	4.09250	2.04429
29	8.85244	4.41700	4.06728	2.03169
30	8.80361	4.39264	4.04472	2.02042
31	8.75990	4.37083	4.02451	2.01033
32	8.72071	4.35128	4.00640	2.00128
33	8.68555	4.33373	3.99014	1.99316
34	8.65399	4.31798	3.97554	1.98586
35	8.62562	4.30383	3.96241	1.97931

10.375% Blended-payment factor for a loan of $1000 — Amortization Periods 1 to 35 years

MONTHLY	SEMIMONTHLY	BIWEEKLY	WEEKLY	YRS AMORT
87.98921	43.90189	40.51252	20.23661	1
46.21770	23.06016	21.27703	10.62820	2
32.34123	16.13654	14.88690	7.43623	3
25.43834	12.69237	11.70801	5.84833	4
21.32468	10.63987	9.81354	4.90201	5
18.60541	9.28310	8.56118	4.27644	6
16.68273	8.32379	7.67563	3.83409	7
15.25769	7.61277	7.01925	3.50622	8
14.16417	7.06716	6.51553	3.25460	9
13.30250	6.63724	6.11857	3.05632	10
12.60922	6.29133	5.79917	2.89677	11
12.04201	6.00832	5.53781	2.76622	12
11.57155	5.77358	5.32102	2.65793	13
11.17690	5.57667	5.13913	2.56707	14
10.84268	5.40991	4.98508	2.49012	15
10.55735	5.26755	4.85355	2.42442	16
10.31210	5.14518	4.74048	2.36794	17
10.10003	5.03938	4.64270	2.31910	18
9.91574	4.94742	4.55770	2.27664	19
9.75487	4.86716	4.48350	2.23957	20
9.61390	4.79682	4.41846	2.20709	21
9.48995	4.73498	4.36127	2.17852	22
9.38064	4.68044	4.31083	2.15332	23
9.28400	4.63222	4.26622	2.13104	24
9.19835	4.58948	4.22668	2.11129	25
9.12228	4.55153	4.19155	2.09374	26
9.05461	4.51776	4.16030	2.07813	27
8.99431	4.48768	4.13244	2.06422	28
8.94049	4.46083	4.10758	2.05180	29
8.89240	4.43683	4.08536	2.04070	30
8.84939	4.41537	4.06547	2.03076	31
8.81086	4.39615	4.04766	2.02187	32
8.77633	4.37892	4.03169	2.01389	33
8.74536	4.36346	4.01737	2.00673	34
8.71755	4.34959	4.00450	2.00031	35

10.500% Blended-payment factor for a loan of $1000 — Amortization Periods 1 to 35 years

YRS AMORT	MONTHLY	SEMIMONTHLY	BIWEEKLY	WEEKLY
1	88.04496	43.92863	40.53704	20.24863
2	46.27307	23.08721	21.30189	10.64049
3	32.39759	16.16426	14.91237	7.44887
4	25.49602	12.72083	11.73418	5.86133
5	21.38380	10.66911	9.84042	4.91538
6	18.66604	9.31312	8.58878	4.29017
7	16.74488	8.35459	7.70395	3.84820
8	15.32135	7.64434	7.04828	3.52068
9	14.22935	7.09951	6.54527	3.26942
10	13.36917	6.67033	6.14901	3.07149
11	12.67736	6.32517	5.83028	2.91228
12	12.11159	6.04289	5.56960	2.78207
13	11.64255	5.80886	5.35346	2.67410
14	11.24928	5.61265	5.17221	2.58357
15	10.91640	5.44656	5.01878	2.50693
16	10.63239	5.30486	4.88786	2.44153
17	10.38840	5.18313	4.77537	2.38534
18	10.17757	5.07793	4.67815	2.33678
19	9.99446	4.98658	4.59370	2.29460
20	9.83473	4.90688	4.52003	2.25779
21	9.69487	4.83710	4.45550	2.22556
22	9.57198	4.77579	4.39880	2.19724
23	9.46369	4.72176	4.34882	2.17228
24	9.36802	4.67402	4.30466	2.15022
25	9.28330	4.63175	4.26555	2.13068
26	9.20812	4.59425	4.23083	2.11334
27	9.14130	4.56091	4.19997	2.09792
28	9.08181	4.53122	4.17249	2.08420
29	9.02876	4.50475	4.14798	2.07195
30	8.98140	4.48113	4.12609	2.06102
31	8.93908	4.46001	4.10652	2.05125
32	8.90121	4.44112	4.08902	2.04250
33	8.86730	4.42420	4.07333	2.03467
34	8.83691	4.40903	4.05928	2.02765
35	8.80965	4.39544	4.04667	2.02135

10.625% Blended-payment factor for a loan of $1000 — Amortization Periods 1 to 35 years

MONTHLY	SEMIMONTHLY	BIWEEKLY	WEEKLY	YRS AMORT
88.10072	43.95535	40.56156	20.26065	1
46.32846	23.11427	21.32675	10.65279	2
32.45398	16.19199	14.93786	7.46152	3
25.55375	12.74932	11.76037	5.87435	4
21.44300	10.69837	9.86733	4.92877	5
18.72675	9.34318	8.61641	4.30393	6
16.80712	8.38544	7.73231	3.86232	7
15.38513	7.67598	7.07736	3.53517	8
14.29465	7.13191	6.57506	3.28427	9
13.43599	6.70350	6.17951	3.08669	10
12.74566	6.35909	5.86147	2.92782	11
12.18135	6.07754	5.60146	2.79795	12
11.71373	5.84423	5.38598	2.69031	13
11.32185	5.64871	5.20537	2.60010	14
10.99033	5.48331	5.05257	2.52378	15
10.70763	5.34227	4.92225	2.45868	16
10.46491	5.22117	4.81035	2.40279	17
10.25531	5.11660	4.71370	2.35451	18
10.07340	5.02584	4.62980	2.31260	19
9.91482	4.94672	4.55665	2.27606	20
9.77606	4.87749	4.49263	2.24409	21
9.65423	4.81670	4.43642	2.21601	22
9.54696	4.76318	4.38691	2.19128	23
9.45226	4.71594	4.34320	2.16944	24
9.36847	4.67413	4.30451	2.15012	25
9.29419	4.63707	4.27021	2.13299	26
9.22821	4.60415	4.23974	2.11776	27
9.16952	4.57487	4.21262	2.10422	28
9.11724	4.54879	4.18847	2.09215	29
9.07060	4.52552	4.16691	2.08139	30
9.02896	4.50475	4.14766	2.07177	31
8.99175	4.48618	4.13046	2.06318	32
8.95845	4.46957	4.11506	2.05549	33
8.92864	4.45469	4.10127	2.04860	34
8.90193	4.44137	4.08891	2.04242	35

10.750% Blended-payment factor for a loan of $1000
Amortization Periods 1 to 35 years

YRS AMORT	MONTHLY	SEMIMONTHLY	BIWEEKLY	WEEKLY
1	88.15646	43.98207	40.58608	20.27266
2	46.38385	23.14133	21.35161	10.66509
3	32.51040	16.21974	14.96336	7.47417
4	25.61152	12.77783	11.78658	5.88737
5	21.50226	10.72767	9.89427	4.94217
6	18.78754	9.37328	8.64409	4.31770
7	16.86946	8.41633	7.76072	3.87646
8	15.44903	7.70766	7.10650	3.54968
9	14.36009	7.16438	6.60492	3.29914
10	13.50294	6.73674	6.21007	3.10192
11	12.81412	6.39308	5.89272	2.94340
12	12.25127	6.11227	5.63339	2.81387
13	11.78509	5.87909	5.41858	2.70657
14	11.39460	5.68487	5.23862	2.61668
15	11.06445	5.52015	5.08644	2.54067
16	10.78307	5.37977	4.95673	2.47588
17	10.54164	5.25932	4.84542	2.42028
18	10.33328	5.15537	4.74934	2.37229
19	10.15256	5.06520	4.66600	2.33066
20	9.99513	4.98666	4.59338	2.29438
21	9.85747	4.91798	4.52987	2.26266
22	9.73671	4.85773	4.47414	2.23483
23	9.63045	4.80472	4.42511	2.21033
24	9.53672	4.75796	4.38184	2.18872
25	9.45386	4.71662	4.34358	2.16961
26	9.38046	4.68000	4.30969	2.15268
27	9.31533	4.64750	4.27960	2.13765
28	9.25744	4.61862	4.25286	2.12429
29	9.20592	4.59292	4.22905	2.11240
30	9.16000	4.57001	4.20783	2.10180
31	9.11905	4.54958	4.18889	2.09234
32	9.08247	4.53133	4.17198	2.08390
33	9.04978	4.51502	4.15686	2.07634
34	9.02055	4.50043	4.14334	2.06959
35	8.99438	4.48738	4.13123	2.06354

10.875% Blended-payment factor for a loan of $1000
Amortization Periods 1 to 35 years

MONTHLY	SEMIMONTHLY	BIWEEKLY	WEEKLY	YRS AMORT
88.21219	44.00879	40.61059	20.28467	1
46.43925	23.16840	21.37648	10.67739	2
32.56684	16.24750	14.98888	7.48683	3
25.66935	12.80636	11.81281	5.90041	4
21.56158	10.75701	9.92124	4.95558	5
18.84842	9.40342	8.67180	4.33150	6
16.93191	8.44728	7.78917	3.89063	7
15.51304	7.73941	7.13568	3.56422	8
14.42566	7.19692	6.63483	3.31405	9
13.57004	6.77005	6.24069	3.11718	10
12.88273	6.42715	5.92405	2.95902	11
12.32136	6.14709	5.66540	2.82983	12
11.85662	5.91523	5.45125	2.72286	13
11.46755	5.72112	5.27195	2.63330	14
11.13876	5.55709	5.12041	2.55760	15
10.85871	5.41738	4.99131	2.49312	16
10.61857	5.29757	4.88059	2.43782	17
10.41145	5.19424	4.78508	2.39011	18
10.23193	5.10468	4.70229	2.34876	19
10.07566	5.02671	4.63020	2.31275	20
9.93911	4.95859	4.56720	2.28128	21
9.81940	4.89887	4.51197	2.25369	22
9.71416	4.84637	4.46340	2.22943	23
9.62141	4.80009	4.42058	2.20804	24
9.53947	4.75921	4.38275	2.18915	25
9.46695	4.72303	4.34926	2.17242	26
9.40266	4.69096	4.31956	2.15759	27
9.34556	4.66247	4.29318	2.14441	28
9.29479	4.63714	4.26972	2.13269	29
9.24960	4.61460	4.24883	2.12226	30
9.20931	4.59450	4.23020	2.11295	31
9.17338	4.57657	4.21359	2.10465	32
9.14129	4.56056	4.19874	2.09724	33
9.11262	4.54626	4.18548	2.09061	34
9.08698	4.53347	4.17362	2.08469	35

11.000% — Blended-payment factor for a loan of $1000, Amortization Periods 1 to 35 years

YRS AMORT	MONTHLY	SEMIMONTHLY	BIWEEKLY	WEEKLY
1	88.26792	44.03550	40.63509	20.29668
2	46.49467	23.19547	21.40135	10.68969
3	32.62332	16.27527	15.01441	7.49950
4	25.72722	12.83492	11.83906	5.91345
5	21.62097	10.78637	9.94823	4.96901
6	18.90938	9.43360	8.69954	4.34531
7	16.99445	8.47827	7.81767	3.90482
8	15.57716	7.77121	7.16492	3.57878
9	14.49135	7.22951	6.66480	3.32898
10	13.63729	6.80343	6.27138	3.13247
11	12.95149	6.46130	5.95545	2.97467
12	12.39162	6.18199	5.69749	2.84582
13	11.92833	5.95086	5.48401	2.73919
14	11.54068	5.75747	5.30536	2.64996
15	11.21327	5.59413	5.15445	2.57458
16	10.93456	5.45508	5.02597	2.51041
17	10.69570	5.33592	4.91585	2.45540
18	10.48984	5.23322	4.82092	2.40798
19	10.31152	5.14426	4.73868	2.36691
20	10.15640	5.06687	4.66712	2.33117
21	10.02096	4.99930	4.60464	2.29995
22	9.90231	4.94011	4.54989	2.27261
23	9.79809	4.88812	4.50179	2.24858
24	9.70630	4.84232	4.45941	2.22742
25	9.62529	4.80191	4.42201	2.20873
26	9.55365	4.76617	4.38892	2.19221
27	9.49019	4.73451	4.35961	2.17757
28	9.43389	4.70642	4.33359	2.16457
29	9.38387	4.68147	4.31048	2.15303
30	9.33938	4.65927	4.28991	2.14275
31	9.29977	4.63951	4.27160	2.13361
32	9.26446	4.62190	4.25527	2.12545
33	9.23297	4.60619	4.24070	2.11817
34	9.20486	4.59216	4.22770	2.11168
35	9.17974	4.57963	4.21607	2.10587

11.125% — Blended-payment factor for a loan of $1000, Amortization Periods 1 to 35 years

MONTHLY	SEMIMONTHLY	BIWEEKLY	WEEKLY	YRS AMORT
88.32364	44.06221	40.65959	20.30869	1
46.55010	23.22255	21.42623	10.70199	2
32.67983	16.30306	15.03995	7.51217	3
25.78515	12.86349	11.86533	5.92651	4
21.68043	10.81576	9.97526	4.98245	5
18.97042	9.46381	8.72733	4.35913	6
17.05709	8.50931	7.84621	3.91903	7
15.64140	7.80306	7.19421	3.59337	8
14.55717	7.26217	6.69482	3.34394	9
13.70467	6.83688	6.30214	3.14780	10
13.02041	6.49552	5.98691	2.99035	11
12.46204	6.21696	5.72965	2.86185	12
12.00022	5.98658	5.51685	2.75556	13
11.61399	5.79390	5.33886	2.66666	14
11.28797	5.63125	5.18859	2.59160	15
11.01060	5.49288	5.06073	2.52774	16
10.77304	5.37437	4.95120	2.47303	17
10.56843	5.27229	4.85685	2.42590	18
10.39131	5.18394	4.77516	2.38510	19
10.23735	5.10713	4.70414	2.34963	20
10.10302	5.04012	4.64216	2.31867	21
9.98544	4.98146	4.58791	2.29157	22
9.88223	4.92997	4.54027	2.26778	23
9.79141	4.88466	4.49834	2.24684	24
9.71132	4.84471	4.46136	2.22836	25
9.64055	4.80940	4.42868	2.21204	26
9.57792	4.77816	4.39975	2.19759	27
9.52241	4.75046	4.37409	2.18478	28
9.47313	4.72588	4.35132	2.17340	29
9.42935	4.70404	4.33108	2.16329	30
9.39039	4.68461	4.31307	2.15430	31
9.35571	4.66731	4.29703	2.14629	32
9.32481	4.65189	4.28274	2.13914	33
9.29725	4.63814	4.26998	2.13278	34
9.27266	4.62587	4.25860	2.12709	35

11.250% — Blended-payment factor for a loan of $1000, Amortization Periods 1 to 35 years

YRS AMORT	MONTHLY	SEMIMONTHLY	BIWEEKLY	WEEKLY
1	88.37935	44.08891	40.68409	20.32070
2	46.60554	23.24963	21.45111	10.71430
3	32.73637	16.33086	15.06550	7.52485
4	25.84312	12.89209	11.89162	5.93957
5	21.73995	10.84519	10.00231	4.99591
6	19.03154	9.49407	8.75515	4.37298
7	17.11983	8.54040	7.87479	3.93326
8	15.70575	7.83497	7.22355	3.60798
9	14.62312	7.29489	6.72491	3.35893
10	13.77220	6.87040	6.33295	3.16315
11	13.08948	6.52982	6.01844	3.00606
12	12.53262	6.25202	5.76188	2.87792
13	12.07228	6.02238	5.54977	2.77197
14	11.68749	5.83042	5.37244	2.68340
15	11.36286	5.66847	5.22281	2.60866
16	11.08684	5.53078	5.09557	2.54511
17	10.85059	5.41292	4.98665	2.49071
18	10.64722	5.31147	4.89287	2.44387
19	10.47132	5.22372	4.81174	2.40334
20	10.31851	5.14749	4.74125	2.36814
21	10.18529	5.08103	4.67979	2.33744
22	10.06877	5.02291	4.62602	2.31058
23	9.96658	4.97193	4.57885	2.28702
24	9.87672	4.92710	4.53736	2.26630
25	9.79755	4.88760	4.50081	2.24804
26	9.72766	4.85274	4.46852	2.23192
27	9.66585	4.82190	4.43997	2.21766
28	9.61112	4.79460	4.41468	2.20502
29	9.56258	4.77039	4.39225	2.19382
30	9.51949	4.74889	4.37233	2.18387
31	9.48120	4.72979	4.35462	2.17503
32	9.44713	4.71280	4.33887	2.16716
33	9.41681	4.69767	4.32484	2.16015
34	9.38980	4.68419	4.31234	2.15391
35	9.36571	4.67218	4.30119	2.14834

11.375% — Blended-payment factor for a loan of $1000, Amortization Periods 1 to 35 years

MONTHLY	SEMIMONTHLY	BIWEEKLY	WEEKLY	YRS AMORT
88.43505	44.11561	40.70858	20.33270	1
46.66099	23.27672	21.47600	10.72661	2
32.79294	16.35868	15.09107	7.53753	3
25.90114	12.92072	11.91794	5.95265	4
21.79954	10.87465	10.02939	5.00938	5
19.09275	9.52437	8.78300	4.38684	6
17.18267	8.57153	7.90342	3.94752	7
15.77022	7.86694	7.25294	3.62262	8
14.68920	7.32767	6.75505	3.37394	9
13.83986	6.90398	6.36383	3.17854	10
13.15870	6.56419	6.05004	3.02181	11
12.60337	6.28716	5.79419	2.89402	12
12.14451	6.05826	5.58276	2.78842	13
11.76117	5.86703	5.40610	2.70018	14
11.43794	5.70579	5.25712	2.62577	15
11.16327	5.56877	5.13050	2.56253	16
10.92833	5.45157	5.02218	2.50843	17
10.72622	5.35075	4.92898	2.46188	18
10.55152	5.26360	4.84841	2.42163	19
10.39988	5.18796	4.77846	2.38669	20
10.26777	5.12205	4.71750	2.35625	21
10.15231	5.06446	4.66422	2.32964	22
10.05113	5.01398	4.61752	2.30631	23
9.96224	4.96964	4.57648	2.28581	24
9.88398	4.93060	4.54034	2.26776	25
9.81495	4.89617	4.50846	2.25184	26
9.75397	4.86574	4.48029	2.23777	27
9.70001	4.83883	4.45535	2.22531	28
9.65221	4.81498	4.43326	2.21428	29
9.60981	4.79383	4.41366	2.20449	30
9.57217	4.77505	4.39625	2.19579	31
9.53872	4.75837	4.38078	2.18806	32
9.50897	4.74352	4.36701	2.18119	33
9.48249	4.73032	4.35476	2.17507	34
9.45891	4.71855	4.34384	2.16962	35

11.500% — Blended-payment factor for a loan of $1000, Amortization Periods 1 to 35 years

YRS AMORT	MONTHLY	SEMIMONTHLY	BIWEEKLY	WEEKLY
1	88.49074	44.14230	40.73307	20.34470
2	46.71645	23.30381	21.50089	10.73892
3	32.84954	16.38651	15.11665	7.55022
4	25.95920	12.94937	11.94427	5.96573
5	21.85919	10.90414	10.05650	5.02286
6	19.15404	9.55471	8.81089	4.40072
7	17.24560	8.60272	7.93209	3.96179
8	15.83480	7.89896	7.28238	3.63728
9	14.75540	7.36052	6.78525	3.38899
10	13.90767	6.93763	6.39477	3.19396
11	13.22808	6.59863	6.08171	3.03760
12	12.67428	6.32238	5.82657	2.91016
13	12.21692	6.09423	5.61583	2.80490
14	11.83502	5.90373	5.43984	2.71700
15	11.51320	5.74319	5.29150	2.64292
16	11.23990	5.60686	5.16552	2.57999
17	11.00626	5.49031	5.05780	2.52619
18	10.80542	5.39013	4.96518	2.47993
19	10.63194	5.30359	4.88517	2.43997
20	10.48146	5.22852	4.81575	2.40529
21	10.35046	5.16317	4.75531	2.37511
22	10.23606	5.10611	4.70252	2.34874
23	10.13588	5.05614	4.65628	2.32564
24	10.04795	5.01227	4.61568	2.30537
25	9.97061	4.97369	4.57996	2.28753
26	9.90244	4.93969	4.54848	2.27180
27	9.84228	4.90967	4.52068	2.25792
28	9.78909	4.88314	4.49610	2.24564
29	9.74201	4.85966	4.47434	2.23477
30	9.70030	4.83885	4.45506	2.22514
31	9.66330	4.82040	4.43795	2.21660
32	9.63046	4.80401	4.42275	2.20901
33	9.60127	4.78945	4.40925	2.20226
34	9.57533	4.77651	4.39724	2.19626
35	9.55224	4.76500	4.38656	2.19093

11.625% — Blended-payment factor for a loan of $1000, Amortization Periods 1 to 35 years

MONTHLY	SEMIMONTHLY	BIWEEKLY	WEEKLY	YRS AMORT
88.54643	44.16899	40.75756	20.35670	1
46.77193	23.33091	21.52578	10.75123	2
32.90617	16.41435	15.14224	7.56291	3
26.01732	12.97803	11.97062	5.97883	4
21.91891	10.93366	10.08364	5.03636	5
19.21540	9.58508	8.83882	4.41462	6
17.30864	8.63395	7.96080	3.97609	7
15.89949	7.93103	7.31187	3.65197	8
14.82173	7.39342	6.81550	3.40406	9
13.97561	6.97136	6.42577	3.20941	10
13.29760	6.63315	6.11345	3.05341	11
12.74535	6.35767	5.85902	2.92633	12
12.28949	6.13028	5.64897	2.82143	13
11.90906	5.94051	5.47366	2.73386	14
11.58865	5.78069	5.32598	2.66010	15
11.31671	5.64504	5.20062	2.59749	16
11.08440	5.52915	5.09351	2.54399	17
10.88482	5.42960	5.00148	2.49803	18
10.71255	5.34367	4.92202	2.45834	19
10.56323	5.26918	4.85314	2.42394	20
10.43334	5.20439	4.79321	2.39401	21
10.32000	5.14786	4.74090	2.36788	22
10.22084	5.09839	4.69513	2.34502	23
10.13386	5.05500	4.65497	2.32496	24
10.05742	5.01687	4.61967	2.30733	25
9.99012	4.98330	4.58858	2.29181	26
9.93077	4.95369	4.56116	2.27811	27
9.87834	4.92755	4.53694	2.26601	28
9.83199	4.90442	4.51551	2.25531	29
9.79096	4.88395	4.49654	2.24583	30
9.75459	4.86582	4.47972	2.23743	31
9.72235	4.84973	4.46480	2.22998	32
9.69372	4.83545	4.45156	2.22337	33
9.66830	4.82277	4.43979	2.21749	34
9.64570	4.81150	4.42933	2.21226	35

11.750% Blended-payment factor for a loan of $1000
Amortization Periods 1 to 35 years

YRS AMORT	MONTHLY	SEMIMONTHLY	BIWEEKLY	WEEKLY
1	88.60211	44.19567	40.78203	20.36869
2	46.82741	23.35801	21.55068	10.76354
3	32.96283	16.44221	15.16784	7.57562
4	26.07548	13.00673	11.99700	5.99193
5	21.97870	10.96321	10.11081	5.04987
6	19.27686	9.61550	8.86679	4.42854
7	17.37177	8.66522	7.98955	3.99040
8	15.96429	7.96316	7.34140	3.66668
9	14.88819	7.42639	6.84581	3.41916
10	14.04369	7.00514	6.45684	3.22488
11	13.36728	6.66774	6.14525	3.06926
12	12.81658	6.39305	5.89154	2.94254
13	12.36224	6.16642	5.68219	2.83799
14	11.98327	5.97738	5.50755	2.75076
15	11.66428	5.81827	5.36053	2.67733
16	11.39372	5.68331	5.23581	2.61504
17	11.16272	5.56808	5.12930	2.56184
18	10.96442	5.46917	5.03786	2.51617
19	10.79336	5.38384	4.95896	2.47677
20	10.64521	5.30994	4.89062	2.44263
21	10.51643	5.24571	4.83120	2.41295
22	10.40415	5.18970	4.77938	2.38707
23	10.30599	5.14074	4.73406	2.36444
24	10.21997	5.09783	4.69435	2.34460
25	10.14443	5.06015	4.65947	2.32718
26	10.07798	5.02700	4.62877	2.31185
27	10.01943	4.99780	4.60172	2.29834
28	9.96777	4.97203	4.57784	2.28642
29	9.92214	4.94927	4.55675	2.27588
30	9.88177	4.92913	4.53809	2.26656
31	9.84604	4.91131	4.52156	2.25830
32	9.81438	4.89552	4.50691	2.25099
33	9.78631	4.88152	4.49392	2.24450
34	9.76141	4.86909	4.48239	2.23874
35	9.73929	4.85806	4.47216	2.23363

11.875% Blended-payment factor for a loan of $1000
Amortization Periods 1 to 35 years

MONTHLY	SEMIMONTHLY	BIWEEKLY	WEEKLY	YRS AMORT
88.65778	44.22235	40.80651	20.38069	1
46.88291	23.38512	21.57558	10.77586	2
33.01952	16.47008	15.19346	7.58832	3
26.13369	13.03544	12.02339	6.00505	4
22.03854	10.99279	10.13800	5.06339	5
19.33839	9.64596	8.89478	4.44247	6
17.43499	8.69655	8.01835	4.00474	7
16.02920	7.99534	7.37099	3.68142	8
14.95477	7.45941	6.87617	3.43428	9
14.11191	7.03900	6.48796	3.24039	10
13.43710	6.70241	6.17712	3.08514	11
12.88797	6.42850	5.92413	2.95879	12
12.43515	6.20263	5.71549	2.85458	13
12.05766	6.01434	5.54153	2.76770	14
11.74010	5.85594	5.39517	2.69460	15
11.47091	5.72167	5.27108	2.63262	16
11.24124	5.60711	5.16519	2.57974	17
11.04420	5.50883	5.07432	2.53436	18
10.87437	5.42412	4.99599	2.49523	19
10.72738	5.35080	4.92818	2.46136	20
10.59971	5.28712	4.86927	2.43194	21
10.48848	5.23164	4.81794	2.40630	22
10.39133	5.18318	4.77309	2.38390	23
10.30626	5.14074	4.73381	2.36429	24
10.23162	5.10352	4.69934	2.34707	25
10.16602	5.07080	4.66904	2.33194	26
10.10828	5.04199	4.64236	2.31861	27
10.05737	5.01660	4.61883	2.30686	28
10.01244	4.99419	4.59806	2.29649	29
9.97275	4.97439	4.57970	2.28732	30
9.93764	4.95688	4.56347	2.27921	31
9.90657	4.94138	4.54909	2.27203	32
9.87904	4.92765	4.53635	2.26567	33
9.85464	4.91548	4.52506	2.26003	34
9.83300	4.90469	4.51504	2.25502	35

12.000% — Blended-payment factor for a loan of $1000, Amortization Periods 1 to 35 years

YRS AMORT	MONTHLY	SEMIMONTHLY	BIWEEKLY	WEEKLY
1	88.71344	44.24903	40.83098	20.39268
2	46.93842	23.41223	21.60049	10.78817
3	33.07623	16.49796	15.21908	7.60104
4	26.19194	13.06418	12.04981	6.01817
5	22.09846	11.02240	10.16523	5.07693
6	19.40000	9.67645	8.92282	4.45642
7	17.49832	8.72792	8.04719	4.01910
8	16.09423	8.02758	7.40063	3.69618
9	15.02147	7.49250	6.90659	3.44944
10	14.18027	7.07292	6.51915	3.25593
11	13.50708	6.73714	6.20906	3.10106
12	12.95952	6.46403	5.95680	2.97507
13	12.50823	6.23893	5.74886	2.87122
14	12.13222	6.05138	5.57559	2.78468
15	11.81610	5.89370	5.42989	2.71191
16	11.54829	5.76012	5.30643	2.65025
17	11.31995	5.64623	5.20115	2.59767
18	11.12419	5.54859	5.11088	2.55258
19	10.95557	5.46448	5.03310	2.51374
20	10.80974	5.39175	4.96583	2.48014
21	10.68318	5.32862	4.90743	2.45097
22	10.57301	5.27367	4.85659	2.42558
23	10.47685	5.22571	4.81220	2.40341
24	10.39273	5.18375	4.77336	2.38401
25	10.31900	5.14697	4.73930	2.36700
26	10.25424	5.11467	4.70939	2.35206
27	10.19729	5.08627	4.68307	2.33892
28	10.14714	5.06125	4.65989	2.32734
29	10.10291	5.03919	4.63944	2.31713
30	10.06387	5.01972	4.62139	2.30811
31	10.02938	5.00252	4.60544	2.30015
32	9.99889	4.98730	4.59133	2.29310
33	9.97190	4.97384	4.57884	2.28686
34	9.94800	4.96192	4.56777	2.28133
35	9.92683	4.95136	4.55797	2.27644

12.125% — Blended-payment factor for a loan of $1000, Amortization Periods 1 to 35 years

MONTHLY	SEMIMONTHLY	BIWEEKLY	WEEKLY	YRS AMORT
88.76909	44.27570	40.85545	20.40466	1
46.99394	23.43934	21.62540	10.80049	2
33.13298	16.52586	15.24472	7.61376	3
26.25025	13.09294	12.07625	6.03131	4
22.15843	11.05205	10.19248	5.09049	5
19.46169	9.70698	8.95089	4.47039	6
17.56174	8.75933	8.07608	4.03348	7
16.15936	8.05987	7.43032	3.71096	8
15.08830	7.52565	6.93707	3.46462	9
14.24876	7.10691	6.55040	3.27150	10
13.57720	6.77195	6.24106	3.11701	11
13.03122	6.49963	5.98953	2.99139	12
12.58147	6.27531	5.78231	2.88789	13
12.20696	6.08851	5.60972	2.80169	14
11.89227	5.93155	5.46468	2.72926	15
11.62585	5.79867	5.34187	2.66792	16
11.39884	5.68544	5.23720	2.61565	17
11.20436	5.58844	5.14752	2.57085	18
11.03696	5.50495	5.07031	2.53229	19
10.89230	5.43279	5.00357	2.49896	20
10.76685	5.37022	4.94568	2.47005	21
10.65773	5.31580	4.89532	2.44490	22
10.56257	5.26833	4.85139	2.42296	23
10.47939	5.22685	4.81298	2.40377	24
10.40655	5.19051	4.77934	2.38697	25
10.34263	5.15863	4.74981	2.37222	26
10.28647	5.13062	4.72386	2.35926	27
10.23706	5.10598	4.70102	2.34786	28
10.19353	5.08427	4.68090	2.33781	29
10.15515	5.06512	4.66314	2.32894	30
10.12127	5.04822	4.64747	2.32111	31
10.09134	5.03330	4.63362	2.31420	32
10.06488	5.02010	4.62138	2.30808	33
10.04148	5.00843	4.61054	2.30267	34
10.02077	4.99810	4.60095	2.29788	35

12.250% Blended-payment factor for a loan of $1000 — Amortization Periods 1 to 35 years

YRS AMORT	MONTHLY	SEMIMONTHLY	BIWEEKLY	WEEKLY
1	88.82474	44.30236	40.87991	20.41665
2	47.04947	23.46646	21.65031	10.81281
3	33.18976	16.55377	15.27038	7.62648
4	26.30860	13.12172	12.10270	6.04445
5	22.21848	11.08172	10.21976	5.10405
6	19.52347	9.73755	8.97900	4.48438
7	17.62525	8.79080	8.10500	4.04788
8	16.22461	8.09221	7.46005	3.72577
9	15.15526	7.55886	6.96760	3.47983
10	14.31739	7.14096	6.58171	3.28710
11	13.64746	6.80683	6.27312	3.13299
12	13.10308	6.53531	6.02234	3.00774
13	12.65488	6.31177	5.81583	2.90460
14	12.28186	6.12572	5.64393	2.81875
15	11.96862	5.96949	5.49956	2.74665
16	11.70359	5.83730	5.37739	2.68563
17	11.47792	5.72474	5.27334	2.63366
18	11.28471	5.62838	5.18424	2.58916
19	11.11854	5.54550	5.10759	2.55088
20	10.97504	5.47393	5.04139	2.51782
21	10.85070	5.41191	4.98401	2.48916
22	10.74263	5.35801	4.93413	2.46425
23	10.64847	5.31104	4.89066	2.44254
24	10.56623	5.27003	4.85269	2.42358
25	10.49427	5.23414	4.81945	2.40698
26	10.43119	5.20268	4.79031	2.39242
27	10.37582	5.17506	4.76472	2.37965
28	10.32714	5.15078	4.74222	2.36841
29	10.28431	5.12942	4.72242	2.35852
30	10.24657	5.11059	4.70496	2.34980
31	10.21329	5.09400	4.68957	2.34211
32	10.18392	5.07935	4.67598	2.33532
33	10.15799	5.06641	4.66398	2.32933
34	10.13507	5.05499	4.65337	2.32403
35	10.11481	5.04488	4.64398	2.31934

12.375% Blended-payment factor for a loan of $1000 — Amortization Periods 1 to 35 years

MONTHLY	SEMIMONTHLY	BIWEEKLY	WEEKLY	YRS AMORT
88.88038	44.32902	40.90436	20.42863	1
47.10501	23.49359	21.67523	10.82514	2
33.24657	16.58170	15.29604	7.63922	3
26.36700	13.15052	12.12918	6.05761	4
22.27858	11.11143	10.24707	5.11763	5
19.58532	9.76816	9.00714	4.49838	6
17.68886	8.82231	8.13397	4.06230	7
16.28996	8.12461	7.48984	3.74061	8
15.22233	7.59213	6.99819	3.49506	9
14.38615	7.17508	6.61308	3.30273	10
13.71787	6.84178	6.30526	3.14900	11
13.17510	6.57107	6.05521	3.02412	12
12.72845	6.34831	5.84942	2.92134	13
12.35694	6.16302	5.67822	2.83584	14
12.04515	6.00751	5.53452	2.76407	15
11.78152	5.87602	5.41298	2.70338	16
11.55718	5.76413	5.30955	2.65172	17
11.36526	5.66841	5.22104	2.60752	18
11.20030	5.58614	5.14496	2.56952	19
11.05797	5.51515	5.07929	2.53672	20
10.93473	5.45369	5.02242	2.50832	21
10.82771	5.40031	4.97303	2.48365	22
10.73454	5.35384	4.93002	2.46217	23
10.65324	5.31330	4.89247	2.44342	24
10.58217	5.27785	4.85964	2.42702	25
10.51992	5.24680	4.83089	2.41266	26
10.46533	5.21957	4.80566	2.40006	27
10.41738	5.19566	4.78349	2.38899	28
10.37523	5.17464	4.76400	2.37926	29
10.33813	5.15613	4.74684	2.37069	30
10.30545	5.13983	4.73172	2.36314	31
10.27663	5.12546	4.71839	2.35648	32
10.25122	5.11279	4.70663	2.35060	33
10.22878	5.10160	4.69624	2.34541	34
10.20897	5.09171	4.68706	2.34083	35

12.500% Blended-payment factor for a loan of $1000
Amortization Periods 1 to 35 years

YRS AMORT	MONTHLY	SEMIMONTHLY	BIWEEKLY	WEEKLY
1	88.93601	44.35568	40.92882	20.44061
2	47.16056	23.52072	21.70015	10.83746
3	33.30340	16.60964	15.32172	7.65195
4	26.42544	13.17935	12.15568	6.07077
5	22.33875	11.14116	10.27440	5.13123
6	19.64725	9.79881	9.03531	4.51240
7	17.75256	8.85386	8.16298	4.07675
8	16.35542	8.15705	7.51967	3.75546
9	15.28953	7.62545	7.02882	3.51033
10	14.45505	7.20927	6.64450	3.31839
11	13.78843	6.87680	6.33745	3.16504
12	13.24727	6.60690	6.08815	3.04054
13	12.80219	6.38492	5.88308	2.93812
14	12.43219	6.20039	5.71258	2.85297
15	12.12185	6.04562	5.56955	2.78154
16	11.85962	5.91483	5.44866	2.72116
17	11.63662	5.80361	5.34585	2.66982
18	11.44598	5.70853	5.25793	2.62591
19	11.28225	5.62688	5.18241	2.58819
20	11.14108	5.55647	5.11728	2.55566
21	11.01895	5.49556	5.06092	2.52752
22	10.91297	5.44270	5.01201	2.50309
23	10.82079	5.39673	4.96945	2.48183
24	10.74043	5.35665	4.93234	2.46330
25	10.67023	5.32164	4.89991	2.44711
26	10.60881	5.29100	4.87153	2.43293
27	10.55499	5.26416	4.84666	2.42051
28	10.50777	5.24061	4.82483	2.40961
29	10.46629	5.21993	4.80565	2.40003
30	10.42982	5.20174	4.78878	2.39161
31	10.39773	5.18573	4.77394	2.38419
32	10.36947	5.17164	4.76086	2.37766
33	10.34456	5.15921	4.74933	2.37190
34	10.32259	5.14826	4.73915	2.36682
35	10.30322	5.13859	4.73018	2.36234

12.625% Blended-payment factor for a loan of $1000
Amortization Periods 1 to 35 years

MONTHLY	SEMIMONTHLY	BIWEEKLY	WEEKLY	YRS AMORT
88.99163	44.38233	40.95326	20.45259	1
47.21612	23.54785	21.72508	10.84979	2
33.36027	16.63759	15.34741	7.66470	3
26.48393	13.20819	12.18220	6.08395	4
22.39898	11.17093	10.30177	5.14484	5
19.70927	9.82950	9.06353	4.52644	6
17.81636	8.88546	8.19204	4.09121	7
16.42100	8.18956	7.54955	3.77034	8
15.35685	7.65884	7.05952	3.52562	9
14.52408	7.24352	6.67599	3.33408	10
13.85913	6.91189	6.36971	3.18112	11
13.31959	6.64281	6.12116	3.05699	12
12.87608	6.42162	5.91682	2.95494	13
12.50760	6.23785	5.74702	2.87014	14
12.19873	6.08381	5.60466	2.79904	15
11.93790	5.95372	5.48442	2.73899	16
11.71624	5.84318	5.38223	2.68795	17
11.52689	5.74874	5.29490	2.64434	18
11.36438	5.66770	5.21994	2.60691	19
11.22437	5.59787	5.15535	2.57465	20
11.10334	5.53751	5.09949	2.54675	21
10.99841	5.48518	5.05106	2.52257	22
10.90721	5.43970	5.00896	2.50154	23
10.82778	5.40008	4.97227	2.48322	24
10.75845	5.36551	4.94025	2.46722	25
10.69785	5.33528	4.91225	2.45324	26
10.64480	5.30882	4.88773	2.44100	27
10.59830	5.28563	4.86623	2.43026	28
10.55749	5.26528	4.84736	2.42084	29
10.52165	5.24741	4.83078	2.41256	30
10.49014	5.23169	4.81620	2.40527	31
10.46242	5.21787	4.80337	2.39887	32
10.43801	5.20569	4.79207	2.39322	33
10.41651	5.19497	4.78212	2.38825	34
10.39756	5.18552	4.77334	2.38387	35

12.750% Blended-payment factor for a loan of $1000
Amortization Periods 1 to 35 years

YRS AMORT	MONTHLY	SEMIMONTHLY	BIWEEKLY	WEEKLY
1	89.04724	44.40897	40.97771	20.46457
2	47.27170	23.57499	21.75001	10.86211
3	33.41716	16.66556	15.37311	7.67745
4	26.54247	13.23706	12.20873	6.09713
5	22.45928	11.20072	10.32916	5.15846
6	19.77136	9.86022	9.09177	4.54050
7	17.88026	8.91711	8.22113	4.10569
8	16.48668	8.22211	7.57948	3.78525
9	15.42428	7.69228	7.09027	3.54093
10	14.59324	7.27783	6.70754	3.34979
11	13.92997	6.94705	6.40204	3.19722
12	13.39206	6.67879	6.15424	3.07347
13	12.95014	6.45839	5.95063	2.97179
14	12.58318	6.27539	5.78153	2.88734
15	12.27577	6.12208	5.63985	2.81658
16	12.01635	5.99270	5.52026	2.75686
17	11.79604	5.88283	5.41868	2.70613
18	11.60797	5.78904	5.33195	2.66281
19	11.44669	5.70861	5.25755	2.62566
20	11.30784	5.63936	5.19349	2.59367
21	11.18791	5.57955	5.13815	2.56603
22	11.08402	5.52774	5.09020	2.54208
23	10.99381	5.48275	5.04854	2.52128
24	10.91529	5.44359	5.01228	2.50317
25	10.84684	5.40945	4.98066	2.48738
26	10.78705	5.37964	4.95303	2.47358
27	10.73476	5.35356	4.92887	2.46151
28	10.68897	5.33072	4.90770	2.45094
29	10.64883	5.31070	4.88913	2.44167
30	10.61360	5.29314	4.87284	2.43353
31	10.58267	5.27771	4.85853	2.42638
32	10.55548	5.26415	4.84594	2.42010
33	10.53157	5.25222	4.83487	2.41457
34	10.51052	5.24173	4.82512	2.40970
35	10.49200	5.23249	4.81654	2.40542

12.875% Blended-payment factor for a loan of $1000
Amortization Periods 1 to 35 years

MONTHLY	SEMIMONTHLY	BIWEEKLY	WEEKLY	YRS AMORT
89.10285	44.43561	41.00215	20.47654	1
47.32729	23.60213	21.77494	10.87444	2
33.47409	16.69354	15.39883	7.69020	3
26.60106	13.26595	12.23529	6.11033	4
22.51964	11.23055	10.35658	5.17209	5
19.83353	9.89099	9.12005	4.55457	6
17.94425	8.94880	8.25026	4.12020	7
16.55246	8.25472	7.60946	3.80018	8
15.49184	7.72579	7.12107	3.55627	9
14.66254	7.31221	6.73914	3.36554	10
14.00096	6.98228	6.43443	3.21336	11
13.46469	6.71484	6.18739	3.08999	12
13.02435	6.49525	5.98451	2.98867	13
12.65892	6.31301	5.81612	2.90458	14
12.35299	6.16044	5.67511	2.83416	15
12.09497	6.03177	5.55617	2.77476	16
11.87602	5.92257	5.45522	2.72435	17
11.68923	5.82942	5.36908	2.68133	18
11.52917	5.74960	5.29524	2.64445	19
11.39149	5.68094	5.23172	2.61273	20
11.27266	5.62168	5.17688	2.58534	21
11.16981	5.57038	5.12940	2.56163	22
11.08057	5.52588	5.08820	2.54106	23
11.00297	5.48719	5.05237	2.52316	24
10.93538	5.45348	5.02114	2.50757	25
10.87640	5.42406	4.99389	2.49396	26
10.82487	5.39836	4.97007	2.48206	27
10.77978	5.37588	4.94922	2.47165	28
10.74030	5.35619	4.93096	2.46253	29
10.70568	5.33893	4.91495	2.45454	30
10.67531	5.32378	4.90090	2.44752	31
10.64865	5.31049	4.88856	2.44135	32
10.62523	5.29880	4.87771	2.43594	33
10.60463	5.28853	4.86817	2.43117	34
10.58652	5.27950	4.85978	2.42698	35

13.000%
Blended-payment factor for a loan of $1000
Amortization Periods 1 to 35 years

YRS AMORT	MONTHLY	SEMIMONTHLY	BIWEEKLY	WEEKLY
1	89.15844	44.46225	41.02658	20.48852
2	47.38288	23.62928	21.79988	10.88678
3	33.53104	16.72153	15.42455	7.70296
4	26.65969	13.29487	12.26187	6.12353
5	22.58006	11.26041	10.38402	5.18574
6	19.89578	9.92179	9.14837	4.56866
7	18.00833	8.98054	8.27944	4.13472
8	16.61836	8.28738	7.63948	3.81513
9	15.55952	7.75935	7.15192	3.57164
10	14.73196	7.34665	6.77081	3.38132
11	14.07208	7.01758	6.46688	3.22953
12	13.53747	6.75097	6.22060	3.10654
13	13.09872	6.53217	6.01846	3.00560
14	12.73483	6.35071	5.85077	2.92185
15	12.43037	6.19888	5.71045	2.85178
16	12.17377	6.07091	5.59216	2.79270
17	11.95617	5.96240	5.49183	2.74260
18	11.77067	5.86989	5.40628	2.69988
19	11.61183	5.79068	5.33301	2.66329
20	11.47530	5.72260	5.27002	2.63183
21	11.35757	5.66388	5.21569	2.60469
22	11.25575	5.61311	5.16869	2.58122
23	11.16749	5.56909	5.12793	2.56087
24	11.09081	5.53085	5.09252	2.54319
25	11.02407	5.49757	5.06169	2.52779
26	10.96590	5.46856	5.03481	2.51436
27	10.91511	5.44324	5.01133	2.50264
28	10.87073	5.42110	4.99081	2.49239
29	10.83189	5.40174	4.97285	2.48342
30	10.79788	5.38478	4.95712	2.47556
31	10.76808	5.36991	4.94332	2.46868
32	10.74193	5.35687	4.93122	2.46263
33	10.71899	5.34543	4.92059	2.45733
34	10.69884	5.33538	4.91126	2.45266
35	10.68113	5.32655	4.90306	2.44857

13.125%
Blended-payment factor for a loan of $1000
Amortization Periods 1 to 35 years

MONTHLY	SEMIMONTHLY	BIWEEKLY	WEEKLY	YRS AMORT
89.21403	44.48888	41.05101	20.50049	1
47.43849	23.65643	21.82482	10.89911	2
33.58802	16.74953	15.45029	7.71573	3
26.71837	13.32380	12.28847	6.13674	4
22.64054	11.29029	10.41150	5.19940	5
19.95811	9.95263	9.17672	4.58277	6
18.07250	9.01232	8.30866	4.14927	7
16.68436	8.32009	7.66955	3.83010	8
15.62732	7.79297	7.18283	3.58704	9
14.80152	7.38116	6.80253	3.39712	10
14.14335	7.05295	6.49939	3.24573	11
13.61039	6.78717	6.25388	3.12313	12
13.17325	6.56918	6.05248	3.02255	13
12.81090	6.38849	5.88551	2.93917	14
12.50792	6.23740	5.74587	2.86943	15
12.25274	6.11014	5.62823	2.81068	16
12.03649	6.00231	5.52852	2.76089	17
11.85228	5.91044	5.44357	2.71846	18
11.69466	5.83184	5.37086	2.68216	19
11.55929	5.76434	5.30840	2.65097	20
11.44265	5.70617	5.25457	2.62408	21
11.34187	5.65591	5.20805	2.60085	22
11.25457	5.61238	5.16774	2.58072	23
11.17880	5.57460	5.13274	2.56324	24
11.11292	5.54174	5.10231	2.54804	25
11.05554	5.51313	5.07579	2.53480	26
11.00550	5.48818	5.05266	2.52325	27
10.96181	5.46639	5.03246	2.51316	28
10.92361	5.44734	5.01479	2.50434	29
10.89020	5.43068	4.99933	2.49662	30
10.86095	5.41609	4.98579	2.48986	31
10.83531	5.40331	4.97393	2.48393	32
10.81284	5.39210	4.96352	2.47873	33
10.79313	5.38227	4.95439	2.47417	34
10.77582	5.37364	4.94637	2.47017	35

13.250% Blended-payment factor for a loan of $1000
Amortization Periods 1 to 35 years

YRS AMORT	MONTHLY	SEMIMONTHLY	BIWEEKLY	WEEKLY
1	89.26961	44.51550	41.07544	20.51245
2	47.49411	23.68358	21.84977	10.91144
3	33.64503	16.77755	15.47604	7.72850
4	26.77709	13.35276	12.31508	6.14997
5	22.70109	11.32021	10.43900	5.21308
6	20.02052	9.99350	9.20510	4.59689
7	18.13677	9.04415	8.33792	4.16383
8	16.75047	8.35285	7.69967	3.84510
9	15.69524	7.82665	7.21379	3.60246
10	14.87120	7.41573	6.83431	3.41295
11	14.21475	7.08838	6.53197	3.26197
12	13.68346	6.82344	6.28723	3.13975
13	13.24793	6.60626	6.08657	3.03954
14	12.88713	6.42634	5.92031	2.95651
15	12.58564	6.27600	5.78135	2.88712
16	12.33187	6.14946	5.66437	2.82870
17	12.11698	6.04230	5.56529	2.77922
18	11.93405	5.95108	5.48092	2.73709
19	11.77766	5.87309	5.40878	2.70106
20	11.64345	5.80616	5.34686	2.67014
21	11.52790	5.74854	5.29353	2.64351
22	11.42814	5.69880	5.24748	2.62051
23	11.34181	5.65575	5.20761	2.60060
24	11.26695	5.61842	5.17304	2.58334
25	11.20191	5.58599	5.14299	2.56833
26	11.14532	5.55777	5.11684	2.55527
27	11.09602	5.53318	5.09405	2.54389
28	11.05301	5.51173	5.07416	2.53396
29	11.01545	5.49301	5.05679	2.52528
30	10.98263	5.47664	5.04160	2.51770
31	10.95392	5.46232	5.02831	2.51106
32	10.92879	5.44979	5.01668	2.50525
33	10.90678	5.43882	5.00649	2.50016
34	10.88750	5.42920	4.99755	2.49570
35	10.87059	5.42077	4.98972	2.49179

13.375% Blended-payment factor for a loan of $1000
Amortization Periods 1 to 35 years

MONTHLY	SEMIMONTHLY	BIWEEKLY	WEEKLY	YRS AMORT
89.32518	44.54213	41.09986	20.52442	1
47.54974	23.71074	21.87472	10.92378	2
33.70207	16.80558	15.50180	7.74128	3
26.83586	13.38174	12.34172	6.16320	4
22.76170	11.35015	10.46653	5.22677	5
20.08300	10.01442	9.23352	4.61103	6
18.20113	9.07602	8.36722	4.17842	7
16.81668	8.38566	7.72984	3.86012	8
15.76328	7.86038	7.24480	3.61790	9
14.94102	7.45036	6.86615	3.42881	10
14.28630	7.12388	6.56460	3.27823	11
13.75668	6.85979	6.32064	3.15640	12
13.32276	6.64341	6.12072	3.05656	13
12.96352	6.46428	5.95518	2.97389	14
12.66351	6.31468	5.81691	2.90485	15
12.41117	6.18885	5.70059	2.84676	16
12.19763	6.08237	5.60213	2.79759	17
12.01600	5.99179	5.51836	2.75575	18
11.86083	5.91442	5.44678	2.72001	19
11.72777	5.84807	5.38538	2.68935	20
11.61331	5.79099	5.33256	2.66297	21
11.51457	5.74176	5.28698	2.64021	22
11.42921	5.69919	5.24756	2.62052	23
11.35524	5.66231	5.21339	2.60346	24
11.29105	5.63030	5.18373	2.58865	25
11.23524	5.60247	5.15794	2.57577	26
11.18667	5.57825	5.13549	2.56456	27
11.14434	5.55714	5.11591	2.55478	28
11.10741	5.53873	5.09883	2.54625	29
11.07517	5.52265	5.08392	2.53880	30
11.04700	5.50860	5.07088	2.53229	31
11.02237	5.49632	5.05947	2.52660	32
11.00082	5.48557	5.04949	2.52161	33
10.98195	5.47617	5.04075	2.51725	34
10.96543	5.46793	5.03310	2.51342	35

13.500% Blended-payment factor for a loan of $1000
Amortization Periods 1 to 35 years

YRS AMORT	MONTHLY	SEMIMONTHLY	BIWEEKLY	WEEKLY
1	89.38075	44.56874	41.12428	20.53638
2	47.60538	23.73791	21.89967	10.93612
3	33.75914	16.83363	15.52758	7.75406
4	26.89468	13.41074	12.36838	6.17644
5	22.82238	11.38013	10.49408	5.24047
6	20.14557	10.04537	9.26198	4.62519
7	18.26558	9.10793	8.39656	4.19302
8	16.88301	8.41853	7.76005	3.87516
9	15.83143	7.89417	7.27587	3.63338
10	15.01096	7.48505	6.89804	3.44470
11	14.35798	7.15945	6.59730	3.29452
12	13.83005	6.89620	6.35412	3.17308
13	13.39775	6.68064	6.15495	3.07362
14	13.04006	6.50229	5.99013	2.99131
15	12.74155	6.35344	5.85255	2.92261
16	12.49064	6.22832	5.73688	2.86485
17	12.27846	6.12252	5.63904	2.81599
18	12.09811	6.03259	5.55587	2.77445
19	11.94416	5.95582	5.48485	2.73899
20	11.81225	5.89005	5.42398	2.70859
21	11.69888	5.83352	5.37166	2.68246
22	11.60116	5.78479	5.32655	2.65994
23	11.51675	5.74270	5.28757	2.64047
24	11.44368	5.70627	5.25382	2.62362
25	11.38032	5.67467	5.22454	2.60900
26	11.32530	5.64724	5.19911	2.59630
27	11.27745	5.62338	5.17699	2.58525
28	11.23579	5.60260	5.15772	2.57563
29	11.19948	5.58450	5.14093	2.56725
30	11.16782	5.56871	5.12628	2.55993
31	11.14018	5.55493	5.11348	2.55354
32	11.11604	5.54289	5.10231	2.54796
33	11.09493	5.53237	5.09253	2.54308
34	11.07648	5.52317	5.08398	2.53881
35	11.06034	5.51512	5.07650	2.53507

Blended-payment factor for a loan of $1000 13.625%
Amortization Periods 1 to 35 years

MONTHLY	SEMIMONTHLY	BIWEEKLY	WEEKLY	YRS AMORT
89.43630	44.59536	41.14869	20.54834	1
47.66103	23.76508	21.92463	10.94846	2
33.81624	16.86169	15.55336	7.76685	3
26.95354	13.43976	12.39505	6.18969	4
22.88311	11.41014	10.52167	5.25418	5
20.20821	10.07636	9.29046	4.63936	6
18.33012	9.13989	8.42594	4.20765	7
16.94943	8.45144	7.79031	3.89023	8
15.89970	7.92802	7.30699	3.64888	9
15.08103	7.51981	6.93000	3.46062	10
14.42980	7.19509	6.63007	3.31084	11
13.90356	6.93269	6.38766	3.18979	12
13.47289	6.71795	6.18924	3.09071	13
13.11677	6.54037	6.02514	3.00876	14
12.81975	6.39228	5.88825	2.94040	15
12.57027	6.26787	5.77324	2.88297	16
12.35944	6.16275	5.67603	2.83443	17
12.18038	6.07347	5.59345	2.79319	18
12.02765	5.99731	5.52299	2.75801	19
11.89689	5.93211	5.46266	2.72788	20
11.78460	5.87612	5.41083	2.70199	21
11.68790	5.82790	5.36619	2.67970	22
11.60444	5.78629	5.32765	2.66046	23
11.53227	5.75030	5.29430	2.64381	24
11.46974	5.71912	5.26541	2.62938	25
11.41548	5.69207	5.24034	2.61686	26
11.36835	5.66857	5.21855	2.60597	27
11.32735	5.64812	5.19959	2.59651	28
11.29167	5.63033	5.18308	2.58826	29
11.26057	5.61482	5.16869	2.58108	30
11.23345	5.60130	5.15613	2.57481	31
11.20979	5.58950	5.14518	2.56934	32
11.18913	5.57920	5.13561	2.56456	33
11.17109	5.57021	5.12725	2.56038	34
11.15532	5.56234	5.11994	2.55673	35

13.750% Blended-payment factor for a loan of $1000 — Amortization Periods 1 to 35 years

YRS AMORT	MONTHLY	SEMIMONTHLY	BIWEEKLY	WEEKLY
1	89.49185	44.62196	41.17310	20.56030
2	47.71670	23.79225	21.94959	10.96080
3	33.87336	16.88976	15.57916	7.77965
4	27.01245	13.46881	12.42175	6.20295
5	22.94391	11.44017	10.54928	5.26791
6	20.27092	10.10738	9.31899	4.65355
7	18.39476	9.17190	8.45536	4.22229
8	17.01596	8.48441	7.82062	3.90532
9	15.96809	7.96193	7.33816	3.66440
10	15.15123	7.55463	6.96200	3.47656
11	14.50176	7.23079	6.66289	3.32720
12	13.97721	6.96924	6.42127	3.20654
13	13.54818	6.75532	6.22360	3.10783
14	13.19362	6.57854	6.06023	3.02625
15	12.89811	6.43119	5.92403	2.95824
16	12.65005	6.30750	5.80967	2.90113
17	12.44059	6.20306	5.71309	2.85290
18	12.26282	6.11442	5.63110	2.81196
19	12.11130	6.03887	5.56121	2.77706
20	11.98169	5.97425	5.50140	2.74719
21	11.87048	5.91880	5.45007	2.72156
22	11.77480	5.87109	5.40589	2.69950
23	11.69228	5.82995	5.36779	2.68047
24	11.62099	5.79440	5.33485	2.66403
25	11.55928	5.76363	5.30634	2.64979
26	11.50579	5.73696	5.28162	2.63744
27	11.45937	5.71381	5.26015	2.62672
28	11.41903	5.69370	5.24150	2.61741
29	11.38395	5.67621	5.22527	2.60930
30	11.35342	5.66098	5.21114	2.60225
31	11.32682	5.64772	5.19882	2.59610
32	11.30363	5.63616	5.18809	2.59074
33	11.28341	5.62607	5.17872	2.58606
34	11.26577	5.61728	5.17054	2.58197
35	11.25036	5.60960	5.16340	2.57841

Blended-payment factor for a loan of $1000 — Amortization Periods 1 to 35 years — 13.875%

MONTHLY	SEMIMONTHLY	BIWEEKLY	WEEKLY	YRS AMORT
89.54739	44.64856	41.19750	20.57225	1
47.77237	23.81943	21.97456	10.97315	2
33.93052	16.91784	15.60497	7.79245	3
27.07140	13.49787	12.44847	6.21623	4
23.00476	11.47024	10.57691	5.28165	5
20.33372	10.13845	9.34754	4.66776	6
18.45949	9.20395	8.48483	4.23696	7
17.08259	8.51743	7.85097	3.92043	8
16.03659	7.99589	7.36938	3.67995	9
15.22155	7.58951	6.99407	3.49254	10
14.57385	7.26656	6.69577	3.34358	11
14.05101	7.00587	6.45493	3.22332	12
13.62362	6.79277	6.25803	3.12499	13
13.27063	6.61677	6.09538	3.04377	14
12.97663	6.47018	5.95987	2.97610	15
12.73000	6.34721	5.84618	2.91933	16
12.52190	6.24345	5.75022	2.87141	17
12.34541	6.15546	5.66883	2.83077	18
12.19511	6.08052	5.59949	2.79614	19
12.06665	6.01646	5.54021	2.76654	20
11.95651	5.96155	5.48938	2.74116	21
11.86184	5.91434	5.44566	2.71933	22
11.78027	5.87367	5.40799	2.70052	23
11.70985	5.83856	5.37546	2.68427	24
11.64896	5.80820	5.34733	2.67022	25
11.59623	5.78191	5.32295	2.65805	26
11.55051	5.75911	5.30182	2.64750	27
11.51083	5.73933	5.28346	2.63833	28
11.47634	5.72214	5.26751	2.63037	29
11.44636	5.70719	5.25363	2.62344	30
11.42027	5.69418	5.24155	2.61740	31
11.39755	5.68285	5.23103	2.61215	32
11.37776	5.67298	5.22186	2.60757	33
11.36051	5.66438	5.21387	2.60358	34
11.34547	5.65688	5.20689	2.60010	35

14.000% Blended-payment factor for a loan of $1000
Amortization Periods 1 to 35 years

YRS AMORT	MONTHLY	SEMIMONTHLY	BIWEEKLY	WEEKLY
1	89.60292	44.67516	41.22190	20.58420
2	47.82805	23.84661	21.99953	10.98549
3	33.98770	16.94594	15.63079	7.80526
4	27.13040	13.52696	12.47520	6.22951
5	23.06568	11.50033	10.60458	5.29541
6	20.39659	10.16954	9.37613	4.68198
7	18.52430	9.23604	8.51433	4.25164
8	17.14933	8.55049	7.88137	3.93557
9	16.10521	8.02990	7.40065	3.69552
10	15.29200	7.62445	7.02619	3.50854
11	14.64607	7.30239	6.72871	3.35999
12	14.12495	7.04256	6.48867	3.24012
13	13.69920	6.83029	6.29252	3.14218
14	13.34780	6.65508	6.13060	3.06132
15	13.05530	6.50925	5.99579	2.99400
16	12.81011	6.38700	5.88275	2.93756
17	12.60336	6.28392	5.78742	2.88996
18	12.42817	6.19656	5.70662	2.84961
19	12.27908	6.12223	5.63784	2.81526
20	12.15176	6.05875	5.57909	2.78593
21	12.04269	6.00437	5.52875	2.76079
22	11.94902	5.95767	5.48550	2.73919
23	11.86839	5.91746	5.44826	2.72060
24	11.79984	5.88279	5.41613	2.70455
25	11.73876	5.85284	5.38837	2.69069
26	11.68679	5.82692	5.36435	2.67869
27	11.64177	5.80447	5.34353	2.66830
28	11.60272	5.78501	5.32547	2.65928
29	11.56884	5.76811	5.30979	2.65145
30	11.53940	5.75343	5.29616	2.64465
31	11.51381	5.74068	5.28432	2.63873
32	11.49155	5.72958	5.27401	2.63358
33	11.47218	5.71992	5.26503	2.62910
34	11.45532	5.71151	5.25722	2.62520
35	11.44063	5.70419	5.25041	2.62180

Blended-payment factor for a loan of $1000 **14.125%**
Amortization Periods 1 to 35 years

MONTHLY	SEMIMONTHLY	BIWEEKLY	WEEKLY	YRS AMORT
89.65845	44.70176	41.24629	20.59616	1
47.88375	23.87380	22.02450	10.99784	2
34.04491	16.97405	15.65663	7.81807	3
27.18944	13.55607	12.50196	6.24280	4
23.12667	11.53045	10.63227	5.30918	5
20.45954	10.20068	9.40475	4.69622	6
18.58921	9.26818	8.54387	4.26634	7
17.21617	8.58361	7.91181	3.95073	8
16.17394	8.06398	7.43197	3.71112	9
15.36258	7.65945	7.05837	3.52456	10
14.71843	7.33829	6.76171	3.37643	11
14.19902	7.07933	6.52246	3.25696	12
13.77493	6.86788	6.32708	3.15940	13
13.42511	6.69347	6.16589	3.07891	14
13.13412	6.54839	6.03177	3.01194	15
12.89037	6.42686	5.91940	2.95583	16
12.68498	6.32446	5.82470	2.90854	17
12.51107	6.23775	5.74449	2.86848	18
12.36320	6.16402	5.67627	2.83442	19
12.23702	6.10111	5.61804	2.80534	20
12.12902	6.04727	5.56819	2.78045	21
12.03635	6.00106	5.52540	2.75908	22
11.95664	5.96132	5.48859	2.74070	23
11.88797	5.92708	5.45686	2.72486	24
11.82870	5.89753	5.42947	2.71118	25
11.77746	5.87199	5.40579	2.69936	26
11.73313	5.84988	5.38529	2.68912	27
11.69473	5.83074	5.36752	2.68025	28
11.66142	5.81413	5.35211	2.67255	29
11.63253	5.79973	5.33874	2.66588	30
11.60743	5.78721	5.32712	2.66007	31
11.58563	5.77634	5.31702	2.65503	32
11.56667	5.76689	5.30824	2.65064	33
11.55019	5.75867	5.30060	2.64683	34
11.53584	5.75152	5.29394	2.64351	35

14.250% Blended-payment factor for a loan of $1000
Amortization Periods 1 to 35 years

YRS AMORT	MONTHLY	SEMIMONTHLY	BIWEEKLY	WEEKLY
1	89.71396	44.72834	41.27068	20.60810
2	47.93945	23.90099	22.04948	11.01019
3	34.10215	17.00218	15.68247	7.83089
4	27.24853	13.58520	12.52873	6.25610
5	23.18771	11.56061	10.65998	5.32296
6	20.52256	10.23185	9.43341	4.71048
7	18.65421	9.30036	8.57345	4.28107
8	17.28312	8.61678	7.94230	3.96591
9	16.24279	8.09811	7.46334	3.72675
10	15.43328	7.69451	7.09060	3.54062
11	14.79092	7.37425	6.79477	3.39290
12	14.27324	7.11616	6.55632	3.27383
13	13.85081	6.90555	6.36171	3.17665
14	13.50258	6.73193	6.20124	3.09653
15	13.21310	6.58760	6.06782	3.02991
16	12.97078	6.46679	5.95611	2.97413
17	12.76676	6.36507	5.86204	2.92715
18	12.59413	6.27901	5.78242	2.88739
19	12.44747	6.20589	5.71476	2.85361
20	12.32243	6.14354	5.65705	2.82479
21	12.21549	6.09023	5.60769	2.80015
22	12.12381	6.04452	5.56536	2.77901
23	12.04504	6.00525	5.52898	2.76084
24	11.97722	5.97144	5.49765	2.74520
25	11.91875	5.94228	5.47062	2.73170
26	11.86826	5.91711	5.44728	2.72005
27	11.82461	5.89535	5.42710	2.70997
28	11.78683	5.87651	5.40962	2.70124
29	11.75411	5.86020	5.39448	2.69368
30	11.72574	5.84606	5.38135	2.68712
31	11.70113	5.83379	5.36996	2.68143
32	11.67978	5.82314	5.36006	2.67649
33	11.66123	5.81389	5.35147	2.67220
34	11.64511	5.80586	5.34400	2.66847
35	11.63111	5.79888	5.33750	2.66523

Blended-payment factor for a loan of $1000 14.375%
Amortization Periods 1 to 35 years

MONTHLY	SEMIMONTHLY	BIWEEKLY	WEEKLY	YRS AMORT
89.76947	44.75493	41.29507	20.62005	1
47.99517	23.92818	22.07446	11.02254	2
34.15942	17.03031	15.70833	7.84371	3
27.30767	13.61435	12.55552	6.26940	4
23.24881	11.59079	10.68773	5.33675	5
20.58566	10.26306	9.46210	4.72475	6
18.71930	9.33258	8.60308	4.29581	7
17.35016	8.64999	7.97283	3.98111	8
16.31175	8.13229	7.49477	3.74240	9
15.50410	7.72963	7.12288	3.55670	10
14.86354	7.41028	6.82789	3.40940	11
14.34760	7.15305	6.59024	3.29073	12
13.92683	6.94328	6.39639	3.19394	13
13.58019	6.77046	6.23666	3.11418	14
13.29223	6.62689	6.10394	3.04791	15
13.05135	6.50680	5.99290	2.99246	16
12.84868	6.40576	5.89945	2.94580	17
12.67734	6.32034	5.82042	2.90634	18
12.53189	6.24782	5.75331	2.87283	19
12.40798	6.18605	5.69613	2.84427	20
12.30211	6.13326	5.64726	2.81987	21
12.21141	6.08805	5.60538	2.79896	22
12.13356	6.04923	5.56942	2.78101	23
12.06660	6.01585	5.53849	2.76556	24
12.00892	5.98709	5.51183	2.75225	25
11.95916	5.96229	5.48883	2.74076	26
11.91618	5.94086	5.46895	2.73084	27
11.87903	5.92234	5.45176	2.72225	28
11.84688	5.90631	5.43689	2.71482	29
11.81904	5.89243	5.42400	2.70839	30
11.79491	5.88040	5.41283	2.70281	31
11.77399	5.86997	5.40313	2.69797	32
11.75584	5.86092	5.39473	2.69377	33
11.74009	5.85307	5.38742	2.69013	34
11.72642	5.84625	5.38108	2.68696	35

14.500% — Blended-payment factor for a loan of $1000
Amortization Periods 1 to 35 years

YRS AMORT	MONTHLY	SEMIMONTHLY	BIWEEKLY	WEEKLY
1	89.82497	44.78151	41.31945	20.63199
2	48.05089	23.95538	22.09945	11.03489
3	34.21671	17.05846	15.73420	7.85654
4	27.36685	13.64352	12.58234	6.28272
5	23.30998	11.62100	10.71550	5.35056
6	20.64884	10.29431	9.49082	4.73904
7	18.78448	9.36485	8.63274	4.31057
8	17.41731	8.68326	8.00341	3.99634
9	16.38083	8.16653	7.52624	3.75807
10	15.57505	7.76481	7.15523	3.57281
11	14.93630	7.44637	6.86107	3.42593
12	14.42210	7.19002	6.62422	3.30767
13	14.00300	6.98108	6.43115	3.21126
14	13.65795	6.80906	6.27215	3.13187
15	13.37150	6.66625	6.14013	3.06594
16	13.13206	6.54688	6.02974	3.01083
17	12.93076	6.44653	5.93692	2.96448
18	12.76070	6.36175	5.85849	2.92531
19	12.61646	6.28983	5.79194	2.89208
20	12.49367	6.22862	5.73527	2.86379
21	12.38886	6.17636	5.68689	2.83963
22	12.29915	6.13164	5.64547	2.81894
23	12.22221	6.09328	5.60993	2.80120
24	12.15610	6.06033	5.57938	2.78595
25	12.09921	6.03196	5.55309	2.77282
26	12.05017	6.00751	5.53042	2.76150
27	12.00787	5.98642	5.51085	2.75173
28	11.97133	5.96821	5.49395	2.74329
29	11.93974	5.95246	5.47933	2.73599
30	11.91242	5.93884	5.46668	2.72967
31	11.88876	5.92705	5.45573	2.72420
32	11.86828	5.91683	5.44624	2.71946
33	11.85052	5.90798	5.43801	2.71535
34	11.83513	5.90031	5.43087	2.71179
35	11.82178	5.89365	5.42468	2.70870

14.625% — Blended-payment factor for a loan of $1000
Amortization Periods 1 to 35 years

MONTHLY	SEMIMONTHLY	BIWEEKLY	WEEKLY	YRS AMORT
89.88046	44.80808	41.34383	20.64393	1
48.10663	23.98258	22.12444	11.04725	2
34.27404	17.08662	15.76008	7.86937	3
27.42607	13.67271	12.60917	6.29605	4
23.37120	11.65124	10.74329	5.36438	5
20.71209	10.32559	9.51958	4.75335	6
18.84974	9.39716	8.66244	4.32536	7
17.48456	8.71657	8.03404	4.01158	8
16.45001	8.20082	7.55777	3.77377	9
15.64611	7.80005	7.18762	3.58895	10
15.00918	7.48252	6.89430	3.44249	11
14.49673	7.22705	6.65827	3.32463	12
14.07930	7.01895	6.46596	3.22860	13
13.73585	6.84773	6.30770	3.14958	14
13.45093	6.70569	6.17638	3.08401	15
13.21293	6.58704	6.06666	3.02922	16
13.01299	6.48736	5.97446	2.98319	17
12.84421	6.40322	5.89662	2.94432	18
12.70117	6.33191	5.83062	2.91136	19
12.57951	6.27126	5.77448	2.88333	20
12.47575	6.21953	5.72658	2.85941	21
12.38702	6.17530	5.68561	2.83896	22
12.31099	6.13739	5.65049	2.82142	23
12.24572	6.10486	5.62033	2.80636	24
12.18961	6.07688	5.59439	2.79341	25
12.14129	6.05279	5.57206	2.78226	26
12.09965	6.03203	5.55280	2.77264	27
12.06372	6.01412	5.53617	2.76434	28
12.03269	5.99865	5.52181	2.75717	29
12.00587	5.98528	5.50940	2.75097	30
11.98268	5.97372	5.49866	2.74561	31
11.96262	5.96372	5.48936	2.74097	32
11.94525	5.95506	5.48131	2.73695	33
11.93021	5.94757	5.47434	2.73347	34
11.91718	5.94107	5.46830	2.73045	35

14.750% Blended-payment factor for a loan of $1000
Amortization Periods 1 to 35 years

YRS AMORT	MONTHLY	SEMIMONTHLY	BIWEEKLY	WEEKLY
1	89.93595	44.83465	41.36820	20.65587
2	48.16238	24.00979	22.14943	11.05960
3	34.33139	17.11480	15.78597	7.88221
4	27.48534	13.70192	12.63602	6.30939
5	23.43249	11.68151	10.77112	5.37821
6	20.77542	10.35691	9.54837	4.76767
7	18.91510	9.42951	8.69218	4.34016
8	17.55191	8.74994	8.06471	4.02685
9	16.51931	8.23517	7.58934	3.78949
10	15.71730	7.83535	7.22007	3.60511
11	15.08220	7.51874	6.92760	3.45907
12	14.57150	7.26415	6.69237	3.34162
13	14.15575	7.05689	6.50084	3.24598
14	13.81390	6.88647	6.34332	3.16733
15	13.53050	6.74519	6.21270	3.10211
16	13.29394	6.62726	6.10364	3.04766
17	13.09536	6.52827	6.01207	3.00193
18	12.92786	6.44477	5.93481	2.96336
19	12.78602	6.37405	5.86937	2.93068
20	12.66549	6.31397	5.81374	2.90291
21	12.56277	6.26276	5.76633	2.87923
22	12.47502	6.21901	5.72580	2.85900
23	12.39989	6.18156	5.69110	2.84167
24	12.33546	6.14944	5.66133	2.82680
25	12.28012	6.12185	5.63575	2.81403
26	12.23251	6.09812	5.61374	2.80304
27	12.19152	6.07769	5.59478	2.79357
28	12.15619	6.06008	5.57844	2.78541
29	12.12571	6.04488	5.56433	2.77837
30	12.09940	6.03176	5.55215	2.77228
31	12.07667	6.02043	5.54162	2.76703
32	12.05703	6.01064	5.53252	2.76248
33	12.04004	6.00217	5.52464	2.75855
34	12.02535	5.99485	5.51783	2.75515
35	12.01263	5.98851	5.51193	2.75220

14.875% Blended-payment factor for a loan of $1000
Amortization Periods 1 to 35 years

MONTHLY	SEMIMONTHLY	BIWEEKLY	WEEKLY	YRS AMORT
89.99142	44.86121	41.39257	20.66781	1
48.21814	24.03700	22.17443	11.07196	2
34.38877	17.14299	15.81188	7.89506	3
27.54465	13.73116	12.66289	6.32273	4
23.49383	11.71180	10.79897	5.39205	5
20.83882	10.38826	9.57719	4.78201	6
18.98054	9.46190	8.72196	4.35498	7
17.61936	8.78335	8.09542	4.04214	8
16.58872	8.26957	7.62096	3.80524	9
15.78861	7.87071	7.25257	3.62130	10
15.15534	7.55502	6.96095	3.47568	11
14.64640	7.30131	6.72653	3.35864	12
14.23234	7.09490	6.53578	3.26339	13
13.89210	6.92529	6.37900	3.18511	14
13.61021	6.78477	6.24908	3.12024	15
13.37510	6.66756	6.14069	3.06612	16
13.17788	6.56924	6.04974	3.02071	17
13.01166	6.48638	5.97307	2.98243	18
12.87101	6.41627	5.90818	2.95003	19
12.75160	6.35674	5.85307	2.92251	20
12.64992	6.30606	5.80613	2.89907	21
12.56314	6.26279	5.76606	2.87906	22
12.48891	6.22579	5.73177	2.86194	23
12.42531	6.19409	5.70238	2.84727	24
12.37073	6.16688	5.67715	2.83467	25
12.32384	6.14350	5.65547	2.82384	26
12.28349	6.12339	5.63681	2.81453	27
12.24876	6.10607	5.62074	2.80650	28
12.21882	6.09115	5.60688	2.79958	29
12.19301	6.07828	5.59493	2.79361	30
12.17073	6.06717	5.58461	2.78846	31
12.15149	6.05759	5.57570	2.78401	32
12.13488	6.04930	5.56799	2.78017	33
12.12052	6.04215	5.56134	2.77684	34
12.10811	6.03596	5.55558	2.77397	35

15.000% Blended-payment factor for a loan of $1000
Amortization Periods 1 to 35 years

YRS AMORT	MONTHLY	SEMIMONTHLY	BIWEEKLY	WEEKLY
1	90.04689	44.88777	41.41693	20.67974
2	48.27390	24.06422	22.19943	11.08432
3	34.44617	17.17119	15.83779	7.90791
4	27.60401	13.76041	12.68978	6.33609
5	23.55524	11.74213	10.82684	5.40591
6	20.90229	10.41965	9.60604	4.79636
7	19.04607	9.49434	8.75177	4.36982
8	17.68692	8.81681	8.12618	4.05746
9	16.65824	8.30402	7.65264	3.82101
10	15.86004	7.90612	7.28513	3.63751
11	15.22861	7.59136	6.99435	3.49233
12	14.72144	7.33854	6.76075	3.37569
13	14.30906	7.13297	6.57078	3.28083
14	13.97043	6.96417	6.41474	3.20292
15	13.69007	6.82441	6.28552	3.13840
16	13.45640	6.70792	6.17780	3.08461
17	13.26054	6.61029	6.08748	3.03952
18	13.09559	6.52807	6.01140	3.00153
19	12.95614	6.45855	5.94706	2.96940
20	12.83784	6.39958	5.89246	2.94214
21	12.73721	6.34941	5.84600	2.91895
22	12.65139	6.30663	5.80637	2.89916
23	12.57805	6.27007	5.77249	2.88224
24	12.51528	6.23878	5.74348	2.86776
25	12.46146	6.21195	5.71860	2.85534
26	12.41526	6.18892	5.69724	2.84467
27	12.37556	6.16913	5.67888	2.83550
28	12.34140	6.15211	5.66307	2.82761
29	12.31200	6.13745	5.64946	2.82081
30	12.28668	6.12483	5.63774	2.81496
31	12.26484	6.11394	5.62762	2.80991
32	12.24601	6.10456	5.61890	2.80555
33	12.22976	6.09646	5.61136	2.80179
34	12.21574	6.08946	5.60486	2.79854
35	12.20363	6.08343	5.59924	2.79574

Index